Martha Rose Shulman's
Feasts & Fêtes

MARTHA ROSE SHULMAN'S

Feasts & Fêtes

Elegantly healthful menus for do-ahead entertaining

By Martha Rose Shulman

❧

With a Foreword by Julee Rosso

Photography by Teri Sandison

CHAPTERS PUBLISHING LTD. SHELBURNE, VERMONT 05482

Other Books by Martha Rose Shulman

Gourmet Vegetarian Feasts
Spicy Vegetarian Feasts
Garlic Cookery
Herbs and Honey Cookery
Fast Vegetarian Feasts
The Vegetarian Feast
Stress, Diet and Your Heart *With Dean Ornish, M.D.*
Dr. Lendon Smith's Teenage Diet *With Lendon Smith, M.D.*
Mediterranean Light
Entertaining Light

❀

Copyright © 1992, 1988 by Martha Rose Shulman

Photographs copyright © 1992 by Teri Sandison

Published by
Chapters Publishing Ltd.
2031 Shelburne Road
Shelburne, Vermont 05482

Originally published in different form in 1988 as
Supper Club Chez Martha Rose: A Cookbook of Parties and Tales From Paris

Library of Congress Cataloging-in-Publication Data
Shulman, Martha Rose.
[Supper club Chez Martha Rose]
Feasts & fêtes: elegantly healthful menus for do-ahead entertaining / by Martha Rose Shulman;
with a foreword by Julee Rosso; photography by Teri Sandison.
p. cm.
Originally published: Supper club Chez Martha Rose. New York: Atheneum, 1988.
Includes index.
ISBN 0-9631591-0-0 : $17.95
I. Cookery, International. 2. Menus. 3. Entertaining.
I. Title. II. Title: Feasts and fêtes.
[TX725.A1S516 1992]   641.59—dc20   92-3613
CIP

Trade distribution by
Firefly Books Ltd.
250 Sparks Avenue
Willowdale, Ontario
Canada M2H 2S4

Printed and bound in Canada by
D.W. Friesen & Sons, Altona, Manitoba

Designed by Hans Teensma/Impress

À ma chère Christine, sans laquelle tout
cela n'aurait pas été possible

Contents

Foreword

I FIRST MET Martha Rose Shulman at a birthday party at a country house in Provence. During the cocktail hour, a vivacious, eclectically dressed woman appeared who suddenly became the life of the party. As Martha and I talked, I learned of her Supper Club in Paris, which she created once a month in her apartment and where visiting and resident Americans gathered regularly. When I at last arrived in Paris, Martha invited me to be her house guest. I quickly realized that Americans in Paris, particularly those who care about food, visit Martha's house much more frequently than on Supper Club evenings.

Martha is a natural hostess, creating great home cooking that everyone loves. Unlike many people, who dread having company for dinner and agonize over special meals for the occasion, Martha understands that the most personal way to entertain is to cook the same way for guests as for family.

She always begins with fresh ingredients and then masterfully combines herbs and spices. Her sense of style and adventure is apparent in all her dishes. Well before the current trends emphasizing grains and produce, Martha loved vegetables. She still does. Her Mediterranean-inspired soups, stews and casseroles have a goodness that reflects their traditional roots, with clean, clear, magnified flavors.

In *Feasts & Fêtes*, Martha shares the secrets of effortless cooking for a crowd. Her menus are well balanced, filled with accessible recipes that are healthful, yet satisfying. As is her fashion, most of them can be made ahead to ensure that the cook has a great time too.

This kind of entertaining is a necessity for Martha. She herself would never, ever be found in the kitchen during a party because everyone would want to be there with her. And as I well know, her cozy Paris kitchen could never accommodate all her friends and admirers.

Julee Rosso
co-author of *The Silver Palate Cookbook*
and *The New Basics Cookbook*
Saugatuck, Michigan
1992

Acknowledgments

ALL OF THE RECIPES in this book were tested by Laurie Dill, and I would like to thank her for her objectivity and good palate. I am also indebted to Laurie for peeling and chopping kilos of onions, garlic and tomatoes, washing and drying dozens of heads of lettuce and bunches of herbs and setting the tables during the years she worked as my assistant.

I am very grateful to Jon Winroth for contributing wine suggestions to each menu in this book. An American wine writer who has lived in Paris for over 30 years, Jon came here on a Fulbright to do research for a history dissertation but found that he was more interested in spending time in wine bars than in libraries. Now he is one of France's most respected wine authorities. He also happens to be my neighbor, a lucky break for me; I met him my first week here. He has taught me much of what I know about wine and has introduced me to all of my favorite wine bistros in Paris. He started L'Académie du Vin, a well-known Parisian wine school, with Steven Spurrier, is the author of *Wine As You Like It*, the wine columnist for *Elle* and *Lui* and a regular contributor to other publications.

The Supper Club would never run so smoothly if it weren't for my assistants. I thank all of the people who have helped me over the years, especially Chase Kennedy and Anne Trager.

I am, as always, indebted to my husband, Bill Grantham, who cedes his office to all of the dinners and parties we give in our apartment and who is such a gracious host and willing opener and server of wine.

Thank you Joyce Johnson for your initial enthusiasm about this book, and for being such a good editor; and thank you Rux Martin and Barry Estabrook for keeping it alive.

Thank you Teri Sandison for your beautiful food photographs. Also many thanks to Norman Stewart for making my recipes come alive for the camera.

To Charles Gautreux, John Nyquist and Kathy Vanderbilt of Vanderbilt and Company, Napa Valley, California, thank you for sharing your tablewares for the photography.

Christine et Lulu, vous deux méritez bien un chapitre chacune, mais je tiens à vous témoigner dès maintenant ma gratitude.

Sabine, thanks for helping me with my French.

Finally, I want to thank all of my Supper Club guests, especially the "regulars." You know who you are. You always leave a little of your warmth and goodwill behind when you go, so it's there to welcome people the next time. Supper Club Chez Martha is what it is because of you.

Martha Rose Shulman
Paris, France

Introduction

Supper Club Chez Martha

ONCE A MONTH, on Thursday nights, 25 people come to my apartment for dinner. They begin to arrive around 8:30 for aperitifs, which I serve in my large, friendly living room, and continue arriving until 9:30 or 10:00, when I begin to lure them away from their cocktail conversations by asking them to find their places at the two long tables.

The tables, which are in different rooms, each seat 12 to 13 people. They have been set with colorful Provençal tablecloths and napkins—red, green, blue or yellow—white porcelain plates, low flower arrangements and candles. There is a handwritten menu, which also serves as a place card, at each setting. In winter, a fire has been lit in the living room; in late spring and summer, when it stays light until 10:00, the French doors leading out onto the balcony are wide open. A tall, extravagant vase of flowers—gladiolas in the fall, tulips and irises in the winter, daisies, roses, hollyhocks and lilies in the spring—decorates the mantle above the fireplace in the living room.

The group is an ever-changing one, although there are many "regulars." Some are French, more are American, and there is usually a smattering of other nationalities. But the mix is always interesting, and my guests all seem to have one thing in common: congeniality. They've heard about my Supper Club through friends who have come, or I've invited them, and they pay what is called here a "participation."

Supper Club Chez Martha is unique; it isn't a dinner party—nobody is obligated to be there—and it isn't a restaurant; it's not open to the public, and the "participation" just covers the cost of the food and wine. It is a soiree, and people choose to come and keep returning because it is a marvelous meeting ground and because of the food, which is never the same from one dinner to the next. The French are fascinated by the concept of the supper club and always tell me what an American phenomenon it is; yet it is not too different from the old-fashioned salon.

I first had the idea for a Supper Club in 1973, when I was living in Austin, Texas, and had decided to make a career out of cooking. The two things I loved to do best were to give parties and cook. I didn't want to open a restaurant—too risky—but I needed to cook for people and expand my repertoire. The Supper Club would allow me to do these things.

I called it Martha's Moon House Supper Club because my house had a big crescent-moon window in the wooden front door. In those days, I did the dinners once a week for 35 people, and they sat on the floor at long, low tables. They paid $1.50 (some paid with food stamps); most of us were hippies and poor in those halcyon days. I operated this Supper

Club for two years and then had to move out of my house and into a smaller one. I didn't have the space for a large group anymore. At that point, I began catering and put the Supper Club away. But I always missed it and hoped that I would be able to start another one.

The notion came alive again when I came to Paris. Supper Club Chez Martha was small at first —only 14 or 15 people. But it caught on so quickly that I had a large table with benches built and arranged my apartment so that the big dining room and the library could each accommodate tables for 12 to 14 people (once I even did a sit-down Thanksgiving dinner for 40).

In September and in January, I send out announcements for the opening of the "season" to everyone on my ever-expanding mailing list, with the dates of the dinners. I urge everyone to call for reservations as soon as possible because the dinners fill up quickly.

I spend a week or two working on the menus and testing recipes. I walk around the city with the menu on my mind, scouting markets, composing plates in my imagination, thinking about combinations of courses. I consider colors, textures and the balance of the meal and always take into account time requirements; cooking for 25 people is not like cooking for 4 to 6, and certain dishes just aren't feasible, even with an assistant. And because I am both hostess and cook, I can't choose dishes that require lots of last-minute preparation or supervision.

Sometimes my meals have a seasonal or an ethnic theme (I am known for my Mexican food and always kick off the season with a Mexican or Tex-Mex meal); sometimes they are Provençal in character; sometimes I'll take a French idea and give the menu an American twist.

Always, my cuisine is healthy and seasonal, inspired by the best products the gorgeous Paris markets have to offer.

The weekend before my dinner, I make lists. I have a notebook for shopping lists and make up a preparation schedule, which I post in my kitchen, so that I can check things off as I get them done. I begin preparations on Monday, xeroxing menus and doing whatever supermarket shopping is necessary, but the real push begins on Tuesday. I go from market to market, searching out ingredients and good buys, and begin, with the help of my assistant, any preparation that can be begun this far in advance. Marketing and preparation continue on Wednesday; that's the day I order my fish, if fish is on the menu, to be picked up early Thursday morning. In the evenings, I work on the seating plans.

Thursday is a nonstop day for my assistant and me in the kitchen. If I am ahead in the morning, I'll work very slowly so that I will have to rush in the afternoon. I seem to thrive on a certain amount of tension; there is something inside of me that wants to rush towards the end.

But by 7:00 or 7:15, I'm out of the kitchen. The next 45 minutes is my quiet time, and it's essential. I take a hot bath and retreat to my bedroom, where I close the door and curtains, unplug the phone, turn off the lights and lie on my back on the floor, my legs over my head. I close my eyes, breathe deeply and let go of the day's tension. In a way, I forget that I was in the kitchen all day. Then I get dressed and go out and join my second assistant, who arrives at 8:00 to help serve, wash dishes and prepare the plates for the first course.

This last half hour is a bit crazed with final details. I set out the menu place cards, making any necessary last-minute changes. My assistant sets out small bowls with radish roses and olives. I prepare the ice bucket and open the aperitif wine or mix up the margaritas if it's a Mexican meal. I explain to my assistant how I want the plates to look for the first course, and he or she begins to uncork wine for the dinner and to cut bread, which goes into pretty napkin-lined baskets.

Then the doorbell begins to ring (if anybody comes early, I make them work): it's show time. I move into my hostess mode, and for the next hour, I'm running track between the kitchen, front door and living room, constantly putting on and taking off my apron, as if I were doing quick costume changes between scenes. Every time the doorbell rings, I wonder, "Who will it be?" The guests bring me new energy; it really is as if somebody else had spent all day in the kitchen. During the cocktail hour, I am busy making introductions and filling glasses, but everybody makes it so easy by being curious and nice. Maybe it's because many of my guests are foreigners who share a passion for the city. "You spend your first year in Paris figuring out how to work it so that you can spend the rest of your life here," I once overheard one of my guests say; she was a woman who has lived here for over 30 years. People are always running into friends and acquaintances from other spheres of their lives, and even making professional connections. The rooms buzz with talk and fun.

By the time everybody has had a drink or two, they are so engaged in conversation that, hungry as they are, they refuse to be torn away from each other. But eventually, they do find their seats at the table, and a new phase of the party—the dinner—begins. I always have as good a time as my guests. I sit at the head of the table in the dining room, only disappearing between courses to do last-minute touches in the kitchen, while my assistant clears the plates. I warn my dinner partners that they will have to put up with my comings and goings, and while I'm in the kitchen, I listen for the crescendo of table talk and laughter, signs that the dinner is a success.

The meals consist of three courses, and I serve a wine that will go with both the first and main dish. The first course is usually some kind of salad, attractively composed on individual plates, which are set at each place before we sit down. We sometimes serve the main course and dessert from the buffet in the dining room and sometimes make up the plates in the kitchen. After dessert, I serve coffee and "infusion" (herb tea: verbena or mint) in the living room. This is phase three of the evening: more mingling. People stay until the last metro, at about 12:30, although some soirees have gone on much later. Before they leave, many guests exchange telephone numbers and addresses. An ever-expanding network of friends is growing out of my Supper Club, and it's been heartwarming to see it begin around my tables.

Come to Your Own Party

MY PARIS APARTMENT has provided the setting for all sorts of events over the last five years, not just Supper Club Chez Martha. There have been innumerable cocktail parties, small dinner parties, brunches and New Year's Eve extravaganzas. Sometimes when I want to give a big party but don't have time to do a lot of cooking, I ask people to bring things to eat, but I always manage to pull off some kind of a buffet. Giving a party is a performance, with a curtain time, a stage set and an audience. It's show biz, it's in my blood, and it's irresistible.

No matter how large or small your guest list, successful entertaining depends on a few simple rules. The most important one is organization. You can't be too organized. Make lists.

Try to do as much as possible in advance. Set tables or prepare the buffet the night before. Even if you fall behind in the kitchen, there is something very reassuring, even calming, about tables that are beautifully set and waiting. Before the guests arrive, set out bowls of radishes and olives or an attractive platter of crudités, so that they'll have something to nibble on even before the first course. Open a good bottle of wine.

Choose menus that don't involve too much last-minute preparation. Otherwise, you'll be in the kitchen the whole time, and your guests will never see you. You will notice that my menus all include dishes that will hold and can be reheated at the last minute or whose final cooking is unsupervised, like Baked Fish Fillets With Salsa Fresca (page 52), lasagna (page 88) and cannelloni (page 125). During summer months, many of my main dishes are cold, so all of the cooking is done in advance. I have noted throughout what can be done ahead of time. You will also find that for the most part, the dishes are not too labor-intensive. That's because the recipes have been multiplied by 3 or 4 for my dinners. I've included other recipes for 4 or 6 that aren't feasible for large groups in the "Menus From Small Dinner Parties" (page 215). The most important thing to take into consideration when you are feeding a crowd is that you will need more time for preparation of the ingredients: whatever you are multiplying the recipe by, figure on that much more time for cutting and chopping. Do as much ahead of time as possible and organize your refrigerator so that you'll have more storage space.

Once you've got the practical matters taken care

of, what are the secrets of being the host or hostess once the evening gets under way? I think that the most important duty is making introductions. I'm always annoyed when I go to a party and the host doesn't fulfill this function. It doesn't take much, but people have to have a springboard from which to jump into conversation. Even if you don't know your guests well, you probably know at least one thing about each of them, like where they're from or what they do. Mention that one thing and let it be the hook.

If you're throwing a really big party, you need to think about how you're going to keep the place in order. Remember to tuck trash cans or boxes with heavy garbage bags away under tables, so that empty bottles and paper plates can be quickly disposed of. If you can possibly hire somebody to help with this, do so. It's too depressing to see a beautiful setting strewn with empty bottles, used paper plates and glasses halfway into a party. All you need to do is make a few rounds every hour or so to keep it under control.

Finally, try to set aside at least a half hour for yourself, before everybody arrives. This time is invaluable for me, even if I sometimes have to rush in the kitchen to get it. If you're hurrying right up until the last minute, you'll have no time to regain your composure, and you'll need that once the party gets under way.

Seating Plans

I DEVOTE HOURS each month to my seating plans. It's always a challenge, mostly because I've got two long tables, each with 12 to 13 people, to deal with. If the tables were round, it would be easier. I have to consider overall configurations, as well as who sits next to whom.

First, I picture the whole group and try to imagine what the dynamic will be. Are they mostly high-energy, fun people? Are there many shy people? (Usually not.) Will there be a big crowd of journalists tonight, or photographers, or musicians? Sometimes there are a lot of newcomers on the list, but usually half the guests are old friends. I think about people who might enjoy each other's company. Then I make a diagram of the table, cut out strips of paper with guests' names on them and start moving the strips around. Often there will be several people in the same profession or overlapping professions, and I'll try to place them near each other. I try to make sure that each table has a few dynamic people, good conversationalists who can talk to anyone. Then there is the language consideration. Almost all the Americans who have lived here for a while speak French, but not all the French people who come to my dinners speak English. I have to make sure that nobody has a dinner partner with whom he or she can't converse.

I try to seat guests who are coming for the first time and don't know anybody near me, unless they are being brought by friends. Then I'll usually seat the members of the party near each other. However, I often split up couples. For one thing, there is always a shortage of men at my dinners, and I try to sprinkle them somewhat evenly among the tables.

Inevitably, I'll get a cancellation or two on Thursday that will mess up my whole arrangement. Perhaps I've placed two people next to each other who have a lot in common, and one of them gets sick. It's usually not too difficult to find replacements, but I have to redo the seating plan. Once I got a last-minute reservation from two men on a night when we happened to have a larger-than-usual surplus of women. I changed the entire seating plan about an hour before the dinner, and then one of the men called me to ask if I was serving anything with cheese in it, as he was deathly allergic. Wouldn't you know that on this night, I had made my spinach lasagna! He cancelled. But faced with having to change the table configuration again (and wanting the extra man), I called him back and offered to make a special dish for him, since nothing but the lasagna contained cheese. Happily, he came after all. This kind of thing happens all the time.

About My Cuisine

Because I live and cook in France, most people assume that I focus on French cuisine. But that isn't really the case. My first year here, I sat in on some cooking classes at La Varenne and Le Cordon Bleu, but not for very long. The fact is, cooking with large quantities of butter, sugar and meat just doesn't interest me. I appreciate haute French cuisine, but I can't handle eating it very often. And since I love to sit down with my guests and indulge in a full plate of food, I cook the kind of food I love to eat.

What I am passionate about is Provençal and other Mediterranean cuisines, which rely on a bounty of vegetables, grains and legumes, fish, olive oil and lots of herbs and garlic. And I'll always love cooking Mexican food, a legacy from the years I lived in Texas. This isn't to say that you won't find some traditional French dishes here, but I always try to reduce the fat and sugar. I use low-fat milk in custard sauces (crème anglaise), for example, and use less sugar than the French would use. I substitute olive oil for butter whenever I can get away with it in cooking and rarely use cream. I tend to use goat cheese more than most other kinds of cheese (except Parmesan, which I also use a lot). I love goat cheese's distinctive, earthy taste and find that a little goes a long way.

As you work through the recipes in this book, you will see that I am an eclectic cook who loves garlic, olive oil (kept at a minimum), vibrant flavors and bright colors: substantial food that will leave you feeling wholesome, healthy and happy.

How to Plan a Balanced, Low-Fat Menu

A low-fat menu doesn't have to be an ascetic menu. The most important thing to think about is balance: if the dessert is rich, make sure the first course and the main dish are light. Dishes can be low in fat and still be hearty. The Provençal-Style Fish Chowder on page 117, for example, serves 6 and has only 2 tablespoons of olive oil in it, yet it's quite filling and substantial, with all the vegetables and fish. It is preceded by a salad with goat cheese (but the cheese slices are thinner than they would be in a traditional dish of the same kind) and followed by Pear Crisp With Ginger Crème Anglaise, which, although lighter than a typical version made with cream or whole milk, is still relatively high in fat and cholesterol. The rich dessert and salad with cheese are counterbalanced by the low-fat, low-cholesterol soup. Similarly, the substantial first course of Black Bean Nachos and Tomatoes Stuffed With Guacamole in the September menu on page 47 are followed by a light main dish of Baked Fish Fillets With Salsa Fresca, and a low-fat sorbet (with higher-fat cookies).

Planning low-fat menus won't pose a problem if you concentrate on fish and vegetables for your main courses with vegetable-based sauces, use a light hand on the olive oil, and serve fruit-based desserts. It's when you get into heavy meats and butter-and-cream sauces that calories and fat can get out of hand.

How to Cook Using a Minimum of Fat

Most recipes call for more fat than is actually necessary for sautéing vegetables or browning meat. One to two tablespoons usually suffice if you use a nonstick or heavy-bottomed saucepan or frying pan. Heat the oil over medium-low heat. Add the vegetables and cook, stirring often, according to the recipe. If they begin to stick, add a little water or wine to the frying pan.

Special Considerations

Increasing recipes for large groups:

With the exception of some of the dishes in the last section of this book, I have made all of the recipes for up to 25 people (and in the case of Mexican food, for 150). All of them can be easily increased up to 35 by multiplying quantities in the recipe by the appropriate factor. (Once you get beyond 35, the factor changes, but it's not within the scope of this book to deal with that.) For 25 people, I multiply by 3, 4 or 5, depending on whether the recipe feeds 4, 6 or 8. If a recipe feeds 6 to 8, I would rather err on the side of more and will multiply by 4 rather than 3; however, if I note that a recipe feeds 6 to 8 "generously," multiplying by 3 suffices.

A note on the metric equivalents in these recipes:

For the purposes of this book, 2 pounds corresponds to 1 kilo (kg); ½ pound to 250 grams; and ¾ pound to 350 grams. In reality, 1 pound equals 455 grams, but when you are marketing in a European market, you wouldn't ask for 455 grams of, say, apples, you'd ask for ½ kilo. Exact weights, rather than approximate ones, are given in some pastry recipes, where measures have to be exact.

A note on honey:

Very few of my dishes are sweetened with sugar; I have always worked with honey. It's important, though, to find a mild-flavored honey, or the flavor will overpower the dish. Mild honeys are lighter in color than strong-flavored types. I recommend acacia or clover as the best all-around types. If you can't find a light honey, substitute sugar or brown sugar.

A note on crème fraîche:

I usually use fromage blanc instead of crème fraîche because the fat content is so much lower. However, where crème fraîche is called for in these recipes, it's because I have found no suitable substitute.

Crème fraîche can be found in many specialty food stores or can be made at home. To make crème fraîche: Stir 1 tablespoon buttermilk into 1 cup (225 ml heavy cream. Cover loosely with plastic and let stand at room temperature for several hours or overnight, until thick and slightly sour. Cover tightly and refrigerate another 4 hours before using. This will keep for several days in the refrigerator.

Part One

SUPPER CLUB
MENUS

Some Basics:
Breads, Pasta and Piecrusts

❦

Sourdough Country Bread

Sourdough Country Bread With Cornmeal and Oats or Bran

Sourdough Country Bread With Raisins

Country Rye Bread With Raisins

Millet and Cornmeal Bread

Mixed-Grains Bread

Cumin and Cornmeal Bread

Sourdough Baguettes

Herbed Whole-Wheat Bread

Country Bread With Olives

Pesto Bread

Texas Cornbread

Homemade Pasta

Whole-Wheat Piecrusts

Homemade Tortillas

Blini

Garlic Croutons

Some Basics: Breads, Pasta and Piecrusts

THESE ARE THE RECIPES that come up repeatedly: breads, pasta and piecrusts. Bread has always been my mainstay, and I never tire of making it. Even though I make the same kinds over and over again, the experience is never the same. I always have Sourdough Country Bread and Mixed-Grains Bread on hand. When I plan my Supper Club menus, I choose a bread that will go with the spirit of the meal: thus, Pesto Bread with the December lasagna dinner, Cumin and Cornmeal Bread with Mexican food, Mixed-Grains Bread for November and Thanksgiving dinners. You might want to try different breads than the ones I've suggested with these menus.

My whole-wheat piecrusts are crumbly and light, not like the cardboard crusts that got vegetarianism off to such a bad start in the early '70s. They aren't as easy to roll out as white-flour crusts, but the extra labor is worth it. The resulting crusts have a rich, nutty taste that I prefer to their refined counterparts.

When I make pasta, I always use part whole-grain (whole-wheat or buckwheat) flour. Like the piecrusts, pasta containing whole-grain flours has a nutty taste. I love the deep green color of spinach pasta and the delicate flecks of green in herb pastas. The more you make pasta, the easier it gets, so that eventually you will think nothing of an impromptu dinner of homemade fettuccine and the sauce of your choice.

A note on freezing bread:
It's best to double-wrap bread before freezing. Allow to cool completely. Wrap first in either plastic wrap or foil, then in foil or plastic bags.

Sourdough Country Bread

❀

THIS VERSATILE BREAD is the one I most often serve at my Supper Club. It has a very hard crust and a tart, earthy flavor and is chewy and dense, with great staying power.

I have three people to thank for getting me going with this recipe. First, Lionel Poilane, who supplies Paris with thousands of loaves of his *pain de campagne* every day; his is made with a more refined flour. The bread is somewhere between whole wheat and white, and I love it for its sour taste, hard crust and moist, chewy texture. Then, Lionel's brother Max, who let me work in his bakery for a month during my first year here. It was there that I began to understand that the dough should be quite wet. And finally, Patricia Wells, for working out a recipe for Poilane's *chef*, or sourdough leavener, which is the only leavener used in real French country bread. Unlike most sourdough starters, the *chef* isn't runny but is more like a spongy dough. I have frozen the *chef*, carried it with me unfrozen from place to place—from Paris to America, from Paris to Yugoslavia in a car and from Yugoslavia back to Italy, to Provence and, finally, home to Paris. Sometimes I use it alone to make authentic *pain de campagne*, which rises for 8 to 12 hours, never gets airy and has a marvelous sour taste. I've combined it with yeast in this version to make a faster-rising, puffier bread that still has the denseness and the sour flavor.

FOR THE STARTER

THE FIRST DAY

⅓ cup (80 ml) water
1 cup (115 g) flour, whole-wheat or unbleached white

AFTER 72 HOURS

½ cup (120 ml) lukewarm water
1 ½ cups (170 g) whole-wheat or unbleached white flour

FOR THE BREAD

All of the sourdough starter

2 cups (450 ml) lukewarm water or 1 cup (225 ml) lukewarm water plus 1 cup (225 ml) coffee
1 scant tablespoon (1 envelope) active dry yeast
1 tablespoon blackstrap molasses (optional)
1 scant tablespoon salt
4 ½ to 5 cups (515 to 575 g) whole-wheat flour
   Cornmeal for the baking sheet

The first day: Mix together the water and flour and knead into a smooth ball on a floured work surface. The dough should be soft and sticky. Flour your hands so you can work with it. Return it to the bowl, cover with a damp towel, and let sit at room temperature for 72 hours. The dough will form a crust on the top and turn a grayish color, which is normal. If you keep wetting the towel, it will reduce the drying. The dough will rise slightly and take on an acidic aroma.

After 72 hours: Add the water to the bowl and blend together. If the crust on the top is like cardboard or wood, you will have to peel it off and discard it. (Try blending it before you resort to this.) Add the flour and stir to blend. Transfer the dough to a floured work surface and knead into a smooth ball.

Return it to the bowl, cover with a damp towel, and let sit in a warm place for 24 to 48 hours. Again, a crust may form on the top. If it is like cardboard or wood, peel it off and discard before proceeding with the recipe.

Mixing the dough by hand: Combine the sourdough starter, the water or the water-coffee mixture and the yeast. Whisk together until the starter and yeast are thoroughly dissolved. Whisk in the molasses and the salt.

Fold in the whole-wheat flour, 1 cup (115 g) at a time. By the time you have added 4 cups (455 g), you should be able to knead. I usually do this right in the bowl, as the dough is sticky and unwieldy. Using a pastry scraper instead of your hands to fold the dough for kneading will help. Knead for 10 minutes, adding flour as necessary.

Mixing the dough in an electric mixer: Combine the sourdough starter, the water or water-coffee mixture, the yeast and the molasses in the bowl of your electric mixer. Use the mixer attachment (not the dough hook and not the wire whip) to combine these ingredients. When the starter and the yeast are thoroughly dissolved, add the salt and 4 cups (455 g) of the whole-wheat flour all at once. Mix together briefly, using the mixing attachment, until everything is amalgamated. Then scrape off the mixing attachment and replace it with the dough hook. Knead at a low speed for 10 minutes, adding up to 1 cup (115 g) of flour if the dough seems very liquid (it should be sticky).

Rising, forming the loaf, baking: Cover the dough and let rise in a warm spot for 1 ½ hours. Flour your hands and wrists and punch down the dough. Knead for 2 or 3 minutes on a lightly floured surface, using a pastry scraper to make it easier. Remove 1 cup of the dough and place in a bowl to use as a starter for your next loaf of bread. Cover the starter and refrigerate after a few hours, if not using again in a day's time.

Dust a clean, dry towel with flour and line a bowl or basket. Form the dough into a ball, dust the surface with flour, and place, rounded side down, in the towel-lined bowl or basket. Cover with a towel and let rise in a warm spot for 1 ½ to 2 hours, until almost doubled in bulk. You can also let the dough rise in the refrigerator for several hours or overnight.

Preheat the oven to 400° F (200° C). Place an empty pan on the bottom shelf of the oven. When the oven is heated, pour 2 cups (450 ml) water into the pan; the steam will help give the bread a thick, hard crust. Turn the dough out onto an unoiled baking sheet (or preferably a baking stone) dusted with cornmeal, peel off the towel and slash the dough with a sharp knife or a razor. Place it in the oven and bake 45 minutes, until it is brown and responds to tapping with a hollow thumping sound. Remove from the oven and cool on a rack.

MAKES 1 LARGE LOAF

Sourdough Country Bread
With Cornmeal and Oats or Bran

❧

THIS IS THE BREAD I most often made in Yugoslavia and Italy when I traveled to these countries during the summer of '85. I had brought my sourdough along, but not enough whole-wheat flour to make more than one big loaf, and as there were five of us, one loaf went quickly. I like a bread with a lot of texture and substance, so I used whatever grains I could find to make up for the absence of whole-wheat flour. These turned out to be polenta and oats. Later, I got the idea of incorporating bran into the bread.

Follow the preceding recipe for Sourdough Country Bread, using the same sourdough starter. Substitute 1 cup (115 g) bran or rolled oats and 1 cup (140 g) cornmeal for 2 cups (225 g) of the whole-wheat flour that is mixed into the dough at the end. Proceed with the recipe.

MAKES 1 LOAF

Sourdough Country Bread With Raisins

✾

THE SWEETNESS and abundance of the raisins make a great contrast with the sour bread. The bread was inspired by Lionel Poilane's dense rye-raisin rolls. My frequent cravings for these rolls are easy to satisfy because his beautiful rue du Cherche-Midi bakery is a half block from my apartment.

See recipe for Sourdough Country Bread (page 26). Substitute 1 ½ cups (170 g) rye flour for 1 ½ cups (170 g) of the whole-wheat flour that is added to the starter after 72 hours.

When forming the loaf, knead in 2 cups (340 g) raisins. Proceed with the recipe.

MAKES 1 LARGE LOAF

Country Rye Bread With Raisins

✾

LESS ACIDIC than the bread of the previous recipe, this rye-raisin loaf takes 2 ½ or 3 days from start to finish. If you begin the starter in the afternoon or evening, you will mix up the sponge the following evening and finish the bread the next day. If you mix the starter in the morning, you will mix the sponge the following morning and finish the bread that night.

FOR THE STARTER

1 teaspoon active dry yeast
1 cup (225 ml) lukewarm water
1 cup (115 g) rye flour

FOR THE SPONGE

All of the starter
1 ¼ cups (285 ml) lukewarm water
2 tablespoons molasses
1 cup (115 g) unbleached white flour
1 ½ cups (170 g) rye flour

FOR THE DOUGH

All of the sponge
½ cup (120 ml) lukewarm water
1 tablespoon salt
1 cup (115 g) whole-wheat flour
2 cups (225 g) rye flour

1 cup (115 g) unbleached white flour, as needed

FOR THE LOAVES

All of the dough
1 pound (500 g) raisins or currants
1 egg yolk, beaten with 1 tablespoon water or milk

Day 1: Making the starter: In a small bowl, dissolve the yeast in the water and whisk in the rye flour. Combine well, cover with plastic wrap, and set in a draft-free spot to rise for 24 hours.

Day 2: Mixing up the sponge: Stir down the starter and scrape it into a bread bowl. Whisk in the water, molasses, the unbleached flour and the rye flour. Blend well, cover with plastic wrap, and set the bowl in a draft-free place for 12 hours.

Day 3: Mixing up the dough, final rising, baking: Fold the lukewarm water, the salt, the whole-wheat flour and 1 cup (115 g) of the rye flour into the dough. Fold in the additional rye flour, ½ cup (55 g) at a time, until the dough can be turned out of the bowl in more or less one piece. Place ½ cup (55 g) unbleached white flour on your kneading surface and scrape out the dough. The dough will be very sticky. Flour your hands well. If the dough is too sticky to handle, use a pastry scraper instead of your hands to fold the dough for kneading. Knead for about 10 minutes, adding unbleached white flour by the handful, as necessary. After about 5 minutes, the dough should give up some of its stickiness and become easier to work with.

Wash out and oil your bowl. Shape the dough into a ball and place in the oiled bowl, seam side up first, then seam side down. Cover with plastic wrap and set in a warm place to rise for 1 hour.

Punch down the dough and turn onto a well-floured work surface. Press out to a 1-inch thickness and spread the raisins or currants over the surface. Fold the dough over and knead several times until they are evenly distributed.

Divide the dough into 3 equal pieces (or for rolls, see note below). Shape into round balls and place on a large, oiled baking sheet. Cover with wax paper or a towel and set in a warm place to rise for 30 minutes. Meanwhile, preheat the oven to 400° F (200° C).

Uncover the loaves, and using a razor blade or a thin, sharp knife, make 2 intersecting Xs across the top of each loaf, so that 8 intersecting lines radiate out from the center like a star. Brush with the eggwash and place in the preheated oven. Bake 45 to 50 minutes, turning the baking sheet around and brushing once more with the egg beaten with the water or milk halfway through the baking.

When the bottom crusts respond to tapping with a hollow thump, remove the loaves from the oven and cool on racks.

MAKES 2 LARGE LOAVES OR 3 SMALLER LOAVES

Note: For rolls: Divide the dough into 2-ounce (55 g) pieces and roll into balls. Place on oiled baking sheets, cover with wax paper and let rise about 1 hour, until doubled in size. Preheat the oven about 20 minutes before baking.

Brush the rolls with egg beaten with water or milk and slash an X across the tops. Bake 25 to 30 minutes, turning the sheets around and brushing again halfway through the baking. Cool on racks or eat while still warm.

Millet and Cornmeal Bread

֎

THIS LOVELY, slightly golden-colored bread is a lot like my Mixed-Grains Bread, but more crumbly. It has a rich, grainy texture.

'FOR THE SPONGE

1   scant tablespoon (1 envelope) active dry
    yeast
3   cups (700 ml) lukewarm water
3   tablespoons mild-flavored honey
2   cups (225 g) unbleached white flour
2   cups (225 g) whole-wheat flour

FOR THE DOUGH

¼   cup (60 ml) safflower oil or melted butter
1   scant tablespoon salt
¾   cup (85 g) rolled oats

1 ½   cups (225 g) ground millet
1   cup (140 g) stoneground cornmeal
2 to 3   cups (225 g to 340 g) whole-wheat flour, as
    necessary

FOR THE LOAVES

1   egg, beaten with 1 tablespoon water
2   tablespoons sesame seeds

Making the sponge: Dissolve the yeast in the warm water in a large bowl. Stir in the honey. Stir in the white and whole-wheat flours, 1 cup (115 g) at a time, and whisk the mixture until smooth, about 100 times. Cover with plastic wrap or a damp towel and set in a warm place to rise for 1 hour.

Mixing the dough and kneading: Fold the oil or

butter and the salt, then the oats, ground millet and cornmeal into the sponge. Begin folding in the whole-wheat flour, 1 cup (115 g) at a time, and as soon as you can turn out the dough, scrape it onto a floured kneading surface. Knead the dough, adding flour as necessary, for 10 minutes, or until stiff and elastic. Wash out and oil your bowl, shape the dough into a ball, and place it in the bowl, seam side up first, then seam side down. Cover and let rise for 1 ½ hours.

Punching down, shaping loaves, baking: Punch down the dough and turn out onto a floured surface. Knead for 1 to 2 minutes, then divide in half and form 2 loaves. Place the loaves in oiled loaf pans, seam side up first, then seam side down. Cover the loaves with a damp towel and let rise in a warm spot for 1 hour, or until the dough rises above the edges of the pans.

During the last 15 minutes of rising, preheat the oven to 350° F (180° C).

Gently brush the loaves with the egg beaten with the water. Sprinkle with sesame seeds, brush again, and slash 3 times across the top with a razor blade or a sharp knife. Bake in the preheated oven for 50 to 60 minutes, brushing again with eggwash halfway through the baking. When the loaves are golden brown and respond to tapping with a hollow thumping sound, remove them from the pans and cool on a rack.

Makes 2 loaves

Mixed-Grains Bread

T HE BREAD that is in my first two cookbooks must be given here because it is my favorite bread, and I still live on it. It is a dense, cakey, slightly sweet, grainy bread, chewy and wholesome. When you eat it, you experience a range of textures and a sweet variation of flavors from the different grains. The only problem I sometimes have with this bread is that it can crumble. When you slice it up for a dinner party, some of the pieces may not look too neat. But this shouldn't matter, since it's a rather rustic bread anyway.

Note: You can vary the grains in this bread, substituting one kind of flake for another; for example, wheat or rye instead of oats, cornmeal for ground millet, chick-pea flour for soy flour.

This bread takes about 5 hours from start to finish, but the dough can be refrigerated after you knead it or punch it down, so you needn't feel tied to the house for all that time.

FOR THE SPONGE

1 scant tablespoon (1 envelope) active dry yeast
3 cups (700 ml) lukewarm water
2 tablespoons mild-flavored honey
2 tablespoons blackstrap molasses
2 cups (225 g) unbleached white flour
2 cups (225 g) whole-wheat flour

FOR THE DOUGH

¼ cup (60 ml) safflower oil
1 tablespoon salt
¾ cup (85 g) oat flakes (may substitute wheat or rye)
¾ cup (130 g) bulgur or cracked wheat
¾ cup (170 g) millet, ground to a flour in a blender, or ¾ cup (115 g) stoneground cornmeal
¾ cup (85 g) soy flour or chick-pea flour
3 cups (340 g) whole-wheat flour, as needed

FOR THE LOAVES

1 egg, beaten with 2 tablespoons water
2 tablespoons sesame seeds

Mixing the sponge: Dissolve the yeast in the warm water in a large bowl. Mix in the honey and molasses. Whisk in the white and whole-wheat flours, 1 cup (115 g) at a time. When all the flour has been added, whisk 100 times, changing directions every once in a while. This really won't take too long. The sponge should have the consistency of thick mud. Cover and set it in a warm place for 1 hour, until bubbly.

Mixing the dough, kneading, first rise: Fold the oil, then the salt into the sponge, using a large wooden spoon and turning the bowl between folds. Fold in the grains, one at a time, and the soy or chick-pea flour.

Now begin folding in the whole-wheat flour. After 2 cups, the dough should hold together in a sticky mass. Place the third cup on your kneading surface and scrape out the dough. Flour your hands and begin kneading the dough. At first, you will have to treat it gingerly, as it is sticky, and you'll have to keep flouring your hands. But after a few minutes, the dough will begin to stiffen and will become easier to work with. Knead, adding more flour as necessary, for 10 minutes. The dough should be elastic and stiff, and the surface slightly tacky. Shape it into a ball. Oil the bowl, place the dough in the bowl, seam side up first, then seam side down. Cover and let rise in a warm spot for 1 hour.

Punching down, shaping loaves, baking: Punch down the dough. At this point, you can cover it, set it in a warm place and let it rise one more time, for 45 to 60 minutes, in the bowl. The extra rise will make a lighter loaf but is not absolutely necessary.

Either with or without the additional rising, turn the dough out onto a lightly floured work surface. Knead it a couple of times and divide the dough roughly in half. Form 2 loaves and place them in oiled 8 x 4 x 3-inch or 9 x 5 x 3-inch loaf pans, seam side up first, then seam side down. Brush the loaves lightly with the beaten egg and water; sprinkle with sesame seeds and brush again. Cover and let rise until the tops of the loaves rise above the edge of the pans. This will take anywhere from 20 to 45 minutes, depending on the weather and the stage at which you shaped the loaves.

When the loaves have risen, preheat the oven to 350° F (180° C). Using a razor blade or a sharp knife, slash the loaves across the top in 3 places and bake on a middle rack for 50 to 60 minutes in the preheated oven. Halfway through the baking, brush again with the eggwash. The bread is done when it is golden brown and responds to tapping with a hollow thumping sound.

Remove from the pans and cool on a rack.

These loaves freeze very well.

MAKES 2 LOAVES

Cumin and Cornmeal Bread

༄

I ALWAYS TRY to serve a bread at my Supper Club that fits in with the spirit of the meal. For my Mexican dinners, I've created this bread, which combines two ingredients that are essential to Mexican cuisine: cumin and cornmeal. This recipe is adapted from one of my herb bread recipes; the dough is moist, and the cornmeal gives the loaf a marvelous grainy texture. The bread has a rich, buttery taste, although there is no butter in it. It's convenient to make because it doesn't require too much rising time.

1 scant tablespoon (1 envelope) active dry yeast
½ cup (120 ml) lukewarm water

1 tablespoon mild-flavored honey
1 cup (225 ml) plain low-fat yogurt, at room temperature
2 large eggs
2 tablespoons safflower oil
1 ½ teaspoons salt
2 tablespoons cumin seeds
1 cup (140 g) stoneground cornmeal
3 cups (340 g) whole-wheat flour
   Unbleached flour, as necessary, for kneading

Dissolve the yeast in the warm water in a large bowl. Stir in the honey and let sit 10 minutes. Add the yogurt, 1 egg, safflower oil, salt and cumin seeds

Black Bean Nachos
page 50

Baked Fish Fillets With Salsa Fresca
page 52

Mixed Plum and Apricot Tart
page 160

36

Herbed Whole-Wheat Bread

THIS SAVORY BREAD is very easy to make. It goes well with Mediterranean dishes.

1   scant tablespoon (1 envelope) active dry yeast
2   cups (450 ml) lukewarm water
1   tablespoon mild-flavored honey
5   tablespoons safflower oil
1   small onion, minced
1   clove garlic, minced or put through a press
1   cup (225 ml) plain low-fat yogurt, at room temperature
1   scant tablespoon salt
2   teaspoons dried thyme
2   tablespoons dried dill weed
2   teaspoons dried sage
6   cups (680 g) whole-wheat flour
2   cups (225 g) unbleached white flour, plus additional for kneading
1   egg, beaten with 2 tablespoons water
    Dill seeds (optional)

Dissolve the yeast in the lukewarm water in a large bowl. Add the honey and let sit for 5 minutes. Meanwhile, heat 1 tablespoon of the safflower oil in a skillet and sauté the onion with the garlic, stirring over medium-low heat until the onion is tender. Remove from the heat.

Stir the yogurt into the yeast mixture, then add the remaining 4 tablespoons safflower oil, the salt, thyme, dill weed and sage. Stir in the sautéed onion and garlic. Whisk in 3 cups (340 g) of the whole-wheat flour and fold in the rest, 1 cup (115 g) at a time. Fold in 1 cup (115 g) unbleached white flour and place the remaining 1 cup (115 g) on your kneading surface. Scrape the dough out onto your kneading surface (you can also knead in the bowl if the dough is too sticky). Knead for 10 minutes, flouring your hands often and using a pastry scraper to scrape up and fold over the dough if it is sticky and hard to work with. When the dough is stiff and elastic, knead it into a ball, wash out and oil your bowl and place the dough in it, seam side up first, then seam side down. Cover with a damp towel or plastic wrap and set in a warm spot to rise for 1 ½ hours, or until doubled in bulk.

Punch down the dough and turn it out onto a lightly floured kneading surface. Oil 2 loaf pans. Knead the dough for a minute or two, cut into 2 equal pieces, and form each piece into a ball. Then roll each ball into a loaf shape, and place the loaves in the oiled loaf pans, seam side up first, then seam side down. Cover with a damp towel and set in a warm place to rise until doubled in bulk, or until the dough rises above the edges of the pans, about 1 hour.

Twenty minutes before you wish to bake, preheat the oven to 375° F (190° C). Brush the loaves gently with the egg beaten with the water, then sprinkle with the optional dill seeds. Brush again, slash the loaves and place in the preheated oven. Bake 45 to 50 minutes, or until they are golden brown and respond to tapping with a hollow thumping sound. Remove from the pans and cool on a rack.

MAKES 2 LOAVES

Country Bread With Olives

❀

THIS BREAD (pictured on page 33) is slightly different from my other Sourdough Country Bread (page 26), in that it is less acidic and a little lighter. You can also make olive bread using that recipe. Just add the olives when you form the loaves, as instructed here.

This is a 3-day bread. You mix the starter on the first day, the sponge on the second and the dough on the third.

FOR THE STARTER

1 scant tablespoon (1 envelope) active dry yeast
1 cup (225 ml) lukewarm water
1 cup (115 g) whole-wheat flour

FOR THE SPONGE

All of the starter
2 cups (450 ml) lukewarm water
3 cups (340 g) whole-wheat flour

FOR THE DOUGH

All of the sponge
1 scant tablespoon salt
3 cups (340 g) whole-wheat flour
Up to 2 cups (225 g) unbleached white flour, as necessary
½ pound (250 g) imported Provençal or Greek olives, pitted and halved or roughly chopped

Day 1: Mixing the starter: Two days before you wish to bake, dissolve the yeast in the water in a bowl and stir in the whole-wheat flour. Mix thoroughly, cover with plastic wrap, and set in a draft-free place for 24 hours.

Day 2: Mixing the sponge: Stir the water into the starter. Whisk in the whole-wheat flour, 1 cup (115 g) at a time. Mix well, cover again, and set in a draft-free place for another 24 hours.

Day 3: Mixing the dough, kneading, rising, shaping, baking: Fold the salt into the sponge, then the whole-wheat flour, 1 cup (115 g) at a time. By the time you add the third cup, you should be able to turn the dough out onto a floured surface. Place ½ cup (55 g) unbleached white flour on your kneading surface and scrape the dough out of the bowl. Knead, flouring your hands often and adding unbleached flour to the kneading surface, for 10 minutes, or until the dough is elastic. It will be sticky, and it will help if you use a pastry scraper to turn the dough. Shape the dough into a ball, wash out and oil your bowl, and place the dough in it, seam side up first, then seam side down. Cover and let rise in a warm place for 1 ½ hours, until doubled in bulk.

Punch the dough down and turn it out onto a lightly floured board. Spread the olives over the surface of the dough, fold the dough in half, and knead for a couple of minutes, until the olives are evenly distributed throughout the dough. Divide the dough in half, if making 2 loaves, and shape into balls, or shape into 1 large ball. Place in baskets or bowls lined with generously floured dishtowels, cover lightly with a dish towel, and let rise for about 2 hours, until doubled in bulk.

Thirty minutes before the end of the rising, preheat the oven to 400° F (200° C) and heat baking stones or a baking sheet in the oven. Also heat an empty pan on a lower rack. Dust your baking stones or sheet with cornmeal and carefully reverse the loaf or loaves onto it. Slash the loaves across the top with a razor blade or a sharp knife and slide them into the preheated oven. Pour 2 cups (450 ml) water into the hot pan, close the oven door, and bake for 50 to 60 minutes, until the bread is dark brown and responds to tapping with a hollow thumping sound. Remove from the oven and cool on a rack.

MAKES 1 LARGE LOAF OR 2 SMALL LOAVES

Pesto Bread

THIS IS INSPIRED by Carol Field's Pesto Bread, which I came across in her lovely book, *The Italian Baker* (Harper & Row, 1985). When I read her recipe, my mouth began to water, as I imagined accompanying an Italian meal with this rich bread. In principle, I like to save my pesto for pasta; I make batches of it every summer and freeze it for winter meals. So in a way, I was a little reluctant to give up some of my precious basil paste for bread; yet I couldn't resist trying the recipe. I have changed Carol Field's version slightly, substituting whole-wheat flour for some of the unbleached white and reducing the oil.

½   cup (100 g) pesto (page 230)
¼   cup (30 g) freshly grated Parmesan
1   scant tablespoon (1 envelope) active dry
      yeast
1   cup (225 ml) plus 2 tablespoons lukewarm
      water
1   tablespoon safflower oil
2   teaspoons salt
2   cups (225 g) whole-wheat flour
2   cups (225 g) unbleached white flour, plus
      additional for kneading
      Cornmeal (optional)

First make the pesto. Stir in the additional ¼ cup Parmesan.

Dissolve the yeast in the water and let sit for 10 minutes. Stir in the pesto and combine thoroughly. Add the safflower oil and salt, and fold in the whole-wheat flour. Fold in the unbleached white flour and turn the dough onto a lightly floured surface.

Knead for 10 minutes, or until the dough is smooth and elastic (this can also be done in a mixer). Shape into a ball.

Wash out your bowl, lightly oil it, and place the dough in it, seam side up first, then seam side down. Cover and let rise in a warm place for about 1 ½ hours, or until doubled in bulk.

Punch down the dough and divide into 2 equal pieces. Knead each piece briefly and shape into a tight round loaf. If you are going to bake on baking stones, first place the dough on a baking sheet sprinkled with cornmeal; otherwise, place it on an oiled baking sheet sprinkled with cornmeal. Cover and let rise in a warm place for 45 minutes to 1 hour, until doubled in bulk.

Preheat the oven to 450° F (230° C). If using baking stones, heat the stones in the oven for 30 minutes and sprinkle with cornmeal just before you slide the loaves onto them. Slash the loaves with a razor blade or a sharp knife and slide them onto the hot stones, or if you are baking on the baking sheet that the loaves have risen on, place this in the oven. Turn down the heat to 400°F (200° C) and spray the loaves with water 3 times in the first 10 minutes. Bake 40 minutes, until the loaves are a deep brown color and respond to tapping with a hollow thumping sound. Remove from the oven and cool on a rack.

MAKES 2 SMALL LOAVES

Texas Cornbread

THIS IS OBVIOUSLY a dish I brought with me to France, and it is one that I'm often inspired to make. The French love it, and so do I. It goes very well with many of the soups and salads I serve. I usually serve it with my Provençal-Style Fish Chowder (page 117).

1 cup (140 g) stoneground cornmeal
½ cup (55 g) whole-wheat flour
1 tablespoon baking powder
¾ teaspoon salt
½ teaspoon baking soda
1 cup (225 ml) plain low-fat yogurt or buttermilk
½ cup (120 ml) low-fat milk
1 tablespoon mild-flavored honey
2 large eggs
3 tablespoons unsalted butter

Preheat the oven to 450° F (230° C).

Sift together the cornmeal, flour, baking powder, salt and baking soda into a large bowl. Beat together the yogurt, milk, honey and eggs in another bowl.

Place the butter in a 9 x 9-inch (22 x 22-cm) baking pan or a 9-inch (22-cm) cast-iron skillet and place the pan in the oven for 3 or 4 minutes, until the butter melts. Remove from the heat, brush the butter over the sides and bottom of the pan, and pour any remaining butter into the yogurt-and-egg mixture. Stir this together well, then fold the liquid mixture into the dry mixture. Do this quickly, with just a few strokes of a wooden spoon or plastic spatula. Don't worry about lumps. You don't want to overwork the batter.

Pour the batter into the warm greased pan, place in the oven, and bake 30 to 35 minutes, until the top is golden brown and a toothpick inserted in the center comes out clean. Let cool in the pan or serve hot.

SERVES 8 TO 10

Homemade Pasta

❀

NOTHING COMPARES to homemade pasta. I learned to make it in a cooking class with Ann Clark in Austin, Texas, years ago, and I can still remember my feeling of discovery when I tasted the fresh, slippery, light noodles. I have worked with many recipes since then, for regular pasta, green pasta, whole-wheat pasta and buckwheat pasta. I've found that, because of the nature of the flour, the proportions of flour and eggs vary according to the kind of flour used. But the method is always the same. Whole-wheat flour absorbs more moisture than refined, so you use slightly less flour in whole-grain pastas. Below are the proportions for regular, whole-wheat, herb, spinach and buckwheat pastas, with instructions that apply to all of them.

Note on quantities: For each additional 2 portions, add 1 egg and increase unbleached white flour quantities by 1 scant cup when using unbleached white flour only; by approximately ¾ cup when using a combination of whole-wheat and other flours; and add ⅛ teaspoon salt.

For the spinach pasta, the spinach replaces 1 of the eggs, so the easiest way to increase quantities is to double the proportions given here; freeze or dry any pasta you don't use.

REGULAR PASTA

Approximately 1 ¾ cups (225 g) unbleached white flour
Heaping ¼ teaspoon salt
2 large eggs
Water, if necessary

WHOLE-WHEAT PASTA

Approximately ¾ cup (90 g) whole-wheat flour
1 scant cup (115 g) unbleached white flour
Heaping ¼ teaspoon salt
2 large eggs
Water, if necessary

SPINACH PASTA

Approximately ¾ cup (90 g) whole-wheat pastry flour, plus 1 scant cup (115 g) unbleached white flour ; or 1 ¾ cups (225 g) unbleached white flour
¼ teaspoon salt
1 large egg

⅓ cup (45 g) spinach, stemmed, washed, thoroughly dried and very finely chopped

Approximately ¾ cup (90 g) whole-wheat pastry flour
½ scant cup (55 g) buckwheat flour
½ scant cup (55 g) unbleached white flour
Heaping ¼ teaspoon salt
1 teaspoon sesame oil
2 large eggs

Ingredients for regular or Whole-Wheat Pasta
4 teaspoons finely chopped fresh herbs, such as parsley or basil

Using the food processor: If you have one, by all means use it. Pasta-making will be a snap. Put the flours, herbs for herb pasta and salt in the bowl of your food processor and mix together by turning on the machine for a few seconds. With the machine off, add the eggs, or the egg and spinach for spinach pasta, and the sesame oil for buckwheat pasta. Now turn on the machine, and in just a few seconds (or maybe half a minute), the dough should either come together on the blades or, instead of coming together, form many little balls in the bowl, which you can then gather together in a solid mass with your hands. In any case, the process shouldn't take more than a minute. If the mixture seems wet, it will dry a little as you knead it, and you can (and should) always dust the pasta with flour before you roll it out. If it seems too dry, add 1 teaspoon of water to the food processor and continue to process a few seconds longer.

Now remove from the food processor and knead the dough for 5 to 10 minutes, until stiff. You can knead it like bread, folding it over and leaning into it on a very lightly floured surface; or you can squeeze the dough from one end to the other, back and forth; or you can slam it down on the work surface, pick it up and slam it down again—whatever seems easiest. The dough is stiff and will be much more difficult to knead than bread. Wrap it in plastic wrap and allow it to rest for 30 minutes before rolling it out. Or refrigerate it for up to 2 days, wrapped in plastic. The dough can also be frozen.

Making the dough by hand: You should probably learn to do this, even if you do have a food processor, just so you know how it's done (and who knows, you may find yourself in a French farmhouse one summer with no food processor!). Sift together the flours and salt, stir in the herbs for herb pasta, and place on a large work surface or in a large bowl, in a mound. Make a depression in the center of the mound and break the eggs into this well, or egg and spinach for spinach pasta, or egg and sesame oil for buckwheat pasta. Using a fork, gently beat the eggs and oil together. When they are lightly beaten, begin brushing flour in from the top of the "walls" of the well and incorporating it into the eggs with your fork. Use your free hand to keep the walls of the well intact while you brush in flour, a little at a time. Don't worry if the egg breaks through the sides of the well; just push the mixture back into the middle, incorporating flour as you do. As soon as it becomes impossible to incorporate any more flour into the mixture with your fork, brush in the remaining flour and incorporate as much as you can with your hands. Now brush away any hard bits of egg and flour that haven't been amalgamated, and gather the mixture into a ball. Knead and let rest as above.

Rolling out the dough: I use a hand pasta machine to roll out my dough. It's a very simple gadget. First cut the dough into quarters, to facilitate rolling. Flatten it down a little, and with the roller set on 1, roll it through. The edges will be very jagged. Fold these jagged edges in toward each other, press down and roll the dough again through the first setting. Repeat this process at each setting, dusting the dough with a little unbleached white flour if it seems damp. With whole-grain doughs, 4 is usually the thinnest setting you can use before the dough tears. If you can roll the dough through at 5 without tearing it, by all means do so, unless you are going to use the noodles for lasagna or a salad (salad noodles need to be more substantial; they will become mushy if they're too thin). For noodles, once you've rolled them to the desired thickness, let rest for 10 to 15 minutes, then attach the noodle-cutting attachment and cut fettuccine or spaghetti. For ravioli, lasagna and cannelloni, roll out wide sheets (see recipes for further instructions).

Let the pasta dry for 15 minutes before cooking it.

At this point, you can either cook the pasta or dry it further by laying it out on a meshed pasta dryer, on flour-dusted wax paper, over the back of a chair or over a dowel, for 24 to 48 hours (it takes longer in a humid climate). When completely dry, store in a tightly covered container. You can also freeze fresh pasta. Once you have rolled it out and cut noodles, dust with unbleached white flour, wrap in plastic, then freeze in a plastic bag. Fresh pasta will keep, well-dusted and wrapped in plastic or sealed in a plastic bag, for 1 day in the refrigerator.

To cook: Fresh pasta cooks in literally seconds. Bring a large pot of water to a rolling boil. Add a generous amount of salt and 1 tablespoon of cooking oil. Add the pasta. It will float to the surface at once. Remove immediately and toss with sauce. If serving cold, rinse with cold water. To cook frozen pasta, transfer it directly from the freezer to the boiling water.

SERVES 4 AS MAIN COURSE, 6 AS A SIDE DISH

Whole-Wheat Piecrusts

❦

I HAVE ALWAYS had a weakness for a good tart crust. There's no reason why a wholesome piecrust can't be delicate. You can avoid the heavy, cardboard texture by using a mixture of whole-wheat and unbleached white or light whole-wheat pastry flours, letting the dough rest for a sufficient amount of time and handling it with a light touch.

These recipes call for unsalted butter. A good-quality margarine will work, but it won't have the same rich flavor.

My dessert crusts contain honey instead of sugar. They aren't as easy to roll out as the more traditional kind, but I love the flavor, which is sweet but not cloying.

I must warn you again that these crusts won't roll out easily, like the ones your mother used to make. You won't be able to roll them around the pin and lift them easily into the pan. Crusts made with whole-wheat flour tend to break apart when you work with them, so you must work briskly and the dough must be cold. I roll them out between pieces of parchment or wax paper. Then I peel off the top piece, reverse the dough into the pan and peel off the bottom piece of paper. Where a traditional dough would normally ease into the edge of a pan, my crust is more likely to break. Then you must spend some time pressing the edges together. Sometimes you have to work the dough up the sides of the pan, pressing out with your hands and patching pieces together. As I said, it takes patience. But the end result will be as beautiful as any crust you've ever seen and will have a rich, full-bodied taste.

GENERAL TECHNIQUE FOR MY PIECRUSTS

1. Mix together dry ingredients (flours, ground nuts, if called for, salt).

2. Cut in the butter, which should be very cold, and cut into small pieces. You can do this in a food processor, using the pulse action, or in an electric mixer, or with forks or two knives, or with your hands. If you use your hands, work quickly; pick up handfuls of the flour and butter with both hands and roll them between your thumbs and first two fingers. Keep picking up handfuls until the butter is evenly distributed through the flour and the mixture resembles oatmeal. Then briskly rub the mixture between the palms of your hands, until it resembles coarse cornmeal. Now add the liquids and gather the dough together in a ball. Press together, without working too much, so the dough is cohesive, and wrap in plastic wrap. Refrigerate several hours, preferably overnight. The dough can also be frozen at this point.

Rolling out the dough: Remove from the

refrigerator and let sit for about 45 minutes before rolling. It helps to have a heavy rolling pin. Place the dough on a piece of wax paper or parchment, lightly dust your rolling pin, and slam the pin down on the dough, *wham!* Don't be alarmed by the noise. Turn the dough a quarter turn and continue to wham it until it is flattened out to about 1 inch (2.5 cm) thick. Lightly flour the top of the dough and roll, from the center out to the edge, turning the wax paper; you may need two pieces of paper underneath, side by side. If the dough is sticky, place a piece of paper on top too, and roll out between the two pieces. When the dough is rolled out enough to fit your tart pan, peel off the top piece of wax paper or parchment, reverse the dough into the pan, and peel off the bottom piece.

The dough may have broken wherever it was supposed to ease into the bends of the pie pan. Not to worry. Use your fingers to press the edges toward each other, then to press them together. If the dough isn't lining the pan evenly, just cut and patch, pressing the edges.

To get a pretty edge around the top of the pan, gently press the dough up the edge from the bottom so that you have some extra at the top, then pinch little creases, using the thumb and index finger of one hand and the index finger of the other, all around the edge of the pan. The crust can be refrigerated or frozen at this point.

SWEET ALMOND PIECRUST

This is delicious with fruit tarts as well as American pies like pumpkin and apple. Because the almonds add oil to the mixture, I have never needed to add the additional tablespoon of water, but I've listed it just in case the crust seems dry to you.

- 1 cup (115 g) whole-wheat flour or whole-wheat pastry flour
- ½ cup (55 g) unbleached white flour
- ½ cup (55 g) finely ground almonds
- ¼ teaspoon salt
- ½ cup (115 g) unsalted butter
- 2 tablespoons mild-flavored honey
- ½ teaspoon almond extract (optional)
- 1 tablespoon ice-cold water, if necessary

Mix together the flours, ground almonds and salt. Cut in the butter. Mix in the honey and almond extract. If the dough comes together, gather it up into a ball. If it seems dry, add the tablespoon of ice-cold water, then gather into a ball. Wrap in plastic wrap and refrigerate several hours, preferably overnight.

Roll out the dough between 2 pieces of wax paper or parchment and line a 12- to 14-inch (30- to 35-cm) tart pan. Proceed with the recipe.

MAKES ONE 12- TO 14-INCH (30- TO 35-CM) CRUST

WHOLE-WHEAT DESSERT CRUST

- 1 cup (115 g) whole-wheat flour
- 1 cup (115 g) unbleached white flour
- ¼ teaspoon salt
- ½ cup (115 g) unsalted butter
- 2 tablespoons mild-flavored honey
- 1 tablespoon ice-cold water, if necessary

Mix together the flours and salt. Cut in the butter. Mix in the honey. If the dough comes together, gather it into a ball. If it seems dry, add the tablespoon of ice-cold water, then gather into a ball. Wrap in plastic wrap and refrigerate for several hours, preferably overnight.

Roll out the crust between pieces of wax paper or parchment and line a 12- to 14-inch (30- to 35-cm) tart pan. Proceed with recipe.

MAKES ONE 12- TO 14-INCH (30- TO 35-CM) CRUST

SAVORY WHOLE-WHEAT CRUST

- 1 cup (115 g) whole-wheat flour
- 1 cup (115 g) unbleached white flour
- ¼ teaspoon salt
- ½ cup (115 g) unsalted butter
- 2 to 3 tablespoons ice-cold water, as necessary

Follow the above technique, omitting the honey.

MAKES ONE 12- TO 14-INCH (30- TO 35-CM) CRUST

Homemade Tortillas

❀

BEFORE I FOUND a reliable source for corn tortillas here in Paris, I used to make my own. That's why I'd brought all the masa harina, the *comal* and the tortilla press, after all. What a labor of love! For nachos, we made cute little round ones, which we fried for chips, and slightly larger ones called chalupas. The first time we catered a *Herald Tribune* party, six of us sat around one night until about 2:00 a.m. rolling out small chalupa crisps—400 of them. It was assembly-line work, although looking back, I am reminded more of a sewing bee. Everyone except me (I was at the stove cooking the tortillas) was sitting around my kitchen table rolling, pressing and jabbering. There was something very satisfying in knowing that we had made all those tortillas and chips from scratch, but it wasn't satisfying enough to keep us from buying them the next year.

Adding a small amount of flour to the masa harina is a trick I learned from my Texas friends. It may not be authentic, but the resulting tortillas are moister and less crumbly than all-masa tortillas.

- 2   cups (225 g) masa harina
- ¼   cup (30 g) unbleached white flour
- ½   teaspoon salt
- 1   cup (225 ml) plus 2 to 3 tablespoons water, as necessary

Mix together the masa harina, flour and salt in a bowl. Pour in 1 cup of the water all at once and mix together quickly with your hands. The dough should not be in a big lump; it should be slightly crumbly but not too dry. If the dough seems too dry, add a little more water, 1 tablespoon at a time. Let rest for 15 minutes.

Take up golf-ball-sized pieces of the dough and form into balls.

Heat a *comal*, griddle or heavy-bottomed frying pan over medium-high heat; have ready 2 zip-lock plastic bags. To press out the tortillas, place 1 of the plastic bags on your tortilla press and a ball of dough on top of this. Press down a little with your thumb, and place the other plastic bag on top. Now press the tortilla, being careful not to press too hard or your tortilla might stick and will be too thin. Lift the press and peel off the top bag. Flip the tortilla gently onto the peeled-off bag and peel off the bottom bag.

Transfer the tortilla to the hot *comal* or frying pan and cook about 1 minute, until it is just beginning to dry around the edges. Turn and cook another minute. Remove from the heat. Wrap loosely in foil or a dish towel to keep warm. Continue making tortillas, stacking and wrapping, until all the dough is used up. If the dough becomes dry, sprinkle on a little water.

Reheat the tortillas, if necessary, by wrapping them in foil and putting them in a low oven.

MAKES 12 CORN TORTILLAS

TORTILLA CHIPS OR CHALUPA CRISPS

For chips, either roll the dough into tiny pea-size balls and press and cook as for normal tortillas or cut cooked tortillas into quarters or sixths. Heat 1 quart (1 L) safflower, vegetable or corn oil to 360° F (180° C) and deep-fry the handmade or cut tortillas in batches until golden. Drain on paper towels in a colander.

Chips and chalupa crisps should be fried on the day you are planning to serve them, as they tend to get stale.

Blini

THESE YEASTED buckwheat pancakes are great for parties (see "New Year's Eve Chez Martha," page 175); they've been the focal point of several soirees at my house, or one dish among many on a buffet table. They're easy to make and keep well, either in the refrigerator or freezer.

Note: These freeze well. Separate between pieces of wax paper, wrap in foil and place in plastic bags. They can be transferred immediately from the freezer, wrapped in the foil, to a 350° F (180° C) oven. They will take about 40 minutes to thaw.

2	tablespoons active dry yeast
4	cups (1 L) warm low-fat milk
4	large eggs, separated
2	teaspoons sugar
1	cup (115 g) whole-wheat flour
1	cup (115 g) unbleached white flour
½	cup (55 g) buckwheat flour
1	teaspoon salt
2	teaspoons unsalted butter, melted

Dissolve the yeast in 2 cups of the milk. Beat in the egg yolks and sugar. Sift together the flours and salt. Stir half of the dry ingredients into the liquid mixture and whisk together until completely smooth. Cover and set in a warm place to rise for 1 hour.

Beat the remaining 2 cups milk into the yeast mixture and add the remaining flour and the melted butter. Combine well. Strain through a medium-fine sieve or a chinois, cover and let rise for another hour in a warm place. At this point, the batter can be refrigerated for several hours or overnight.

Just before cooking, beat the egg whites to stiff peaks and fold them into the batter.

Heat a crepe pan or nonstick skillet over medium-high heat. Brush with butter (it should sizzle). Cook the blini, using about ¼ to ⅓ cup (60 ml to 90 ml) batter per pancake for large blini and 2 tablespoons for finger-food size. Cook 30 seconds to 1 minute on the first side, until bubbles break through, then turn and cook 30 seconds on the other side. Stack and keep warm in a low oven. If not using them right away, wrap the blini tightly in foil. Reheat in a medium oven.

MAKES 12 LARGE OR 24 TO 36 SMALL BLINI

Garlic Croutons

THESE ARE GREAT with Tapenade (page 61), with melted goat cheese in a salad or cut into cubes and added to a salad or soup.

Thin slices of Sourdough Country Bread (page 26) or baguette
1 or 2   cloves garlic, cut in half lengthwise
Olive oil (optional)

Toast the bread in a toaster or under a broiler until lightly browned. Remove from the heat and immediately rub one or both sides (depending on your taste for garlic) with the cut side of a garlic clove. Brush lightly with olive oil, if you wish.

September

❧

Opening Night: A Mexican Soiree

APERITIF: MARGARITAS

BLACK BEAN NACHOS

TOMATO HALVES STUFFED WITH GUACAMOLE

BAKED FISH FILLETS WITH SALSA FRESCA

MEXICAN RICE

PAN-FRIED CUCUMBERS

CUMIN AND CORNMEAL BREAD (PAGE 31)

PEACH SORBET WITH PEACH GARNISH

HONEY-LEMON REFRIGERATOR COOKIES

WINE SUGGESTIONS: BEAUJOLAIS, BROUILLY, CÔTES DE VENTOUX
OR MEXICAN BEER

SERVES 6

September

THE SEPTEMBER SUPPER CLUB is the first one of the fall season. Paris is upbeat. During the first week of the month, called *la rentrée* because so many Parisians are away during July and August, the calm of the summer gives way to a back-to-school, back-to-work bustle.

I always serve Mexican food on "opening night." It ensures (or perhaps the tequila ensures) a lively evening. Guests loosen up quickly with a zesty margarita, and the colorful, vibrant food is a welcome change from French cuisine. When I first served this menu, in September 1985, we had been having a beautiful Indian summer. It was warm enough to stand on the balcony and drink margaritas while we watched the almost-full moon come up.

For this meal, I wanted to do fish fillets with salsa. We marinated the fillets in lemon juice and olive oil with garlic and fresh cilantro, then baked them in a tightly covered baking dish. We ran the glistening red salsa along the side of the fish on the plate and served bright saffron-tinted Spanish rice and sautéed cucumbers on the side. The crunchy cucumbers made a perfect garnish; I wanted a green vegetable but didn't want to complicate the course or confuse the palate.

For this dish, you need a fish with a firm texture. Cod will do, but even better is red snapper or redfish. I picked up the firm, pink-white fillets in the morning and had them all laid out in their lemon-olive oil marinade in the baking dishes by the afternoon.

The colorful first course was something I'd visualized for a while: five generous black bean nachos around a portion of guacamole in a tomato half, in the center of the plate. By the time we sat down at the table, the nachos had cooled off considerably, but everyone enjoyed them just the same.

I'd always been reluctant to serve sorbet for my Supper Clubs, since I don't have a large ice cream maker and my freezer capacity is limited. But finally, after reading all the ice cream and sorbet recipes in Alice B. Toklas's cookbook—and I know she didn't use newfangled gadgets—I decided to try it the good old-fashioned way, letting the sorbet freeze in baking dishes and breaking up the ice crystals once or twice. I used an adaptation of a recipe from *Cooking From an Italian Garden* (Harcourt, Brace, Jovanovich, 1985), by Paola Scaravelli and Jon Cohen, and was very pleased with the results. I tested the recipe a few weeks before the dinner and discovered that the sorbet held very well in the freezer, so I knew it was one of those desserts I could make a few days in advance. After Mexican food, sorbet is delightfully refreshing. I froze the sorbets in small ramekins, then unmolded them into small soup bowls and garnished them with sliced peaches and mint. The honey-lemon cookies were passed on plates.

The Côtes de Ventoux, which I always buy by the case in Apt when I visit Christine Picasso in Provence, was an excellent accompaniment to the meal. This light, fruity wine should be served chilled.

Margaritas

❁

THERE IS ONLY ONE secret to a great margarita: fresh lime juice, squeezed, if possible, just before serving time. The juice will hold, if necessary, for a couple of hours, but then the taste begins to sour.

A margarita is a very congenial drink, perhaps because of all that lime juice consumed with the alcohol. Of course, you don't want people to drink too much, but one before dinner has always contributed to a very animated table.

FOR EACH DRINK

1 ½ ounces (45 ml) tequila
1 ounce (30 ml) fresh lime juice
⅔ to ¾ ounces (20 ml to 25 ml) Triple Sec or Cointreau, to taste (I use the larger

amount, as people seem to prefer the slightly sweeter version)

Mix together the tequila, lime juice and Triple Sec. For a margarita that is less potent but still delicious, though obviously a bit more diluted, you can blend up the mixture with ice. Or you can shake the margaritas with ice and pour them off or serve them on the rocks. For the Supper Club, I blend them with ice; it makes the tequila go further and keeps the guests from getting too "animated."

For a large batch, just remember:

1 part lime juice
1 ½ parts tequila
⅔ to ⅛ part Triple Sec or Cointreau, depending on how sweet you like it

Black Bean Nachos

❁

THE BEANS for these nachos (pictured on page 34) have a rich, earthy flavor, redolent of garlic, cumin and chili, and that's the reason they are so popular.

1 cup Refried Black Beans (page 51; freeze any leftovers)
1 pound (500 g) ripe tomatoes, diced small
1 to 2 fresh jalapeño or serrano peppers, to taste, seeded and minced
3 tablespoons minced fresh cilantro
2 tablespoons minced red onion
1 to 2 tablespoons red-wine vinegar, to taste
Salt, to taste
30 corn tortilla chips (see note below)
¾ cup (85 g) grated Cheddar (3 ounces)
½ cup (120 ml) crème fraîche (page 20) or plain low-fat yogurt
Additional fresh cilantro leaves for garnish

First make the refried beans.

Make a salsa by combining the tomatoes, hot peppers, minced cilantro, red onion, vinegar and salt, to taste. Set aside.

Sprinkle the tortilla chips with the grated Cheddar and melt the cheese under the broiler or in a hot oven.

Spread the refried beans over each chip and heat through under the broiler. Remove from the heat, place on a serving platter or plates, and top with small dabs of crème fraîche or plain low-fat yogurt, then a small spoonful of the salsa (you may substitute a commercial brand of bottled salsa or Mexican-style hot sauce, but it's not as good or as pretty). Garnish with fresh cilantro leaves and serve.

Note: You can make your own chips (page 44), or you can quarter and deep-fry prepared corn tortillas, then drain them on paper towels.

To prepare ahead of time: If you are making your

own tortilla chips, prepare them on the day of the dinner, so they will be fresh.

The beans can be prepared well in advance and, to make things easier for you, should be. They will hold for up to 3 days in the refrigerator, and they freeze well. Save some of the cooking liquid—refrigerate it in a jar—so you can moisten them, as they tend to dry out. Reheat them, covered, for 20 to 30 minutes, in a 325° F (170° C) oven. The remaining ingredients can be prepared early in the day and held in the refrigerator in covered bowls or containers.

Assemble the nachos close to serving time, or the chips will become soggy.

MAKES 30 NACHOS

Refried Black Beans

❦

THIS RECIPE MAKES twice as much as you need for the nachos. Freeze what you don't use. Use bottled water if your water is very hard.

1	pound (500 g) black beans
3	tablespoons safflower or vegetable oil
1	large onion, chopped
4 to 6	large cloves garlic, to taste, minced or put through a press
16	cups (4 L) water
	Salt, to taste
3	tablespoons chopped fresh cilantro
2 to 3	teaspoons ground cumin
2 to 3	teaspoons mild chili powder

Wash and pick over the beans and soak them overnight or for several hours in 8 cups (2 L) water. Heat 1 tablespoon of the oil in a large, heavy-bottomed saucepan or Dutch oven and sauté the onion with 2 cloves of the garlic until the onion is tender. Add the beans and 8 cups (2 L) fresh water and bring to a boil. Add the remaining garlic, reduce the heat, cover, and simmer 1 hour. Add salt to taste and more garlic, if you wish, and the cilantro, and continue to simmer until the beans are soft and the liquid thick and aromatic, about 1 more hour. Adjust seasonings and remove from the heat.

Allow the beans to cool a while, then drain off about ⅔ of the liquid, retaining it in a separate bowl (use some of it later to moisten the beans). Mash the beans coarsely, in batches, in a food processor or blender or with a potato masher. Make sure you do not puree them; you want texture.

Heat the remaining 2 tablespoons oil in a large, heavy-bottomed frying pan and add the cumin and chili powder. Sauté for 1 minute and add the mashed beans (this can be done in batches, depending on the size of your skillet). Fry the beans, stirring often, until they begin to get crusty and aromatic. If they seem too dry, add some of the reserved cooking liquid. Mash and stir the beans as they cook. There should be enough liquid so they bubble as they cook, while at the same time, a thin crust forms on the bottom. Cook for about 15 to 20 minutes, then, if you are serving the beans on their own, transfer to an oiled serving dish.

SERVES 6 TO 8

Tomato Halves Stuffed With Guacamole

❧

GUACAMOLE IS ONE of those dishes that should be made close to serving time. The color will fade a little no matter what, but lemon juice will keep the guacamole from becoming brown. If the color does change too much for your liking, stir in a small amount of crème fraîche (page 20). It's important to use the right kind of avocado: the knobby, dark-skinned California Haas variety. The thin-skinned Florida type is too watery for a good guacamole.

These are lovely in the center of a plate, surrounded by Black Bean Nachos (page 50).

3	ripe medium-sized or large Haas avocados (the knobby, dark-skinned kind)
5	ripe tomatoes (2 chopped, 3 fairly large ones sliced in half)
	Juice of 1 to 2 lemons, to taste
½	small red onion, very finely minced
1	small clove garlic, minced or put through a press
¼	teaspoon ground cumin or more, to taste
¼	teaspoon ground chili powder or more, to taste
	Salt, to taste
	Fresh cilantro and tortilla chips (page 44 for homemade) for garnish

Cut the avocados in half, pit and scoop out the flesh. Mash, using a pestle or a heavy wooden spoon. Add the chopped tomatoes and lemon juice and continue to mash. Stir in the onion, garlic, cumin, chili powder and salt to taste. Correct the seasoning and refrigerate.

Scoop out the pulp from the halved tomatoes. Correct the guacamole seasonings once again and fill the tomatoes. Place on a plate. Garnish with cilantro and a few corn tortilla chips.

If serving with the Black Bean Nachos, place the nachos around the tomatoes and use some of the salsa from that recipe to garnish the guacamole.

SERVES 6

Baked Fish Fillets With Salsa Fresca

❧

THIS IS A GOOD DISH for a dinner party, (pictured on page 35) because all of the ingredients can be prepared well in advance. The fish bakes quickly, so it's just a question of watching it carefully once you put it in the oven. This dish has a very clean taste; the lemony fish fillets go nicely with the vibrant salsa. It's light, lovely to look at and would be appropriate during any season, as long as you can find good fresh tomatoes.

FOR THE FISH

6	fish fillets (about 1 ½ pounds, 750 g), either cod, snapper, sea bass or a more delicate fish like sole; or small whiting, deboned
	Salt and freshly ground pepper, to taste
¼	cup (60 ml) fresh lemon juice
2	tablespoons olive oil
1 to 2	cloves garlic, to taste, minced or put through a press
1	tablespoon minced fresh cilantro

FOR THE SALSA

1	recipe Salsa Fresca (page 53)

Salt and pepper the fish fillets. Mix together the lemon juice, olive oil, garlic and cilantro in a shallow ovenproof casserole. Marinate the fish in this mixture while you prepare the salsa.

Combine all the ingredients for the salsa in a

bowl. Correct seasonings. Chill until 30 minutes before you are ready to bake the fish.

Preheat the oven to 400° F (200° C). Cover the casserole tightly with foil or a lid and bake for 12 minutes, or until the fish flakes. Remove from the heat and transfer to warm plates with a slotted spatula. Place a generous helping of salsa along the side of the fish and serve.

To prepare ahead of time: The fish can marinate for several hours. Prepare the marinade, add the fish and cover the casserole tightly with aluminum foil. Refrigerate until 30 minutes before baking, turning the fillets once or twice. The salsa will hold for several hours; refrigerate in a covered bowl.

SERVES 6

Salsa Fresca

❦

THIS VIBRANT FRESH tomato salsa, piquant with fresh hot peppers and pungent with cilantro, comes up in virtually all of my Tex-Mex menus. It will hold for a few hours in the refrigerator.

2 pounds (1 kg) ripe tomatoes, chopped
½ small yellow or Bermuda onion, finely minced

1 to 3 jalapeño or serrano peppers, to taste, minced
4 tablespoons chopped fresh cilantro
1 tablespoon red-wine vinegar or more, to taste
Salt, to taste

Combine all the ingredients in a bowl and chill until ready to serve.

MAKES ABOUT 2 CUPS

Mexican Rice

❦

THIS FRAGRANT, saffron-hued rice is one of my most frequent side dishes in meals with Mexican flavors.

4 cups (1 L) chicken or vegetable stock
1 tablespoon unsalted butter or safflower oil
½ medium-sized onion, minced
2 large cloves garlic, minced or put through a press
1 ½ cups (340 g) long-grain rice
1 sweet green or red pepper, seeded and cut into thin strips
¾ pound (350 g) ripe tomatoes, seeded and chopped
¼ cup (60 ml) dry white wine
½ teaspoon saffron threads
1 cup (170 g) fresh or thawed frozen peas
Salt and freshly ground pepper, to taste

Have the stock simmering in a saucepan.

Heat the butter or oil over medium heat in a large, heavy-bottomed, lidded frying pan or flameproof casserole and add the onion and garlic. Cook, stirring, until the onion is tender. Add the rice and cook, stirring, for 1 minute. Add the pepper and tomatoes and stir together for a couple of minutes.

Add the wine and cook, stirring with a wooden spoon, until the liquid has just about evaporated. Begin adding the simmering stock, a ladleful at a time. Add the saffron with the first ladleful. Cook, stirring all the while, until each ladleful of stock is almost completely absorbed. Continue adding and stirring until the rice is cooked al dente—just until firm to the bite—which should take 20 to 30 minutes. Add the peas halfway through the cooking, so that they cook 10 to 15 minutes in all. Add salt and freshly ground pepper to taste.

To prepare ahead of time: The rice will hold for several hours. You can transfer it to an oiled casserole, cover and reheat for 30 minutes in a moderate oven, or you can hold it in the frying pan, covered with foil so it won't dry out. Shortly before serving, uncover, add a little oil to the pan, and reheat, stirring, on top of the stove.

SERVES 6

Pan-Fried Cucumbers

THESE DELICATE sautéed cucumbers go nicely with spicy main dishes. Be careful not to overcook them.

1 to 2 tablespoons butter, as necessary
     1 clove garlic, minced or put through a press (optional)
     2 long European-style cucumbers, peeled and sliced ¼ inch (0.75 cm) thick
        Salt and freshly ground pepper, to taste
     1 tablespoon minced fresh parsley

Heat the butter in a large skillet and add the optional garlic. Sauté over medium heat for 1 minute, then add the cucumbers and increase the heat to medium-high. Sauté, stirring, for 5 minutes. The cucumbers should become translucent but should not brown. Add salt and freshly ground pepper to taste and transfer to a warm serving dish. Sprinkle with minced fresh parsley and serve.

SERVES 4 TO 6

Peach Sorbet
With Peach Garnish

IN SEPTEMBER, the Paris markets are still bounteous with the last of the summer fruit, including ripe, juicy peaches from Provence, Italy and Spain. The touch of almond in this luscious sorbet enhances the sweet flavor of the peaches.

FOR THE SORBET

     2 pounds (1 kg) fresh, ripe peaches
     ¼ teaspoon almond extract
     ⅓ cup (80 ml) fresh lemon juice
     1 cup (225 ml) water
     ⅓ cup (80 ml) mild-flavored honey

FOR THE GARNISH

Juice of ½ orange

Juice of ½ lemon
     1 tablespoon mild-flavored honey (optional)
     3 fresh, ripe peaches, pitted and sliced

Making the sorbet: Bring a large pot of water to a boil and blanch the peaches for 20 seconds. Drain, run them under cold water, and remove the skins. Pit and place in a blender or food processor, along with the almond extract and lemon juice. Blend to a puree and set aside in the refrigerator.

Combine the water and the honey in a large saucepan at least twice their volume (honey bubbles up dramatically) and bring to a boil. Reduce the heat and simmer 10 minutes. Remove from the heat and allow to cool.

Blend together the honey syrup and the peach

puree. Transfer to an ice cream maker or sorbetière and freeze according to instructions (see note). Transfer the sorbet to individual molds or an attractive bowl, cover with plastic, then tightly with foil (if the foil is in direct contact with the sorbet, the aluminum will react with the acid in the fruit). Work quickly to cover and return to the freezer before the mixture melts to a liquid, or ice crystals will form again when it freezes.

Making the garnish: Mix together the orange juice, lemon juice and honey. Toss with the peaches and marinate for at least 1 hour in the refrigerator.

About 30 minutes before serving, place the sorbet in the refrigerator to soften. Unmold or scoop out and serve in individual bowls, garnished with the fresh peaches and mint leaves.

Note: You can also transfer the mixture to a shallow baking dish or ice-cube trays, cover with foil, and place in the freezer for 2 hours, or until almost frozen. Remove from the freezer and blend in a food processor or electric mixer to break up the ice crystals. Return to the baking dish or ice trays, cover and freeze for another 2 hours, or until solid. Break up the ice crystals once more, then mold and freeze the sorbet as directed in the recipe.

To prepare ahead of time: The nice thing about this sorbet is that it will hold for weeks in the freezer. You could even make it in September and surprise guests with it later in the fall, although you will have to use frozen peaches for garnish if you can't find fresh. The garnish will hold for several hours in a covered bowl in the refrigerator.

SERVES 6

Honey-Lemon Refrigerator Cookies

❦

THESE COOKIES are great for entertaining because you can make up the dough days in advance. They are tangy and not too sweet.

10	tablespoons (150 g) unsalted butter
⅔	cup (160 ml) mild-flavored honey
2	teaspoons vanilla
1	large egg
	Pinch of salt
2	tablespoons fresh lemon juice
2	tablespoons grated lemon zest
1	cup (115 g) whole-wheat pastry flour
1 ½	cups (170 g) unbleached white flour
¼ to ½	teaspoon ground cloves, to taste

In a food processor or electric mixer, cream the butter and honey. Beat in the vanilla, egg, salt, lemon juice and zest. Gradually add the flours and cloves. The dough will be very soft and sticky.

Divide the dough in half and, using a spatula, spread it on 2 long pieces of wax paper or plastic wrap. Don't be intimidated by how wet the dough is; use the spatula to spread the dough on the paper, then carefully shape it into a cylinder about 2 inches (5 cm) in diameter and roll it up in the paper. Don't worry if your cylinder isn't perfectly round; these cookies usually have very irregular shapes. Place the dough in the freezer for 2 hours, or refrigerate it overnight.

About 45 minutes before baking time, put the dough, if refrigerated, in the freezer to facilitate cutting. Preheat the oven to 350° F (180° C). Butter 4 baking sheets.

Unwrap the chilled dough, cut off ¼ of the log, and return the rest of the dough to the freezer so it doesn't soften. Cut the dough in very thin slices, about ¼ inch (0.75 cm) thick or even thinner, if possible. Place the slices on the baking sheets, about ½ inch (1.5 cm) apart. Bake for 10 to 15 minutes, until golden brown around the edges and crisp. While the first batch is baking, slice more cookies and place them on the remaining baking sheets. When the cookies are done, transfer them to a rack and allow to cool. Store in a tightly sealed tin.

MAKES 4 DOZEN COOKIES

October

❀

A Provençal Dinner

MIXED PROVENÇAL HORS D'OEUVRES
Zucchini and Rice Tian
Roasted Sweet Red Peppers
Vegetables and Eggs With Tapenade
Salad of Mâche (Lamb's Lettuce)

PROVENÇAL VEGETABLE SOUP WITH PISTOU

SOURDOUGH COUNTRY BREAD (PAGE 26)

BAKED FRESH FIGS WITH CRÈME ANGLAISE
OR
FIG TART WITH GREEN GRAPES

WINE SUGGESTIONS: CÔTES DE PROVENCE ROSÉ, TAVEL,
COTEAUX DU TRICASTIN

SERVES 6 TO 8

October

GORGEOUS FALL weather persisted through September and October of 1985, and the night I served this meal, everybody was in a marvelous mood. I hadn't even been too hassled that morning when the French union that controls the electric company called a strike. I just called my guests and told them to bring candles.

I'd been thinking Provençal since the beginning of the month, when Laurie and I had gone down to the Provençal winery, Domaine Tempier, for the end of the harvest. We had eaten Lulu Peyraud's delicious food, had helped make bouillabaisse for 35 people, had breakfasted on figs, which we picked ourselves, and had visited inspiring, colorful Mediterranean markets. With all of the lusty Mediterranean flavors still fresh in my mouth, I wanted to create a meal with lots of garlic, herbs, olive oil, olives, basil and figs. In anticipation of the soup, I'd been freezing basil for months.

Mixed Provençal Hors d'Oeuvres is my version of an appetizer served at a Niçoise restaurant. I especially love their tian, a mold of zucchini, rice, Parmesan and egg, and found I could replicate it, or

nearly, with my recipe. I also adore roasted red peppers with lots of garlic. My assistant arranged all the plates, and they looked gorgeous with the colorful combination of tian; roasted red peppers; dark green mâche (lamb's lettuce) tossed with a mild vinaigrette; and pungent, glistening tapenade spread on tomato halves, raw red pepper slices and hard-boiled eggs.

The soup was hot, heady with basil, garlic and Parmesan. Unfortunately, the green beans and sliced zucchini cooked a little too long. I learned my lesson: now when I serve this soup in quantity, I steam the green vegetables separately and add them to the bowls as I serve them. The soup needs that bright green color.

Figs are one of my great weaknesses and have been ever since I lived in Austin, Texas, where fig trees grow in everybody's backyard. They do in Provence as well. I have made both the fig tart and the baked figs to go with this meal. Baked Fresh Figs With Crème Anglaise was inspired many years ago by a heavenly dessert of roasted figs, just beginning to caramelize, which I ate at l'Archestrate, then a three-star restaurant owned by chef Alain Senderens.

Mixed Provençal Hors d'Oeuvres

❀

On each plate, arrange a slice of the Zucchini and Rice Tian, a portion of Roasted Sweet Red Peppers, a tomato, one or two wide slices of red pepper, a zucchini slice, half an egg and a crouton, each with the tapenade; and a small portion of the Salad of Mâche tossed with mild vinaigrette.

Zucchini and Rice Tian

❀

This is a simple but extraordinary vegetable terrine named after the casserole in which it is traditionally cooked. It is one of my favorite Provençal dishes. The satisfying, chewy texture of the rice contrasts nicely with the zucchini.

3 tablespoons olive oil
1 onion, minced
2 pounds (1 kg) zucchini, finely chopped
1 to 2 cloves garlic, to taste, minced or put through a press
2 large eggs
½ cup (55 g) Gruyère cheese, grated (2 ounces)
2 tablespoons freshly grated Parmesan
½ cup (15 g) chopped fresh parsley
½ cup (100 g) raw short-grain brown or Italian Arborio rice, cooked in 1 ½ cups water, according to directions on page 73
¼ to ½ teaspoon dried thyme, to taste
Salt and freshly ground pepper, to taste
2 heaping tablespoons homemade breadcrumbs

Preheat the oven to 375° F (190° C) and butter a 9 x 5 x 3-inch (22 x 12 x 8-cm) loaf pan or a 1 ½ quart (1.5 L) casserole.

Heat 2 tablespoons of the olive oil in a large, heavy-bottomed skillet and sauté the onion until tender over medium-low heat. Add the zucchini and the garlic, and sauté, stirring often, for 10 minutes over a low flame. Remove from the heat.

Beat the eggs in a large bowl and stir in the cheeses, parsley, rice, thyme and sautéed vegetables. Add salt and freshly ground pepper to taste. Turn into the prepared baking dish. Sprinkle the breadcrumbs over the top and drizzle with the remaining tablespoon of olive oil. Bake 40 to 60 minutes, until firm. The dish will take a little longer, maybe up to 1 hour, in a loaf pan, because it is deeper.

Remove from the heat and cool for at least 20 minutes before serving. Serve warm or cold, cut into slices or squares.

To prepare ahead of time: The ingredients for this can be prepared the day before you make it. Store them in plastic bags or covered containers in the refrigerator. The baked terrine will hold for up to 1 day in the refrigerator, tightly covered. It does not freeze well.

Serves 6 to 8

Roasted Sweet Red Peppers

❧

I DON'T KNOW anybody who doesn't love this dish, although some like it more garlicky than others. My Yugoslavian friend Zoran Mojsilov is used to lots of garlic and a fair amount of vinegar, whereas Christine Picasso uses no vinegar or garlic at all, just olive oil and salt. My version is toned-down Yugoslavian style, with a hint of Provence if I have fresh basil on hand.

6 to 8	medium-sized sweet red peppers
2	large cloves garlic, minced or put through a press, or more, to taste
½	cup (120 ml) olive oil
3	tablespoons red-wine vinegar or more, to taste
	Salt, to taste
1 to 2	tablespoons fresh chopped basil, to taste

There are several ways to roast peppers. You can place them directly over a gas flame or below a broiler. Or you can put them in a dry skillet over an electric or gas burner or in a baking dish in a hot oven. You want all the skin to blister and blacken. Keep turning the peppers until they are uniformly charred, then place them in a paper bag or wrap in a dishtowel until cool enough to handle.

Peel off the blackened skin, split the peppers in half, and remove the seeds and inner membranes. Rinse them quickly under cool water and pat dry. Cut the halved peppers in half again lengthwise or in wide strips. Place them in a bowl or serving dish and toss with the garlic, olive oil, vinegar and salt to taste. Cover and refrigerate until ready to serve. Toss with the basil shortly before serving.

To prepare ahead of time: These will hold for several days in the refrigerator in a covered bowl. But don't add the basil until shortly before you serve.

SERVES 6 TO 8

Tapenade

❧

THIS IS INTENSE Provençal olive paste, heady with garlic, capers and anchovies. It will keep for weeks in the refrigerator and makes a convenient hors d'oeuvre, spread thinly on Garlic Croutons (page 45) or on raw vegetables.

½	pound (250 g) imported black Provençal olives (use Greek if these cannot be found)
2	cloves garlic, minced or put through a press
1 ½	tablespoons capers
4 to 6	anchovy fillets, to taste
¼ to ½	teaspoon dried thyme, to taste
¼ to ½	teaspoon dried rosemary, to taste, crumbled
4	tablespoons olive oil
2	tablespoons fresh lemon juice
1 to 2	tablespoons Cognac (optional)
1	teaspoon Dijon mustard
	Lots of freshly ground black pepper

Pit the olives and puree them, along with the garlic, capers, anchovies, thyme and rosemary in a mortar and pestle or in a food processor. Add the remaining ingredients and continue to process until you have a smooth paste. Place in a bowl, cover, and refrigerate until ready to use.

Spread on croutons or raw vegetables and serve as an hors d'oeuvre.

To prepare ahead of time: This will hold for weeks

in the refrigerator. Keep it in a jar or covered container, and pour a thin film of olive oil over the surface to prevent it from drying out.

SERVES 10 AS AN HORS D'OEUVRE

Vegetables and Eggs With Tapenade

❦

THE TAPENADE is stretched here with the yolks of the hard-boiled eggs, resulting in a slightly milder-tasting version. This makes a wonderful first course as well as a beautiful hors d'oeuvres platter. I also recommend it for picnics (see the menu for "A Picnic on the Seine," page 183).

6   large eggs, hard-boiled
1   recipe Tapenade (page 61)
6   small or medium tomatoes, cut in half
3   small zucchini, cut in half lengthwise, then into 3-inch (8-cm) lengths
2   sweet red peppers, seeded and cut into wide strips

FOR THE GARNISH

Chopped fresh parsley
Lemon rounds or wedges
Radishes

Peel the hard-boiled eggs and cut them in half lengthwise. Carefully remove the yolks and reserve the whites. Mash the yolks with the tapenade and blend together thoroughly.

Turn the tomatoes upside down on a rack and let them drain 15 minutes.

Blanch the zucchini pieces in a large pot of boiling salted water, refresh them under cold water and scoop out the seeds.

Spread a generous portion of tapenade over the tomatoes, zucchini pieces and red pepper slices. Fill the reserved egg whites. Place the stuffed vegetables and eggs on a large platter or on individual plates and garnish with chopped fresh parsley, lemon and radishes.

To prepare ahead of time: The egg yolks make this dish more perishable than tapenade made without them, but it will still hold for 4 or 5 days in the refrigerator, in a covered container. You can prepare the eggs and vegetables several hours before you wish to serve them and hold them in the refrigerator on a platter, in covered containers or in plastic bags.

SERVES 6 TO 8

Salad of Mâche (Lamb's Lettuce)

❦

MÂCHE, which is also called lamb's lettuce in the United States, has small, delicate, soft-textured dark-green leaves, which should not be overpowered by a sharp vinaigrette. This simple salad, with its uncomplicated taste, was a welcome complement to the other items on my Provençal hors d'oeuvres plate.

Make sure you wash the leaves and stems of the mâche thoroughly, as a lot of sand tends to get trapped at the bottom of the stems.

¾   pound (350 g) mâche
2 to 3   tablespoons red-wine vinegar, to taste
½   teaspoon Dijon mustard
  Salt and freshly ground pepper, to taste
6 to 8   tablespoons good-quality olive oil, to taste

Wash and dry the mâche.

Mix together the vinegar, mustard, salt and pepper. Whisk in the olive oil. Toss with the mâche just before serving.

To prepare ahead of time: The dressing will hold for several hours, in or out of the refrigerator, and if the mâche is carefully dried, it will also hold in the refrigerator for several hours.

SERVES 6 TO 8

Provençal Vegetable Soup With Pistou

❀

THIS IS A Provençal minestrone, with the special addition of pistou, a kind of pesto without the nuts that is enriched with tomato and more cheese than Italian pesto. It's a complete meal in itself.

Note: Cooking Parmesan rinds in the soup gives flavor without much fat.

FOR THE SOUP

1	cup (250 g) white or navy beans, washed and picked over
4	quarts (4 L) water
2	tablespoons olive oil
2	medium-sized onions, chopped
4	cloves garlic, minced or put through a press
1	bouquet garni (made with 1 stalk of celery, 1 bay leaf, 2 sprigs of fresh parsley and 2 sprigs of fresh thyme, tied together)
2	Parmesan rinds (optional)
¾	pound (350 g) new or russet potatoes, scrubbed and diced
1	leek, white part only, cleaned and sliced
¾	pound (350 g) carrots, thinly sliced
1	pound (500 g) tomatoes, peeled and quartered or 1 28-ounce (765 g) can, with juice
¾	pound (350 g) zucchini, half chopped, half thinly sliced
½	pound (250 g) green beans, trimmed, cut in 1-inch (2.5-cm) lengths
1	cup (55 g) broken spaghetti or elbow macaroni
	Salt and freshly ground pepper, to taste

FOR THE PISTOU

2 to 4	cloves garlic, or more, to taste
2	cups (60 g) fresh basil, tightly packed
½	cup (120 ml) fruity olive oil
1	small tomato, peeled, seeded and chopped
1	cup (100 g) freshly grated Parmesan, or a mixture of Gruyère cheese and Parmesan
	Salt and freshly ground pepper, to taste

Making the soup: Soak the beans overnight or for several hours in 1 quart (1 L) of the water (use bottled if your water is hard). Drain.

Heat the 2 tablespoons olive oil in a heavy-bottomed soup pot and add the onions and half the garlic. Sauté over medium heat until the onions are tender and add the beans, the bouquet garni and 2 quarts (2 L) water. Bring to a boil, reduce the heat, cover, and cook 1 hour. The beans should be almost tender and the broth aromatic.

Add the remaining 1 quart (1 L) water and 2 cloves garlic, the optional Parmesan rinds, potatoes, leek, carrots, tomatoes and the chopped, but not the sliced, zucchini, and salt to taste. Cover and simmer 1 hour. Adjust seasonings.

Making the pistou: While the soup is simmering, pound together the garlic and basil in a mortar, or puree in a food processor. Drizzle in the oil, continuing to pound or process until you have a smooth paste. Work in the tomato and the cheese. Taste and add salt and freshly ground pepper to taste. Set aside.

Completing the soup: 10 to 15 minutes before you

wish to serve the soup, add the sliced zucchini, green beans and pasta. Simmer until the vegetables are tender but still bright green and the pasta is cooked al dente, just until firm to the bite. Taste the soup, adjust the salt, and add ground pepper to taste. Remove the Parmesan rind and the bouquet garni.

The pistou is added to the soup at the last minute. It can either be stirred into the soup pot or added to each individual serving. Another alternative is to serve the soup and pass the pistou in its mortar, allowing your guests to stir in their own. Serve with a crusty country-style bread, such as Country Bread With Olives (page 38) and a crisp green salad.

To prepare ahead of time: This soup will hold for several days in the refrigerator. It's actually best if made the day before you serve it (see note). Allow it to cool, then cover and refrigerate. The pistou enrichment can be made several days in advance, just up to the adding of the cheese and tomato, and stored in a covered container in the refrigerator. Without the cheese and tomato, it freezes well.

Note: If the soup is made the day before, proceed up to the adding of the sliced zucchini, green beans and pasta. Reheat the soup before serving and adjust seasonings. Ten to 15 minutes before serving, add the sliced zucchini, green beans and pasta and proceed as above, adding the pistou at the last minute. If you are making this soup in quantity, steam the zucchini and green beans separately and add them to the soup when you serve it.

SERVES 6 TO 8

Baked Fresh Figs With Crème Anglaise

❧

I FIRST DEVELOPED this dish to go with a Moroccan meal. The figs are poached in a mixture of red wine, honey and cinnamon. They are then removed from the wine, and the wine is strained and reduced by about ⅓. The poached figs can sit all day, until shortly before serving, they are baked in a moderate oven for about 15 minutes.

Meanwhile, you will have made a crème anglaise, seasoned with vanilla and nutmeg. To serve, first the wine syrup goes on a plate or in a bowl, then the hot figs, then the crème anglaise, which you can also dot around the edges of the syrup. The crème anglaise melts into the syrup, and it is beautiful and insanely delicious.

It really doesn't matter in what order you do this. The crème anglaise can be made before or after you poach the figs.

FOR THE FIGS

3 cups (700 ml) red wine, not too full-bodied
½ cup (120 ml) mild-flavored honey
½ teaspoon ground cinnamon or more, to taste
½ teaspoon vanilla

1½ to 2 pounds (750 g to 1 kg) fresh ripe figs, preferably black

FOR THE CRÈME ANGLAISE

4 large egg yolks
½ cup (120 ml) mild-flavored honey
1½ cups (350 ml) low-fat milk
1 teaspoon vanilla
Pinch of freshly grated nutmeg

Poaching the figs: Combine the wine, honey, cinnamon and vanilla and bring to a boil in a large, heavy-bottomed saucepan. Meanwhile, make a lengthwise incision in each fig, but do not cut them in half all the way. The inside as well as the outside will now become infused with the spicy wine-and-honey mixture.

Turn the wine to a simmer and drop in the figs. If they are very ripe, turn off the heat immediately and infuse for 5 to 10 minutes. If they are slightly hard, poach over low heat for 15 minutes. Carefully remove the figs from the wine with a slotted spoon and place in a buttered flat baking dish. Strain the wine through a fine sieve and return it to the pot.

Bring to a boil and reduce by about ⅓. Set aside. Set the dish aside and cover after the figs have cooled.

Making the crème anglaise: With an electric mixer, beat together the egg yolks and honey at high speed until they are thick, lemon colored and ribbony. At the same time, heat the milk to a simmer. Remove the milk from the heat and beat slowly into the egg yolks. Turn this mixture into a heavy-bottomed saucepan or the top of a double boiler or a saucepan set over a flame tamer, and stir over low heat until it thickens. Do not allow it to come to a simmer, or the egg yolks will curdle. When the mixture coats the front and back of your spoon like thick cream, remove it from the heat and continue to stir for a minute to cool. Stir in the vanilla and nutmeg and set aside. You can serve this on the figs at room temperature, chilled or warm.

About 25 minutes before you wish to serve, preheat the oven to 375° F (190° C). Place the figs in the oven and heat through for 10 to 15 minutes, until they are just beginning to dry. Remove them from the oven and pour on the wine.

To serve: Spoon the wine into serving bowls, then add the figs and top with the crème anglaise.

To prepare ahead of time: Each part of this dish—the poached figs, the wine syrup and the crème anglaise—will hold for several hours, in or out of the refrigerator. The crème anglaise can be made 1 day ahead of time. Allow it to cool, cover tightly, and refrigerate.

Serves 6 to 8

Fig Tart With Green Grapes

❧

THE LIGHT GREEN GRAPES are beautiful alongside the figs in this tart. If you can find the big, sweet Muscat grapes—they are often imported from Italy and France in the fall—use them. Otherwise, use California seedless.

Sweet Almond Piecrust (page 43) or
   Whole-Wheat Dessert Crust (page 43)
Crème Anglaise (page 64)
2   cups (500 ml) red wine, not too full-
      bodied
½   cup (120 ml) mild-flavored honey
½   teaspoon ground cinnamon or more, to
      taste
½   teaspoon vanilla
1   pound (500 g) fresh ripe figs
½   pound (250 g) large green grapes,
      preferably Muscat, or California
      seedless
1   egg, beaten

First make the crust. Refrigerate or freeze it until ready to prebake and assemble the tart.

The crème anglaise can be made before or after you prepare the figs. You can serve it on the tart at room temperature, chilled or warm.

Making the figs: Combine the wine, honey, cinnamon and ½ teaspoon vanilla and bring to a boil in a large, heavy-bottomed saucepan. Meanwhile, cut the figs in half lengthwise. Reduce the wine to a simmer and drop in the figs. Poach them for 5 minutes, then carefully remove from the wine with a slotted spoon and place in a flat baking dish. Strain the wine through a fine sieve and return it to the pot. Bring to a boil and reduce by half. Set aside.

Assembling and completing the tart: If you object to leaving the seeds in the grapes, cut the grapes in half and remove the seeds. Otherwise, leave whole.

Preheat the oven to 375° F (190° C). Brush the crust with beaten egg and prebake it for 15 to 20 minutes, until golden brown. Arrange the figs, cut side up, and grapes, cut side down if you've removed the seeds, on the baked tart shell in an attractive pattern. Brush with the reduced wine.

Preheat the broiler. Place the tart under the broiler for 10 minutes, until the figs begin to caramelize.

(Watch carefully so it does not burn.) Remove from the heat and serve hot or cool, passing the crème anglaise or spooning a little over or alongside the tart.

To prepare ahead of time: The crust can be made days in advance, covered with foil and frozen. The crème anglaise will hold for a day in the refrigerator, and the figs will hold for several hours. For best results, don't let the tart sit too long once it is assembled, as the crust will become soggy.

SERVES 8

November

❦

A Salute to Beaujolais Nouveau

APERITIF: BEAUJOLAIS NOUVEAU

SALAD OF WILD AND ITALIAN RICE WITH GREEN BEANS

MIXED-GRAINS BREAD (PAGE 30)

BROCCOLI PUREE

MUSHROOM TART

PUMPKIN, SWEET POTATO AND APPLE PUREE

PUCKER-UP CRANBERRY RELISH

CRISP ALMOND COOKIES

PEARS POACHED IN BEAUJOLAIS

WINE SUGGESTIONS: ZINFANDEL, GAMAY PRIMEUR

SERVES 6

November

THIS MEAL was a kind of pre-Thanksgiving dinner without the turkey. It also happened to fall on the Beaujolais nouveau day in 1985. Beaujolais nouveau is the first wine made from the year's harvest that is ready to drink, and the government sets a date upon which it can legally be sold, which is usually the third Thursday in November. All the cafés post signs that say, *"Le Beaujolais nouveau est arrivé!"* and all over Paris, people stop at watering holes to taste it. Cafés and wine bars that normally close at 8:00 p.m. are packed with people and stay open until 9:00 or 10:00. During the day, business people—executives, shopkeepers, secretaries and beauticians—open bottles at work so they and their employees can taste the year's wine. Some years, the Beaujolais is smooth, fruity and promising; other times, it tastes rough and unfinished. But whatever the quality of the wine, I love the way all of Paris gets involved.

Naturally, Beaujolais nouveau was the aperitif at the Supper Club. It should be drunk slightly chilled, and on this unseasonably cold, snowy evening, I kept the wine on the balcony, which often serves as a refrigerator for me in the winter. My guests sat around the fireplace drinking the Beaujolais.

This was a fall/winter meal with earth tones and flavors and delicious combinations of savory and sweet. The pale green broccoli puree, bright yellow-orange sweet potato and pumpkin puree and red cranberry relish looked exquisite side by side on the plate, next to the fragrant mushroom tart. The shimmering pears poached in Beaujolais with the hard, almondy biscotti, meant to be dipped into the wine, completed the Beaujolais nouveau theme and provided a refreshing finish to the meal. Many of the American guests commented that the dinner had all the elements of Thanksgiving without the stuffed feeling you have at the end.

Steamed Fish Fillets With Tomato-Caper Sauce
page 149

Salad With Warm Green Beans and Walnuts
page 88

Sopa de Tortilla
page 97

71

Ravioli and Broccoli Salad
page 104

Salad of Wild and Italian Rice With Green Beans

❋

I ALWAYS HAVE wild rice on hand in Paris because my relatives and friends from Minneapolis send it to me regularly. I consider the grain a luxury, but I've seen some French people turn up their noses because it looks funny, even ugly, to them. This salad combines wild rice with brown or Italian Arborio rice; each rice is cooked separately in vegetable stock, and then they are tossed together with walnut oil. Shortly before serving, the grains are tossed in a vinaigrette with walnuts or pecans and mushrooms, bright green beans and herbs, then spooned over a bed of lettuce. What an exciting contrast of textures, flavors and colors! Sweet red peppers garnish the dish and add one more complementary taste.

The dressing for the rice is not very acidic, because the grains themselves taste so good and the mushrooms are tossed separately in lemon juice. But if you prefer a sharper vinaigrette, feel free to add more vinegar and/or mustard. Also, you can vary the herbs. Sometimes, I use the rosemary and thyme; at other times, I go for sweeter herbs like chervil, tarragon or chives.

FOR THE RICE

4 cups (1 L) vegetable stock or bouillon
1 cup (175 g) wild rice
½ cup (100 g) short-grain brown rice or Italian Arborio rice
  Salt
½ cup (120 ml) walnut oil

FOR THE VINAIGRETTE

3 tablespoons red-wine vinegar
1 teaspoon Dijon mustard
1 small clove garlic, minced or put through a press (optional)
6 tablespoons olive or safflower oil
  Salt and freshly ground pepper, to taste

FOR THE SALAD

½ pound (250 g) mushrooms, cleaned and sliced

Juice of 2 large lemons
½ pound (250 g) green beans, ends trimmed
½ cup (55 g) walnuts or pecans, broken
¼ cup (10 g) chopped fresh parsley
1 to 2 teaspoons finely minced fresh rosemary, if available
1 teaspoon fresh thyme leaves, if available, or ¼ teaspoon dried
1 small sweet red pepper, sliced into thin strips
1 bunch fresh chervil, if available
  Lettuce leaves, either green leaf or red-tip

Preparing the rice: Bring 2 ½ cups (570 ml) of the vegetable stock or bouillon to a boil in a large saucepan and add the wild rice and a little salt. When the liquid comes back to a boil, reduce the heat, cover and simmer 35 minutes. If the grains are tender but not mushy, remove from the heat and drain off the excess stock. If still not tender, cook another 10 minutes, adding more water if necessary. Remove from the heat and pour off the excess stock.

Meanwhile, in another saucepan, bring the remaining 1 ½ cups (350 ml) stock or bouillon to a boil and add the brown or Italian rice and a little salt. Bring to a second boil, cover, reduce the heat, and simmer 35 to 40 minutes, until the rice is tender but not mushy (pour off any liquid that remains). Toss the two rices together in a large bowl with the walnut oil and set aside.

Preparing the vinaigrette: Mix together the vinegar, mustard, optional garlic and the olive or safflower oil for the vinaigrette. Add salt and freshly ground pepper to taste and blend well.

Preparing the salad: Slice the mushrooms and toss with the lemon juice. Set aside. Blanch the green beans in boiling water for 1 to 2 minutes, drain, and rinse with cold water. Just before serving, toss the beans with the vinaigrette, then toss this mixture, along with the mushrooms, nuts and all the chopped parsley, rosemary and thyme, with the rice. Taste and correct seasonings, adding salt, pepper, garlic or vinegar to taste.

To serve: Line individual plates with lettuce leaves, top with the salad and place the optional chervil sprigs on the top. Garnish with the strips of sweet red pepper. Or line a salad bowl or platter with the lettuce leaves, top with the salad and decorate with the optional chervil and red peppers.

To prepare ahead of time: The rices can be cooked 1 day ahead and tossed with the walnut oil. Place in a bowl, cover and refrigerate.

You can make the dressing several hours ahead. Hold it in or out of the refrigerator.

The green beans can be blanched up to 1 day ahead and stored in a plastic bag in the refrigerator.

The herbs can be chopped up to 1 day ahead. Make sure they are dry before you chop them. Place in a bowl or plastic container, cover tightly and refrigerate.

The mushrooms can be sliced several hours ahead and held in the refrigerator in a covered bowl. Do not add the lemon juice until close to serving, as the flavor changes after about ½ hour.

SERVES 6

Broccoli Puree

❀

THIS BRIGHT green puree is an adaptation of a *Silver Palate* recipe for pureed broccoli with crème fraîche. I've reduced the amount of crème fraîche and substituted plain low-fat yogurt for the sour cream. This is a light, subtle dish—so subtle, in fact, that people often ask me what the vegetable is.

3 pounds (1.5 kg) broccoli, stems peeled and chopped, tops separated into florets
½ cup (120 ml) crème fraîche (page 20)
¾ cup (180 ml) plain low-fat yogurt
½ cup (55 g) freshly grated Parmesan (2 ounces)
¼ teaspoon freshly grated nutmeg
Salt and freshly ground pepper, to taste
2 tablespoons unsalted butter

Preheat the oven to 350° F (180° C). Butter an ovenproof serving dish.

Steam the broccoli until tender, about 8 to 10 minutes. Drain and refresh under cold water, then puree in a food processor or through a food mill. Add the crème fraîche and continue to puree until smooth. Stir in the yogurt, Parmesan, nutmeg, salt and pepper. Taste and adjust seasonings.

Transfer the puree to the prepared serving dish and dot with butter. Bake for 25 minutes in the preheated oven, or until steaming hot. Serve at once.

To prepare ahead of time: The broccoli can be trimmed and steamed 1 day in advance. Drain it thoroughly and hold in the refrigerator in a plastic bag or covered bowl. The puree can be made several hours before baking and held in the refrigerator.

SERVES 6

Mushroom Tart

❀

THIS IS A HEARTY and heartwarming combination of sweet browned onions and savory mushrooms. The mushrooms are chunky and meaty. The night after I served this at the Supper Club, I was at a French dinner party where the conversation inevitably led to food, and a woman asked me whether it wasn't terribly difficult to produce a satisfying meal without meat. I found myself using this tart to illustrate how certain vegetable dishes can satisfy in the same way that meat satisfies.

I have cut the tart into small pieces and used it as an hors d'oeuvre as well as a main course. Try to make up the crust the day before. Or do it several days before and freeze it.

If fresh wild mushrooms are available, use an assortment. If not, use dried wild mushrooms and fresh cultivated ones.

	Savory Whole-Wheat Crust (page 43)
3	tablespoons butter
2 to 3	tablespoons olive oil, as necessary
4	medium or large onions, chopped
2	cups (55 g) dried cèpes (porcini) or other wild mushrooms
	Boiling water to cover (optional)
2	pounds (1 kg) fresh cultivated mushrooms
3 to 4	cloves garlic, to taste, minced or put through a press
¼	cup (60 ml) dry white wine
1 to 2	tablespoons soy sauce or more, to taste
½	teaspoon dried thyme
½ to 1	teaspoon dried rosemary, to taste, crumbled
	Salt and freshly ground pepper, to taste
4	large eggs
½	cup (120 ml) low-fat milk or (for a richer version) crème fraîche (page 20)
⅔	cup (85 g) grated Gruyère cheese (3 ounces)
3	tablespoons chopped fresh parsley

Make the crust. Refrigerate until ready to prebake.

Making the filling: Heat 2 tablespoons of the butter and 1 tablespoon of the oil in a large, heavy-bottomed skillet and sauté the onions, stirring occasionally, over medium-low heat for 30 to 40 minutes, or until browned and caramelized.

While the onions are browning, prepare the mushrooms. Place the dried cèpes, if using, in a bowl and pour on boiling water to cover. Let them sit for about 20 minutes, or until softened; drain and rinse thoroughly. Squeeze dry. Save the soaking liquid for vegetable stock.

Trim the fresh mushrooms, wash them quickly and wipe dry. Cut into quarters if large, in half if they are small.

When the onions are ready, transfer to a bowl and set aside. Add the remaining tablespoon of butter and 1 tablespoon oil to the skillet and heat over medium heat. Add the mushrooms and sauté, stirring, for about 5 minutes, until they begin to release their liquid. Add the garlic, dried mushrooms and more oil if necessary. After about 10 minutes, add the wine and soy sauce and continue to sauté, stirring from time to time, for another 5 to 10 minutes. Stir in the thyme and rosemary and add salt and freshly ground pepper to taste. Raise the heat and cook, stirring, until the liquid is reduced by about ¾, so that the mushrooms are glazed and a little liquid remains in the pan. Taste and adjust the seasonings, adding a little salt, pepper, soy sauce or garlic if you wish, and transfer to the bowl with the browned onions.

Baking the tart: Preheat the oven to 375° F (190° C). Beat the eggs in a bowl. Prick the tart crust with a fork and brush with some of the beaten egg; this will prevent the crust from becoming soggy. Place it in the preheated oven for about 8 minutes, or until just crisp on the bottom, and remove from the heat.

Stir the milk or crème fraîche into the beaten eggs, along with the cheese and parsley. Add the mushrooms and onions and combine thoroughly. Adjust seasonings.

Turn the mushroom mixture into the crust and bake in the preheated oven for 30 to 40 minutes, until firm. Remove from the heat. Serve hot or at room temperature.

To prepare ahead of time: The unbaked crust can be made several days in advance and stored, covered with foil, in the refrigerator or freezer.

The filling, without the eggs and milk or crème fraîche, can be made 1 day in advance. Let it cool, transfer to a bowl, cover and refrigerate. Allow to come to room temperature before baking.

The tart can be cooked 1 to 2 hours before you wish to serve it and reheated at the last minute.

SERVES 6 TO 8

Pumpkin, Sweet Potato and Apple Puree

O F ALL THE DISHES I serve for my Thanksgiving or Thanksgiving-type meals, this one gets the biggest raves. The contrast of tart and sweet is sublime, the texture is smooth and light, and the color is gorgeous. It's a beguiling combination; my guests always ask me what's in it (and it's so simple!). The puree contrasts nicely with savory dishes.

1	pound (500 g) sweet potatoes
2	tart apples
1	pound (500 g) pumpkin, seeds and strings removed
	Unsalted butter
	Juice of 1 lime
¼	cup (60 ml) plain low-fat yogurt or crème fraîche (page 20)
2	tablespoons melted unsalted butter
1	tablespoon mild-flavored honey
	Salt, to taste (optional)

Preheat the oven to 425° F (220° C). Rub the skins of the sweet potatoes and apples and the surface of the pumpkin with butter, and pierce the sweet potatoes and apples in a few places with a knife. Place the vegetables, with the pumpkin cut side down, on an oiled baking sheet or baking sheets and bake until they are all tender. The apples will be done first, after about 30 minutes, then the pumpkin, after about 45 minutes, and finally the sweet potatoes, after about 50 minutes. Remove them from the oven as they are done; then, when cool enough to handle, remove the skins from the potatoes and pumpkin and the skins and cores from the apples.

Cut the sweet potatoes, pumpkin and apples into chunks and puree in a food processor or through the fine blade of a food mill. Add the remaining ingredients and blend together well. Place in a buttered serving dish and warm in a 350° F (180° C) oven until steaming. Serve hot.

To prepare ahead of time: The sweet potatoes, pumpkin and apples can all be baked, skinned and pureed 1 day in advance and held in the refrigerator.

SERVES 6

Pucker-Up Cranberry Relish

M Y FRIEND Stewart McBride, a journalist who once lived in Paris, gave this tart mixture of cranberries, oranges, nuts and honey its name. In my local Saint-Germain market, there is one woman who sells Ocean Spray cranberries. I don't know where she gets them, but in the fall, I'm one of her best customers.

This cranberry sauce is so much more refreshing than the usual sweet, cooked variety. It makes a great leftover. Eat it in the morning with yogurt.

1	pound (500 g), or 1 ½ 10-ounce bags fresh cranberries, washed and picked over
1	whole navel orange, skin included, washed and cut in eighths
½	cup (55 g) walnuts or pecans
¼	cup (60 ml) mild-flavored honey

Place all the ingredients in a food processor and blend until you have a uniform, very finely chopped mixture. The texture will be crunchy. Chill until ready to serve.

To prepare ahead of time: This can be made 1 day in advance, although it's best made the day you are going to serve it.

SERVES 8

Crisp Almond Cookies

✦

AN ITALIAN MIGHT be scandalized by my version of this well-known Tuscan almond cookie, for mine is half as sweet, made with honey, not sugar, and with whole-wheat flour. I cut the cookies much thinner than the traditional biscotti, and they aren't heavy. But like Italian biscotti, they are very hard and crunchy, with a deep roasted-almond flavor. They are perfect for dipping in sweet red wine, the way the Italians do, and for this reason, I usually serve them with wine-poached or marinated fruit.

This dough becomes very stiff when you are incorporating the almonds, but with persistence, you can work them all in. The cookies should be made a few days before you wish to serve them. They will keep in a well-sealed container for weeks.

¼	pound (115 g) almonds (1 heaping cup)
2	large eggs plus 1 egg white
½	cup (120 ml) mild-flavored honey
2 ¾	cups (310 g) whole-wheat pastry flour or unbleached white flour
½	teaspoon baking soda
¼	teaspoon salt

Preheat the oven to 375° F (190° C). Place the almonds on a baking sheet and roast them for about 10 minutes, until lightly golden and toasty-smelling. Remove from the oven. Grind ¼ heaping cup (1 ounce, 30 g) of the almonds fine and chop the rest into coarse pieces. Set aside.

In a mixer or a large bowl, blend together the whole eggs and honey. Mix in 2 ½ cups (280 g) of the flour, the baking soda and salt. When all the ingredients are mixed together, place the remaining ¼ cup (30 g) flour on a work surface, place the dough on the flour, and knead for 10 to 15 minutes. The dough will be stiff.

The ingredients can also be mixed together like pasta. Place 2 ½ cups (280 g) of flour in a mound on a board and make a well in the center. Break in the eggs, add baking soda and salt, then add the honey. Beat together with a fork, then mix in the remaining ¼ cup (30 g) flour, as needed. Gather into a ball and knead as above.

Now incorporate the ground and chopped almonds into the dough. This will seem difficult at first because the dough is so stiff. The easiest way to do it is to press the dough out flat, add a handful of almonds, fold and knead a few minutes, then press out again and continue with this procedure until all the almonds have been added. You will get a good workout.

Divide the dough in half and shape it into 2 long logs, about 2 inches (5 cm) wide. Place them on a buttered and flour-dusted baking sheet, not too close to each other. Beat the egg white until foamy and brush it over the logs. Bake in the preheated oven for 20 minutes, until golden brown and shiny. Remove from the oven and turn the oven heat down to 275° F (150° C).

Cut the logs into thin slices, about ¼ to ½ inch (0.75 to 1.5 cm) thick, at a 45-degree angle. Use a bread knife or a sharp chef's knife. Place the cookies on the baking sheet (or on 2 baking sheets) and bake again for about 40 minutes in the slow oven, until dry and hard. Remove from the heat and cool. Keep in a covered container. These last a long time.

MAKES ABOUT 5 DOZEN COOKIES

Pears Poached in Beaujolais

THIS DISH doesn't taste as strange as its combination of ingredients may sound. Despite the quantity of peppercorns, their flavor is subtle, giving the wine, which has been sweetened with honey, a unique spicy taste that is altogether different from the usual sweet spice flavorings like cinnamon and nutmeg. You can put the peppercorns in a cheesecloth bag if you want to remove them after cooking. The dessert is perfect after a rich meal. It is served chilled, so you must make it a few hours ahead of time. It looks beautiful when served from a cut-glass or white porcelain bowl.

6   Comice pears, firm but ripe
     Water acidulated with the juice of 1 lemon
1   bottle (750 ml) Beaujolais
½   cup (120 ml) mild-flavored honey
2   tablespoons peppercorns

Peel the pears with a sharp knife, making sure to leave the stems intact. Drop them into a bowl of acidulated water. This will keep the pears from turning brown.

Combine the wine, honey and peppercorns in a large saucepan and bring to a simmer. Simmer 10 minutes and carefully drop in the pears. Simmer, never letting the wine boil, for 10 minutes and remove from the heat. Chill the pears in their liquid for several hours. Place the pears in a serving dish and strain in the wine. Discard the peppercorns.

Serve in wide bowls or sherbet dishes, with some of the wine ladled over the top.

SERVES 6

November, continued:
More Thanksgiving Delights

❧

APERITIF: CHAMPAGNE

CROUTONS WITH CAVIAR

CROUTONS WITH TAPENADE (PAGE 61)

SWEET AND SOUR CHERRY PICKLES

RADISHES, OLIVES

SALAD OF WILD AND ITALIAN RICE WITH GREEN BEANS (PAGE 73)

MIXED-GRAINS BREAD (PAGE 30)

ROAST TURKEY

CORNBREAD STUFFING

MUSHROOM RAGOUT GRAVY

BROCCOLI PUREE (PAGE 74)

PUMPKIN, SWEET POTATO AND APPLE PUREE (PAGE 76)

PUCKER-UP CRANBERRY RELISH (PAGE 76)

PECAN PIE

PUMPKIN PIE

WINE SUGGESTIONS: GAMAY PRIMEUR OR ZINFANDEL

SERVES 8

November, continued:

More Thanksgiving Delights

L E FANKSGEEVING," which is what Art Buchwald calls Thanksgiving in his famous column run faithfully by the *International Herald Tribune* every turkey day, is always a special feast in Paris. My French friends, mystified as some of them may be by pumpkin pie, seem to love the holiday as much as Americans do, although they don't stuff themselves the way Americans tend to. Right up to feast time, you see Americans scouring the markets and crowding Fauchon, the Paris equivalent of New York's Balducci's, in search of cranberries, sweet potatoes and mincemeat. If you are alone in Paris and want to find someone to share the meal with, just go to the market, listen for English, and strike up a conversation: somebody will invite you.

Of course, I always serve turkey; I'm not a fanatic vegetarian, and tradition prevails. But the Supper Club occasionally calls for baking feats beyond the capabilities of my apartment's oven. At times like that, I call on my poultry purveyor in the Saint-Germain market, Madame Decots. According to Jon Winroth and his wife, Doreen, who never seem to be wrong when it comes to gastronomy, Madame Decots sells the best poultry and eggs in Paris. Every November, she puts up a big sign for the Americans. I don't know who writes it for her, but it says: "Order Your Thanksgiving Turkey

Now." She was mighty pleased the year I ordered five big ones for the Supper Club—and also perplexed when I brought her my cornbread stuffing. When I ran into the Winroths a little later that day at a neighborhood wine bar, they told me that Madame Decots, looking confused and worried, had taken them aside, shown them the "farce" and asked them, confidentially, if all this bread was indeed a stuffing. Was it typically American? In France, they stuff their birds with livers, veal and sausage (not exactly my style). Doreen reassured Madame Decots that it was not only typically American, but quite delicious. Madame was skeptical. Nonetheless, every year she has dutifully stuffed and roasted my birds. I accompany the meat with a thick, savory mushroom ragout instead of a fatty gravy. The ragout is fabulous with the stuffing as well as the turkey and is even great all by itself.

My desserts are traditional: pecan and pumpkin pies (I ask every American friend coming to Paris to bring me pecans). Although there are sweet pumpkin pies to be found in France, particularly in the Soulogne region, many French people scorn pumpkin served as dessert, and some refuse to eat it. To them, pumpkin is strictly soup material. But pumpkin pie is one of my favorites, and the fresh pumpkin here is so good.

Sweet and Sour Cherry Pickles

I MAKE THESE PICKLES in June or early July, when the markets abound with Bing cherries, black cherries and Queen Annes. They can be stored for a year in a cool pantry, so they make a perfect hors d'oeuvre with drinks at fall and winter dinners.

1	pound (500 g) firm, ripe sweet or sour cherries
5 to 6	sprigs fresh tarragon, if available, rinsed and dried
2	cups (450 ml) good-quality white-wine vinegar, sherry vinegar or Champagne vinegar
⅓	cup (80 ml) mild-flavored honey
1	teaspoon salt

Pick over the cherries, discarding any with blemishes or soft spots. Rinse, drain and gently roll them in a towel. Cut the stems with scissors to ½ inch (1.5 cm).

Place the tarragon in a dry, sterilized quart canning jar and fill with the cherries.

Heat the vinegar, honey and salt together in a saucepan to simmering. Stir together to mix the honey with the vinegar. Remove from the heat and cool completely.

Pour the vinegar solution over the cherries, covering them (add more vinegar and a little honey if not completely covered). There should be ½ inch (1.5 cm) of headspace. Remove any bubbles by running a knife or chopstick around the inside edge of the jar. Seal the jar with a new sterilized canning lid, according to the manufacturer's directions and store in the refrigerator for no longer than 1 month. Or, process in a boiling-water bath for 10 minutes and store in a cool, dark place for at least 1 month before serving.

MAKES 1 QUART (1 L)

Cornbread Stuffing

WHETHER IT's baked inside or outside a bird, this is my favorite stuffing, especially when it's served with Mushroom Ragout Gravy (page 82). This is the stuffing that the poultry lady, Madame Decots, thought so bizarre. But over the years, she has gotten used to my strange "farce."

Note: This stuffing is even tastier if the sage is added to the cornbread when you make the bread.

2	tablespoons safflower oil or butter
2	cloves garlic, minced or put through a press
1	onion, minced
2 to 3	medium-sized stalks celery, to taste, chopped
4	cups (340 g) crumbled Texas Cornbread (page 39)
1	teaspoon rubbed sage
1 ½	teaspoons dried thyme
½	teaspoon dried rosemary, crumbled
	Freshly ground pepper, to taste
1	tablespoon pink peppercorns (optional)
½	cup (15 g) chopped fresh parsley
3	tablespoons low-fat milk, as necessary, to moisten

Heat the oil or butter in a wide, heavy-bottomed skillet and sauté the garlic and onion until the onion begins to soften. Add the celery and continue to sauté another 1 to 2 minutes. Add the cornbread, sage, thyme, rosemary and pepper and stir together thoroughly. Remove from the heat and stir in the optional pink peppercorns and the chopped parsley. Adjust the seasonings. Moisten with a little milk and use as a stuffing, or place in a buttered casserole, dot with butter, cover with foil, and heat through in a 325° F (170° C) oven.

To prepare ahead of time: The cornbread can be made 1 to 2 days before you make the stuffing, and the stuffing can be made 1 day before you wish to serve it and held in the refrigerator in a covered bowl or container.

SERVES 8 TO 10 OR STUFFS AN 8-POUND (4-KG) TURKEY

Mushroom Ragout Gravy

❧

THIS MAKES a savory, rich sauce for meat, stuffings or grains, as well as a delicious ragout on its own. If you can get fresh wild mushrooms, it will be truly special, but it is marvelous with regular mushrooms, as long as you can also get dried mushrooms, which are necessary for the strong, "meaty" broth.

1	cup (55 g) dried imported wild mushrooms, such as cèpes (porcini) or chanterelles
	Boiling water to cover
2	tablespoons unsalted butter
2	large shallots or 1 medium onion, minced
1	tablespoon olive or safflower oil or more, as needed
1	pound (500 g) fresh cultivated mushrooms, cleaned, trimmed and thickly sliced
3 to 4	cloves garlic, minced or put through a press
½	cup (120 ml) dry red wine
1 to 2	tablespoons soy sauce, to taste
2	cups (450 ml) vegetable stock or bouillon
1	teaspoon dried thyme
½	teaspoon dried rosemary, crumbled
	Salt and freshly ground pepper, to taste
2	tablespoons heavy cream or crème fraîche (page 20), optional

Place the dried mushrooms in a bowl and cover with boiling water. Let sit for 30 minutes while you prepare the remaining ingredients.

Heat the butter in a large, heavy-bottomed skillet and add the shallots or onion. Cook over medium-low heat, stirring often, for about 20 minutes, or until golden brown. Add the olive or safflower oil and the sliced fresh mushrooms. Stir together and sauté for 5 to 10 minutes, until the mushrooms begin to release their liquid.

Meanwhile, drain the dried mushrooms and reserve the liquid. Rinse the mushrooms thoroughly to remove sand, squeeze dry and add to the skillet, along with the garlic. Stir together and sauté for a few minutes, adding oil if necessary. Add the wine and soy sauce and bring to a simmer.

Strain the soaking liquid from the mushrooms through a strainer lined with cheesecloth or through a coffee filter. Measure out 1 cup (225 ml) and add it to the mushrooms, along with the stock, thyme and rosemary. Bring to a simmer, cover and simmer 20 minutes. Uncover and raise the heat to high. Reduce the liquid by half. Taste and adjust seasonings, adding salt, pepper, garlic or herbs to taste.

Remove a cupful of the mushrooms and puree them in a blender or food processor, then stir them back into the ragout. For a creamier mixture, add 2 tablespoons cream or crème fraîche.

To prepare ahead of time: This dish holds well and can be made up to 2 days in advance and kept in the refrigerator in a covered bowl. Reheat before serving.

SERVES 8

Pecan Pie

THIS IS DIFFERENT from the cloyingly sweet traditional pecan pie. Sweet it is, but there's just honey and a hint of molasses.

Whole-Wheat Dessert Crust (page 43)
- 4 eggs
- 4 tablespoons unsalted butter
- ½ cup (120 ml) mild-flavored honey
- 1 tablespoon molasses
- 1 tablespoon rum
- 1 ½ teaspoons vanilla
- ¼ teaspoon freshly grated nutmeg
- ¼ teaspoon salt
- 2 cups (225 g) pecans
  Nutmeg-flavored whipped cream

Prepare the piecrust. Preheat the oven to 375° F (190° C). Beat the eggs, then brush the crust with some of the beaten egg, prick and prebake 8 minutes. Remove from the oven, leaving the oven on.

Cream together the butter, honey and molasses. Beat in the remaining eggs and add the rum, vanilla, nutmeg and salt. Combine well. Fold in the pecans.

Turn the filling into the prebaked pie shell. Bake for 35 to 45 minutes, until a knife comes out clean when inserted in the center. The pie will puff up almost like a soufflé, but then, alas, it will fall.

Remove from the oven and cool on a rack. Serve with the nutmeg-flavored whipped cream.

SERVES 8

Pumpkin Pie

THIS IS A SPICY pumpkin pie with a touch of molasses.

Note: To make fresh pumpkin puree, preheat the oven to 425° F (220° C). Remove the seeds and strings from a 2-pound (1-kg) pumpkin, place it, cut side down, on an oiled baking sheet, and bake until thoroughly soft, about 45 minutes. Peel away the skin, scraping off any pumpkin that adheres, and puree all the pumpkin in a food processor or blender until smooth. Measure 2 cups (450 ml) for the recipe; freeze any left over.

Sweet Almond Piecrust (page 43), omitting almond extract
- 3 eggs
- 2 cups (450 ml) pumpkin puree, canned or fresh
- 1 cup (225 ml) low-fat milk
- 2 tablespoons unsalted butter, softened
- ½ cup (120 ml) mild-flavored honey
- 1 ½ tablespoons molasses
- 1 to 2 tablespoons rum, to taste
- 1 ½ teaspoons vanilla
- 2 teaspoons ground cinnamon
- 1 teaspoon grated fresh ginger or ½ teaspoon ground ginger
- ½ teaspoon freshly grated nutmeg
- ¼ teaspoon ground mace
- ¼ teaspoon ground cloves
- ¼ teaspoon salt
  Vanilla-flavored whipped cream or plain low-fat yogurt

Prepare the piecrust. Preheat the oven to 375° F (190° C). Beat the eggs and brush the piecrust with some of the beaten egg. Prebake the crust for 5 minutes, or until the bottom is just beginning to be crisp, and remove from the oven. Turn up the oven heat to 450° F (230° C).

Blend together the remaining beaten eggs, pumpkin puree, milk, butter, honey, molasses, rum, vanilla, spices and salt. Pour into the prebaked pie shell. Place in the preheated oven. After 10 minutes, turn the heat down to 350° F (180° C). Bake 45 to 50 minutes, or until firm to the touch. If the crust begins to burn on the edges, cover lightly with aluminum foil. Cool completely and serve with vanilla-flavored whipped cream or with plain low-fat yogurt.

SERVES 8

December

❧

An Italian Menu With Christmas Colors

APERITIF: CRÉMANT DE BOURGOGNE OR CHAMPAGNE

SALAD WITH WARM GREEN BEANS AND WALNUTS

PESTO BREAD (PAGE 39)

SOURDOUGH COUNTRY BREAD (PAGE 26)

GREEN LASAGNA WITH SPINACH FILLING

SAUTÉED FENNEL AND RED PEPPERS

TANGERINE SORBET

CORNMEAL AND ALMOND SHORTBREAD

WINE SUGGESTIONS: SAINT-JOSEPH, COTEAUX DU TRICASTIN

SERVES 6

December

My December Supper Club often feels like one of the first in a long string of holiday fêtes. That's one of the reasons I serve a sparkling wine as an aperitif—that and the fact that in December, the sun goes down at around 4:30 in the afternoon. By 8:30 or 9:00, a glass of Crémant de Bourgogne or Champagne is just what one needs to lift one's spirits.

A sensuous Italian meal might also do the trick. Every few months, I like to serve an Italian dinner, but for 25 people, I can't choose a pasta dish that is cooked and served at the last minute. So I serve dishes like the lasagna in this menu, Deep-Dish Eggplant Torte (page 109) or Cannelloni With Chard, Herb and Ricotta Filling (page 125). Good Italian food isn't easy to come by in Paris, and these dishes fulfill my cravings for garlicky, savory tomato sauces, pasta and Parmesan cheese.

This meal is beautifully balanced. The main dish is rich and filling, perfect for a cold, wet December night. It needs to be preceded and followed by a light first course and dessert. The salad is an elegant combination of mixed winter greens and tangy warm green beans and walnuts. The lasagna is set off by the lightly sautéed vegetables served on the side; the fennel, with its anise taste, is especially refreshing. After the lasagna, the Tangerine Sorbet, garnished with marinated tangerines and served with small squares of the almond-scented Cornmeal and Almond Shortbread, is exquisite. When you follow a delicious meal with an ineffable, light dessert, everybody remembers the dinner.

Salad With Warm Green Beans and Walnuts

✿

THIS IS a wonderful winter salad (pictured on page 70), with its warm green beans and slightly sweet and nutty dressing. The dressing contrasts beautifully with the bitter lettuces.

½   pound (250 g) mixed winter lettuces, such as red chicory or radicchio, curly endive, arugula and watercress

12   sprigs of fresh chervil or 1 tablespoon chopped fresh parsley

2   tablespoons chopped fresh chives

3   tablespoons balsamic vinegar

1 ½   teaspoons Dijon mustard

1   small clove garlic, minced or put through a press

¼   teaspoon dried tarragon

     Salt and freshly ground pepper to taste

6   tablespoons sunflower or olive oil, or a combination of the two

3   tablespoons walnut oil

1   teaspoon salt

½   pound (250 g) green beans, trimmed

½   cup (55 g) coarsely chopped walnuts

     Radishes for garnish

Wash, dry and toss together the lettuces, chervil or parsley and chives.

To make the dressing, stir together the vinegar, mustard, garlic, tarragon, salt and freshly ground pepper. Whisk in the oils and mix well.

Bring a large pot of water to a rolling boil. Add 1 teaspoon of salt and blanch the beans for 1 to 2 minutes. Drain the beans and rinse briefly with cold water. Place in a bowl.

Just before serving, toss the lettuce mixture with ⅓ of the dressing. Heat the remaining dressing in a saucepan and add the nuts. Stir together, and when the nuts are heated through, toss with the green beans. Place the dressed greens on individual plates and top with the warm dressed beans and walnuts. Garnish with radishes and serve at once.

To prepare ahead of time: The lettuces can be washed and dried thoroughly a day in advance and refrigerated in plastic bags.

The beans can be trimmed and blanched a day in advance. Reheat at the last minute by dumping them into boiling water for a couple of seconds. Drain and toss in the hot salad dressing with the nuts, as instructed in the recipe.

The dressing can be made a few hours before serving and held in or out of the refrigerator.

SERVES 4 TO 6

Green Lasagna With Spinach Filling

✿

I DON'T KNOW anybody who doesn't like a lasagna, especially this one. I have fond memories of making it for a late-night party on a Saturday afternoon in Austin, Texas, while listening to *Madame Butterfly* on the radio. It was the first time I'd ever listened to an opera in its entirety, which gives you an idea of how long it takes to make this lasagna if you're making it for a crowd. The music was perfect for the sensual activity: handling the light, slippery pasta and the rich spinach-ricotta-goat cheese filling, sprinkling the soft, freshly grated Parmesan and

watching the layers of green, red and milky white pile up on top of one another.

Lasagna can often be heavy and too rich, but this one isn't. For one thing, there is so much spinach and parsley in it that you are eating a garden of greens along with the tomato sauce, pasta and cheese. And the pasta itself is rolled very thin, unlike the thick, commercial variety. However, I wouldn't exactly call this dish "light," which is why I accompany it with a very simple salad and vegetable side dish and an ethereal fruit sorbet.

Note: The cheese filling here calls for goat cheese, and it's very important to find one that isn't too salty. Fresh local goat cheeses, if available, are your best bet. You can also use packaged dried lasagna noodles. The lasagna will be heavier. Cook them al dente, just until firm to the bite, according to the instructions on the box. This will take longer than fresh pasta, and you can cook 6 to 8 noodles at a time.

FOR THE TOMATO SAUCE

1	tablespoon olive oil
1	small onion, chopped
4 to 5	cloves garlic, minced or put through a press
4	pounds (2 kg) fresh tomatoes, seeded and chopped, or 4 28-ounce (765-g) cans, drained, seeded and chopped
2	tablespoons tomato paste
	Pinch of sugar
1	tablespoon chopped fresh basil or 1 teaspoon dried
1	teaspoon dried oregano or more, to taste
½	teaspoon dried thyme or more, to taste
	Salt and freshly ground pepper, to taste
	Pinch of ground cinnamon

FOR THE PASTA

3-egg Spinach Pasta (homemade, increased according to the note on page 40)
Salt
Vegetable or olive oil

FOR THE FILLING

1 ½	pounds (750 g) spinach
2	eggs
1	pound (500 g) part-skim ricotta
¼ to ½	pound (115 g to 250 g) fresh goat cheese, to taste, not too salty
½	cup (15 g) plus 2 tablespoons chopped fresh parsley, preferably flat-leaf
¼	cup (15 g) chopped fresh basil, if available
2	cloves garlic, minced or put through a press
1 ½	cups (170 g) freshly grated Parmesan (6 ounces)
⅛	teaspoon freshly grated nutmeg
	Salt and freshly ground pepper, to taste (optional)
¾	pound (350 g) part-skim mozzarella, thinly sliced
¼	cup (30 g) fresh or dry breadcrumbs, fine or coarse
2	tablespoons unsalted butter or olive oil

Making the tomato sauce: Heat the olive oil in a heavy-bottomed saucepan or Dutch oven and sauté the onion with half the garlic over medium heat until the onion is tender, about 5 minutes. Add the tomatoes, tomato paste and sugar and bring to a simmer. Simmer, uncovered, for 30 minutes. Add the remaining garlic, the herbs, salt and freshly ground pepper to taste and continue to simmer another 30 minutes. Add the cinnamon, then taste and adjust seasonings, adding more garlic, salt, pepper or herbs. Set aside.

Making the pasta: Mix up the pasta dough according to the directions on page 41. Knead, wrap in plastic, and set aside to rest for 30 minutes.

Making the filling: Stem and wash the spinach, but do not dry it. Wilt it in the water remaining on its leaves in a large, heavy-bottomed skillet over medium-high heat. Remove from the heat and squeeze dry in a towel. Chop fine.

Beat the eggs in a large bowl and beat in the ricotta, goat cheese, parsley, basil and garlic, ½ cup of the Parmesan and the spinach. Add the nutmeg and combine thoroughly. Taste and add a little salt and pepper, if you wish. Set aside.

Rolling out the pasta: You will roll out the pasta and cook a few strips at a time, assembling the casserole as you go along. You have to work quickly once you drain the pasta, because the lasagna strips become sticky and difficult to work with.

Oil a large baking dish and bring a large pot of water to a boil.

Meanwhile, roll out the pasta according to the instructions on page 41, into thin strips, 4 to 5 inches (10 cm to 12 cm) wide and a few inches longer than the pan. Allow to dry for 15 minutes or longer before cooking.

Cooking the pasta, assembling the lasagna: Have all your ingredients lined up in this order: pasta, tomato sauce, ricotta-spinach mixture, mozzarella, remaining 1 cup Parmesan and breadcrumbs.

Cook 3 or 4 strips of pasta at a time as follows: When the water reaches a boil, add 1 teaspoon of salt and 1 teaspoon of vegetable or olive oil. Add the fresh pasta, and after about 10 seconds, remove it from the water with a slotted spoon or skimmer, transfer to a bowl of cold water, then drain at once on kitchen towels.

Depending on the amount of pasta you have, you will be making 3 or 4 layers. Spoon a very small amount of tomato sauce over the bottom of the baking dish. Lay 3 sheets of pasta across the bottom of the dish so the edges overlap the sides of the pan. Spread a layer of the tomato sauce over the pasta. Top with a layer of the ricotta-spinach mixture, then a layer of mozzarella and finally a layer of Parmesan. Continue cooking the pasta and layering the lasagna like this, ending with an added layer of pasta, tomato sauce and Parmesan. Take the overlapping edges of the pasta and fold them over the top like a package. Sprinkle the breadcrumbs over the top and dot with butter or drizzle on the olive oil. Cover with foil and set aside or refrigerate until shortly before baking time.

Preheat the oven to 350° F (180° C). Remove the foil and bake the lasagna 40 minutes, or until it is bubbling and starting to brown on the top. Remove from the oven, sprinkle with the additional parsley and serve.

To prepare ahead of time: The tomato sauce can be made up to 2 days in advance. Refrigerate in a covered bowl or container.

The pasta dough can be made 1 day in advance, wrapped tightly in plastic and held in the refrigerator overnight. Don't roll it out, however, until you are ready to assemble the lasagna.

The ricotta-spinach filling can be made 1 day in advance and held in the refrigerator in a covered bowl or container.

The entire lasagna can be assembled up to 1 day in advance, covered with plastic wrap, then aluminum foil and held in the refrigerator. Uncover and allow to come to room temperature before baking.

Serves 6 to 8

Sautéed Fennel and Red Peppers

THIS LIGHT, crunchy sauté is a great accompaniment for rich, complicated dishes. The night I served it with lasagna, one of my guests was allergic to cheese, so I tossed a large portion of the sauté with homemade spinach fettuccine noodles, and he was delighted. It looked as beautiful as it tasted.

2   tablespoons olive oil
3   sweet red peppers, cut into thin strips
1   pound (500 g) fennel, thinly sliced
1   large clove garlic, minced or put through a
      press
    Salt and freshly ground pepper, to taste

Heat the oil in a large, heavy-bottomed skillet and sauté the peppers with the fennel and garlic for 10 to 15 minutes over medium-high heat, stirring often. The vegetables should retain their crunch. Add salt and pepper to taste, and serve as a side dish.

To prepare ahead of time: The vegetables can be prepared and held in the refrigerator several hours ahead of time. They should be cooked just before serving.

Serves 6

Tangerine Sorbet

THIS POPULAR dessert is very easy to prepare, but it will work only if you can find good, juicy tangerines.

FOR THE SORBET

½ cup (120 ml) mild-flavored honey
1 cup (225 ml) water
2 cups (450 ml) strained fresh tangerine juice (juice of about 2 pounds, 1 kg, tangerines)
Juice of 1 orange, strained
½ cup (120 ml) strained fresh lemon juice
Finely minced grated zest of 1 orange (optional)

FOR THE TANGERINE GARNISH

6 tangerines, peeled and sectioned
¼ cup (60 ml) tangerine or mandarin liqueur or Cointreau
2 tablespoons chopped fresh mint leaves

Making the sorbet: Combine the honey and water in a large saucepan and bring to a boil. Reduce the heat and simmer 10 minutes. Remove from the heat and cool.

Stir the juices and optional orange zest into the cooled syrup. Either freeze in an ice cream freezer or sorbetière or still-freeze according to the instructions in the note on page 55.

After freezing by any method, spoon the frozen mixture into individual molds and cover each one with plastic wrap, then foil, and freeze. Or oil a loaf pan and line it with plastic wrap. Spoon in the sorbet mixture, cover tightly with plastic, then foil, and freeze. Work quickly so the frozen mixture doesn't melt, or ice crystals will form again when it freezes.

Making the garnish: Toss together the tangerine sections and the liqueur or Cointreau. Add the fresh mint leaves. Set aside or refrigerate until ready to serve.

Twenty minutes before serving, place the sorbet in the refrigerator to soften. If you froze the sorbet in the loaf pan, unmold it onto a platter. Cut slices with a sharp knife. If you froze it in individual molds, unmold into bowls. Top each serving with the tangerine garnish.

To prepare ahead of time: The sorbet can be made several days or even weeks before you wish to serve it. The garnish can be made several hours ahead of serving time and held in the refrigerator in a covered bowl.

SERVES 6

Cornmeal and Almond Shortbread

THIS IS BASED on Carol Field's recipe for *fregolata veneziana*, a sort of crumbly shortbread made in Venice. It's another terrific recipe that I came across in *The Italian Baker* and have modified, substituting honey for most of the sugar and unbleached white or whole-wheat pastry flour for all-purpose flour. Mine is a denser cookie/cake than the traditional version, and for this reason, I cut it into tiny squares, which I serve with sorbets or marinated fruit.

Note: Malt syrup is found in health-food stores.

1 ¼ cups (125 g) raw almonds
3 tablespoons raw brown sugar (Turbinado)
1 stick (115 g) unsalted butter, melted and cooled
¼ cup (60 ml) mild-flavored honey
1 tablespoon malt syrup

2   large egg yolks
1   tablespoon fresh lemon juice
    Grated zest of 1 lemon
1   teaspoon vanilla
¼   teaspoon almond extract
1   scant cup (100 g) either light whole-wheat pastry flour or unbleached white flour
⅞   cup (100 g) fine yellow cornmeal
    Pinch of salt

Preheat the oven to 350° F (180° C). Butter a 9 x 9-inch (22 x 22-cm) cake pan or a 9- or 10-inch (22- to 25-cm) pie plate.

Grind 1 scant cup (100 g) almonds to a fine powder, along with 2 tablespoons of the sugar, in a nut grinder or a food processor fitted with the steel blade. Transfer to a mixing bowl and beat in the butter. Add the honey and malt syrup and cream together until well blended. Beat in the egg yolks, lemon juice, zest and the vanilla and almond extract.

Sift together the flour, cornmeal and salt. Stir this into the liquid mixture and mix just until the dough comes together. It will be sticky. Do not overwork.

Spoon the dough into the prepared baking dish and spread it out in an even layer with your hands. Chop the remaining ¼ cup (25 g) almonds and sprinkle over the dough, along with the remaining tablespoon of sugar.

Bake 20 minutes in the preheated oven. Turn down the heat to 300° F (150° C) and bake another 20 minutes, or until the top is beginning to brown and a tester comes out clean. Cool completely on a rack and cut into squares. These will keep for several days if well covered.

MAKES 12 TO 24 SQUARES

January

❀

Viva Mexico!

Aperitif: Margaritas (page 50)

Guacamole Nachos

Sopa de Tortilla

Cumin and Cornmeal Bread (page 31)

Marinated Cod in Escabeche

Blue Corn Masa Crepes

Refried Black Beans (page 51)

Salsa Fresca (page 53)

Texas Tea Cakes

Pineapple-Orange-Banana Sorbet With Mint

Wine Suggestions: Hermitage Blanc, Crozes-Hermitage Blanc,
Coteaux du Tricastin

Serves 6

January

WITH THE EXCEPTION of the dessert, most of this menu was inspired by a two-week vacation in the Yucatán. I made the meal just after the trip, when all the flavors of southern Mexico were still vivid. A friend and I had spent our Christmas holiday in a small hotel south of Cancún. Our bungalow was right on the beach, and we ate our meals in an open-air dining room with a thatched roof. I particularly enjoyed the soups I ate every night under the stars: a tangy lime soup with bits of chicken and chili peppers in a light broth seasoned with fresh cilantro and lime juice; a tomatoey tortilla soup; and black beans. This course preceded fish or enchiladas, the fish most often being grilled red snapper with a spicy tomato sauce. Dessert was always fresh fruit: sweet, juicy pineapple, luxurious mango, subtle papaya. When I got back to Paris that dull, gray January, I couldn't wait to liven things up with a Mexican dinner party. The dining room was bright and cheery with colorful new tablecloths, napkins, baskets and pottery I'd bought in Mexico.

When I serve Mexican food at my dinners, there are certain dishes I feel I must include, and it is always a challenge to come up with an original menu while not leaving out the traditional favorites: guacamole, tortillas, refried beans, salsa fresca and, of course, margaritas. For this meal, I include an extra course, Guacamole Nachos, which are easy to assemble while the guests are drinking their margaritas and which look beautiful on the plate, garnished with radish roses or thin strips of red pepper. They are followed by the soup, which isn't a heavy one, so that people won't be too full for the main course, which is marinated cod with zucchini served on a soft masa crepe. Here's where I fit in the salsa, a colorful garnish, and the savory, shiny refried black beans: they go perfectly with the light, pungent fish. The crepes are delicate and delicious, whether made with regular masa harina or blue masa from New Mexico, which has a coarser texture. One of the reasons I serve them, one to a plate, gently folded over the fish, is that the fish often falls apart in the marinade. The crepes serve as a kind of container and make a neater-looking dish. You can leave them out, however, if you want.

Dessert should be light. The zingy pineapple-orange-banana-mint sorbet is a refreshing, tasty palate cleanser. Like all my sorbets, it's also convenient because you can make it days in advance. Each dessert ramekin is served on a plate, with two Texas Tea Cakes. The lemony cookies are fun; everybody sits around determining where Dallas, Houston, El Paso and Austin are before they take their first bite.

Guacamole Nachos

❧

I HAVE SERVED THESE on my own homemade round tortilla chips, as well as on quartered, deep-fried, commercially made corn tortillas. The round ones are cute but time-consuming.

- 1 quart (1 L) safflower or peanut oil for deep-frying
- 30 to 36 small, round Homemade Tortillas (page 44) or 8 to 10 large corn tortillas, quartered
- ½ cup (55 g) Cheddar, grated (2 ounces) Guacamole (page 52)
- ½ cup (120 ml) plain low-fat yogurt or crème fraîche (page 20) Salsa Fresca (page 53) Radish roses or thin slices of sweet red pepper, sliced tomato and sliced lime for garnish

Heat the oil in a wide saucepan, wok or deep fryer to 360° F (180° C). Deep-fry the tortilla chips until golden brown; remove with a skimmer or slotted spoon and drain on paper towels. This should take a few seconds for each batch; allow the oil to come back up to 360° F (180° C) between batches.

Preheat the broiler. Sprinkle the cheese on the nacho chips and heat under the broiler just until the cheese melts. (The melted cheese forms a kind of barrier between the chip and the guacamole so the chips won't get soggy as quickly.)

Shortly before serving, arrange the chips on a platter, if serving as an appetizer, or arrange 5 to 6 to a plate, if serving as an entree, and top with the guacamole, a dab of yogurt or crème fraîche and a spoonful of the salsa.

Garnish with the radishes or red pepper strips, tomato slices and lime and serve, with more hot sauce on the side.

To prepare ahead of time: You can make the chips hours in advance. The chips with the cheese melted on them will hold for a couple of hours. The salsa can be made several hours ahead and stored in a covered bowl in the refrigerator. Make the guacamole as close as possible to serving time and hold in a covered bowl in the refrigerator.

SERVES 4 TO 6

Garlic Broth

❧

THIS MAKES a marvelous stock. It can also serve as a soup in its own right, with the addition of toasted croutons, a little grated cheese and beaten or poached eggs.

- 2 quarts (2 L) water
- 2 large heads garlic, cloves separated and peeled
- 1 bouquet garni (made with 2 sprigs of parsley, 1 bay leaf and 1 or 2 sprigs of thyme) Salt to taste

Combine all the ingredients in a large, heavy-bottomed soup pot or Dutch oven and bring to a simmer. Cover and simmer 2 hours. This will keep in the refrigerator for a few days and freezes well.

MAKES 2 QUARTS (2 L)

Sopa de Tortilla

❀

THIS DISH (pictured on page 71) brings me right back to the Yucatán, even if I can't get pasilla chilies in Paris. But with the savory broth, the spicy cayenne and the rich flavor of fried tortillas and fresh cilantro, I don't miss them.

It's important to take the time to make Garlic Broth for this soup; the flavor depends on it.

1	tablespoon olive oil
1	small onion, minced
4	cloves garlic, minced or put through a press
1	14-oz. (380-g) can tomatoes, with their liquid, pureed
6	cups (1.5 L) Garlic Broth (page 96)
3	tablespoons tomato paste
1	small dried cayenne pepper or ¼ to ½ teaspoon hot chili powder
1	bay leaf
¼	teaspoon dried oregano
¼	teaspoon dried thyme
	Salt and freshly ground pepper, to taste
1 to 2	tablespoons fresh lime juice
1	quart (1 L) safflower or peanut oil for deep-frying
10	slightly stale tortillas, cut into narrow strips
¼	cup (10 g) fresh cilantro leaves
2	eggs
¾	cup (85 g) Gruyère cheese, grated (3 ounces)

Heat the olive oil in a heavy-bottomed soup pot or Dutch oven and sauté the onion with half the garlic until the onion is tender. Add the pureed tomatoes and bring to a simmer. Cook, stirring occasionally, for about 10 minutes. Add the broth, the remaining minced garlic, the tomato paste, the cayenne pepper or chili powder, bay leaf, oregano and thyme, and bring to a simmer. Cover and simmer for 30 minutes. Season to taste with salt and freshly ground pepper. Add the lime juice.

Puree the soup through the medium blade of a food mill and return it to the pot.

While the soup is simmering (or you can do this well in advance), heat the safflower or peanut oil in a wide saucepan, wok or deep fryer to 360° F (180° C), and deep-fry the tortilla strips just until crisp. Drain on paper towels and set aside.

Just before serving, heat the soup to a simmer, correct the seasonings and add the fresh cilantro. Beat the eggs in a bowl and stir in some of the soup, then stir this back into the soup pot. Do not boil.

Place a generous handful of the crisp-fried tortilla strips in each soup bowl, ladle in the soup, top with a handful of grated Gruyère and serve at once.

To prepare ahead of time: The Garlic Broth can be made 1 or 2 days in advance and refrigerated. The soup will hold for 1 day in the refrigerator, without the coriander or eggs. The tortilla strips can be fried several hours in advance.

SERVES 6

Marinated Cod in Escabeche

❀

THIS IS BASED ON a recipe by Diana Kennedy. Hers is more authentic and calls for sierra or striped bass. I couldn't get either of those fish in Paris, and sea bass was too expensive, so I experimented with other fish and found that cod did perfectly well for this dish. Kennedy has you fry the fish slices or fillets before you marinate them, but when I did that, they fell apart too easily, so I tried baking the fillets. They fell apart anyway in the marinade, but I prefer baking them, as it requires less fat and is less time-consuming.

The dish was quite a hit at the Supper Club; the marinade is pungent with spices and tangy with vinegar. It's great for a dinner party because you make it in advance and you can serve it hot or cold. If you're serving it hot, you just reheat it at the last minute on top of the stove. The combination of the fish on the masa crepes, with the crunchy zucchini and salsa and with refried black beans on the side, is sensational.

6	large cod fillets (1 ½ to 2 pounds, 750 g to 1 kg)
2 ¼	cups (400 ml) water
¼	cup (60 ml) fresh lime juice
	Salt
½	teaspoon peppercorns
½	teaspoon coriander seeds
½	teaspoon cumin seeds
2	cloves
⅛	teaspoon ground cinnamon
12	cloves garlic, 2 peeled and 10 toasted and peeled (see note below)
1 ¼	cups (285 ml) wine vinegar
¼	teaspoon dried oregano
2	bay leaves
	Salt to taste
⅓	cup (80 ml) olive oil
4	shallots or 1 red onion, thinly sliced
1	medium-sized zucchini, thinly sliced
12	Blue Corn Masa Crepes (page 99) or hot corn tortillas (homemade, page 44)
	Salsa Fresca (page 53)

Place the fish in a baking dish. Combine 1 cup (225 ml) of the water with the lime juice and 1 teaspoon salt and pour over the fish. Marinate for 1 hour, turning once. Drain, leaving the fish with some of the liquid in the baking dish, and cover the baking dish tightly with foil.

Preheat the oven to 400° F (200° C). Bake the fish 10 to 15 minutes, or until it is just baked through and flakes easily with a fork. Remove from the oven.

Meanwhile, grind the spices together in a spice mill. Mash the peeled raw and toasted garlic together in a mortar and pestle. Add the ground spices and work with the pestle until you have a smooth paste. Combine in a saucepan with ½ cup (120 ml) each of vinegar and water, and the oregano, bay leaves and salt to taste. Bring to a boil. Add the remaining ¼ cup (60 ml) each vinegar and water and the olive oil and bring to a second boil. Boil 1 minute and remove from the heat.

Pour the hot marinade over the baked fish. Add the shallots or onion and the zucchini, toss together gently and marinate 2 hours (or longer), turning, gently and carefully, once or twice. Adjust salt before serving.

If serving hot, heat just to a simmer on the stove right before serving; don't let the liquid boil or the fish will cook more and become tough and dry. Dish out with a slotted spoon and serve over the crepes or hot corn tortillas. Garnish with the salsa.

To prepare ahead of time: The entire dish needs to be started at least 3 hours in advance and can be done the morning of the evening you wish to serve it.

The crepes can be made days in advance and frozen, stacked between squares of wax paper or parchment and sealed in a plastic bag. They will thaw in 3 hours, or thaw them overnight in the refrigerator.

Note: To toast garlic, place the unpeeled cloves in a hot, dry skillet and cook, stirring with a wooden spoon, until the skin is uniformly charred and the flesh slightly transparent on the outside. Remove from the heat, and when cool enough to handle, remove the skins.

SERVES 6

Blue Corn Masa Crepes

❀

A FRIEND OF MINE found this recipe in an issue of *Sunset Magazine* years ago. The crepes are a delightful change from corn tortillas and are excellent served on the side with any Mexican-style fish dish. I think they're best of all with Marinated Cod in Escabeche (page 97). I have made these with both blue corn masa from New Mexico and regular masa harina. The blue corn masa has a much coarser texture than masa harina, so the crepe has a different texture, taste and color. Both versions are good.

Note: Masa harina, which is much more readily available than the blue corn masa, is specially processed cornmeal used specifically for corn tortillas. Do not substitute cornmeal. You can find the Quaker brand wherever Mexican ingredients are sold, and if you live in the Southwest, you can often buy masa harina from tortilla factories.

    2   large eggs
    ¾   cup (180 ml) low-fat milk
    1   tablespoon safflower oil
    ½   cup (55 g) blue corn masa or masa harina
    2   tablespoons whole-wheat pastry flour
    ¼   teaspoon salt
         Unsalted butter for cooking

Beat together the eggs, milk and safflower oil. Beat in the masa, the whole-wheat flour and the salt and blend well (this can be done in a blender). Let the batter rest in the refrigerator for about 30 minutes, to allow the flour to swell and soften.

Heat a crepe pan or nonstick omelet pan over medium-high heat and brush with butter. Spoon in approximately 2 tablespoons batter for each crepe, and swirl the pan to distribute the batter evenly. Cook for about 1 minute, or until the crepe can be turned without breaking. Flip and brown for about ½ minute on the other side. Turn onto a plate and continue until all the batter is used up, stacking the crepes as they are done.

To prepare ahead of time: The crepes will hold for a day in the refrigerator and can be frozen as for blini (see page 45).

MAKES 10 TO 12 CREPES

Texas Tea Cakes

❀

THESE ARE honey-lemon cookies, much like the ones on page 55, but a little crisper and shaped like Texas. To be "authentic," you will need a Texas cookie cutter, which you can find in some kitchen-supply stores. You can, of course, use any shape cutter you want.

    1 ½   sticks (170 g, 6 ounces) unsalted butter
    ⅔   cup (160 ml) mild-flavored honey
    1   large egg
    3   tablespoons fresh lemon juice
    2   tablespoons finely chopped lemon zest
    2   teaspoons vanilla
    1   teaspoon baking powder
         Pinch of salt
    2   cups plus 2 tablespoons (280 g) sifted
             unbleached white flour
    1   cup (115 g) sifted whole-wheat pastry flour

In an electric mixer, cream the butter and honey. Beat in the egg, lemon juice, lemon zest, vanilla, baking powder and salt. Add the flours. The dough will be soft and sticky.

Scrape the dough onto a piece of plastic wrap, wrap well and refrigerate overnight, or freeze for 2 hours.

Preheat the oven to 350° F (180° C). Cut the dough into small pieces and roll out each piece on a floured board or between pieces of wax paper. Keep the dough that you aren't working with in the freezer so it doesn't become too soft. The dough should be ⅛ to ¼ inch (0.25 to 0.75 cm) thick, depending on whether you like your cookies thin or fairly thick. Because the dough is wet, you must work quickly and briskly so it doesn't stick. It helps if you keep brushing the top of the dough and the board with flour. Cut in shapes with a cookie cutter. Using a spatula, transfer to buttered cookie sheets.

Bake the cookies 8 to 12 minutes, until beginning to brown on the edges. Cool on a rack. These will keep several days in tightly sealed containers.

MAKES 4 DOZEN COOKIES

Pineapple-Orange-Banana Sorbet With Mint

❁

THE PREDOMINANT flavors in this refreshing sorbet are pineapple, mint and orange. There's just a little bit of banana, which adds sweetness and body. The mint is what makes this dish sing.

FOR THE SORBET

⅓ cup (90 ml) mild-flavored honey
1 cup (225 ml) water
1 ripe pineapple, peeled, cored and coarsely chopped
3 tablespoons chopped fresh mint leaves
½ small ripe banana
2 cups (450 ml) strained fresh orange juice (juice of about 2 pounds, 1 kg, oranges)
  Juice of 1 large lime, strained

FOR THE ORANGE-MINT OR PINEAPPLE-MINT GARNISH

6 oranges, peeled and sectioned, or ½ ripe pineapple, peeled, cored and chopped
¼ cup (60 ml) Grand Marnier or Cointreau
2 tablespoons chopped fresh mint leaves

Making the sorbet: Combine the honey and water in a large saucepan and bring to a boil. Reduce the heat and simmer 10 minutes. Remove from the heat and cool.

Puree the pineapple, mint leaves and banana in a food processor or blender, using some of the orange juice to moisten it. Combine with the remaining orange and lime juice.

Stir the pineapple mixture into the cooled syrup. Either freeze in an ice cream freezer or sorbetière, or still-freeze in a covered bowl according to the directions in the note on page 55.

After freezing by any method, spoon into individual molds, cover with plastic, then foil, and freeze. Or oil a loaf pan and line it with plastic wrap. Pour in the sorbet mixture, cover tightly with plastic wrap, then foil, and freeze. Work quickly so that the sorbet doesn't melt, or ice crystals will form again when it freezes.

Making the garnish: Toss together the orange sections or chopped pineapple and the Grand Marnier or Cointreau. Add the fresh mint leaves. Set aside or refrigerate until ready to serve.

Twenty minutes before serving, place the sorbet in the refrigerator to soften. If you froze it in the loaf pan, unmold onto a platter. Cut slices with a sharp knife. If you froze it in individual molds, unmold into bowls. Serve, topping each serving with the orange or pineapple garnish.

To prepare ahead of time: This sorbet, like all my others, will hold, covered tightly, for weeks in the freezer. The garnish can be made several hours ahead and held in a covered bowl in the refrigerator.

SERVES 6 TO 8

February

❦

A Warming Italian Menu for a Rainy Winter Night

APERITIF: VOUVRAY PÉTILLANT

RAVIOLI AND BROCCOLI SALAD

SOURDOUGH COUNTRY BREAD (PAGE 26)

DEEP-DISH EGGPLANT TORTE

SAUTÉED RED AND YELLOW PEPPERS

CITRUS AND DATE GRATIN

WINE SUGGESTIONS: BANDOL RED, CÔTES-DU-RHÔNE

SERVES 6

February

EVERYTHING in this menu is showy: the ravioli tossed with bright green broccoli florets and little wild mushrooms; the extravagant eggplant torte, which is like an eggplant Parmesan in a crust; the colorful red and yellow peppers; and the hot fruit gratin, with its tangy citrus, sweet caramelized dates and gratinéed crème anglaise. For this reason, I once chose the menu for some food photographs. The meal looked truly elegant, served on 100-year-old Italian porcelain dishes. We set the table with silver and crystal on a lace tablecloth, poured the deep red Bandol wine into cut-glass carafes and filled vases with extravagant red roses.

After this heartwarming, decidedly Italian dinner, one of my guests wrote in my Supper Club guest book that it had been "a fitting meal for a cold and rainy winter night." In February, that's about the only kind of night we get, but who cares when the table looks beautiful and the food tastes so good.

Ravioli and Broccoli Salad

❀

THIS DISH (pictured on page 72) was initially inspired by a Craig Claiborne recipe, which a friend clipped from *The New York Times*. I added small dried mushrooms, which can be replaced by dried shiitake mushrooms. It's not too difficult to find cheese-filled ravioli or tortellini, with all the pasta shops now springing up around the country. I use ravioli with a delicious basil-cheese filling. Ravioli has less dough than tortellini, and because it's lighter, I think it works better here.

FOR THE SALAD

¾	cup (20 g) small dried mushrooms, such as chanterelles or shiitakes
1	pound (500 g) broccoli florets
1	tablespoon unsalted butter or olive oil
1	clove garlic, minced or put through a press
1	teaspoon soy sauce
	Salt
1	tablespoon vegetable or olive oil
¾	pound (350 g) small ravioli or tortellini with cheese or cheese-and-herb filling (available in most pasta shops)
3 to 4	scallions, sliced very thin
1	tablespoon chopped fresh chives (optional)
2	tablespoons chopped fresh basil or parsley
2 to 3	tablespoons freshly grated Parmesan

FOR THE DRESSING

3 to 4	tablespoons good-quality red- wine vinegar or balsamic vinegar, to taste
1	teaspoon Dijon mustard
1	clove garlic, minced or put through a press
¼	teaspoon dried tarragon
	Salt and freshly ground pepper, to taste
¾	cup (180 ml) good-quality olive oil

FOR THE GARNISH

Watercress and radishes

Making the salad: Place the dried mushrooms in a bowl and pour on boiling water to cover. Let them sit while you prepare the remaining ingredients, about 20 to 30 minutes.

If the broccoli florets are very large, break or cut them into smaller pieces. Steam 5 minutes, or until crisp-tender, and refresh under cold water. Set aside.

Drain the mushrooms, saving the soaking liquid, and rinse them thoroughly. Strain the soaking liquid through a coffee filter or a sieve lined with a double thickness of paper towels and set aside (you will add it to the pasta water). Squeeze the mushrooms dry and remove their woody stems. Heat the butter or oil in a skillet and add the garlic and mushrooms. Sauté for about 5 minutes and add the soy sauce. Remove from the heat.

Fill a large pot with fresh water and the soaking liquid from the mushrooms. Bring to a rolling boil, add a generous amount of salt, a spoonful of oil and the ravioli or tortellini. Cook al dente, just until firm to the bite, which should take from 3 to 5 minutes for fresh pasta and up to 10 minutes for dried. Drain and rinse with cold water. Shake out the excess water and transfer to a salad bowl. Add the other salad ingredients and gently toss together.

Making the dressing: Mix together the vinegar, mustard, garlic, tarragon and salt and pepper, and whisk in the oil.

Just before serving, toss the salad with the dressing. Garnish each serving with a few sprigs of watercress and some radish roses.

To prepare ahead of time: All the components for the salad can be prepared several hours in advance. Hold in covered containers in the refrigerator. If you are holding the dish in the refrigerator, toss the cooked ravioli with a couple of tablespoons of olive oil so they don't stick together, and cover.

SERVES 6 TO 8

Pasta With Sweet Peas and Herb Butter
page 153

Artichokes With Tomatoes, Garlic and Herbs
page 200

Pasta Primavera With Roasted Red Peppers
page 158

Mangoes, Peaches and Berries in Sweet Wine
page 174

106

Deep-Dish Eggplant Torte

THIS RICH, double-crusted torte has very good staying power, which was confirmed when I made it to be photographed. Food photography takes hours, and the torte continued to look beautiful throughout the day. We ate it for dinner that night; the following night, we ate the back-up one, which was even better, although the crust had begun to get a little soggy. The torte also freezes well. It is very hearty and makes a warming, filling winter meal.

The one drawback to this dish is that it is time-consuming, so you shouldn't plan to make it for dinner after work. You can, however, make some of the components, like the crust and the tomato sauce, in advance. This is what I did for the Supper Club, and the assembly went fairly quickly. You can make the torte hours before you bake it; keep it in the refrigerator or freezer until you put it into the oven.

Note: The dried mushrooms here are optional. They add a distinctive flavor that surprises the palate, but the torte is still good without them.

FOR THE CRUST

2 cups (225 g) whole-wheat pastry flour plus 1 cup (115 g) unbleached white flour or use 3 cups (340 g) whole-wheat pastry flour in all
½ teaspoon salt
1 ½ sticks (170 g) butter (6 ounces)
1 large egg yolk
4 to 6 tablespoons ice-cold water, as necessary

FOR THE EGGPLANT

4 medium-sized eggplants, sliced ¼ inch (0.75 cm) thick
Salt
Olive oil, as necessary

FOR THE TOMATO SAUCE

1 tablespoon olive oil
1 onion, finely chopped
4 to 5 cloves garlic, minced or put through a garlic press

3 pounds (1.5 kg) fresh tomatoes, peeled, seeded and chopped, or 3 28-ounce (765-g) cans, drained, seeded and chopped
¼ cup (60 ml) tomato paste
Salt and freshly ground pepper, to taste
¼ teaspoon mild-flavored honey or sugar
¼ teaspoon dried thyme
1 teaspoon dried oregano
1 tablespoon chopped fresh basil or 1 teaspoon dried
Pinch of ground cinnamon
Tiny pinch of cayenne (optional) for a piquant sauce

FOR THE MUSHROOMS (OPTIONAL)

½ to ¾ cup (15 g to 20 g) dried cèpes (porcini) or other dried wild mushrooms
2 teaspoons butter
1 clove garlic, minced or put through a press
Soy sauce to taste

FOR ASSEMBLING THE TORTE

4 eggs
6 ounces (170 g) part-skim mozzarella, sliced thin
½ cup (55 g) whole-wheat breadcrumbs (2 ounces)
1½ cups (170 g) freshly grated Parmesan (6 ounces)

Making the crust: Mix together the flours and salt, then cut in the butter. When the mixture has the consistency of coarse cornmeal, add the egg yolk, then the water by tablespoons. Gather into a ball, wrap tightly in plastic, and refrigerate for 2 hours or overnight.

Preparing the eggplant: Slice the eggplant, salt the slices and place in a colander or on an oven rack over the sink. Set a board on top of the slices weighted with a pot of water or another heavy object and let sit for 1 hour while you prepare the sauce and dried mushrooms, if using.

Preparing the sauce: Heat the olive oil in a large, heavy-bottomed Dutch oven and sauté the onion with half the garlic until the onion begins to turn golden. Add the tomatoes, tomato paste, remaining garlic, salt (¾ to 1 teaspoon or more, to taste) and honey or sugar and bring to a simmer. Simmer, covered, for 1 hour. Remove the lid, taste, and add more salt and garlic if you wish, then add the thyme, oregano and basil. Continue to cook, uncovered, stirring occasionally, for another 30 minutes or so, until the sauce is no longer watery. Add the cinnamon and the optional cayenne and remove from the heat.

Preparing the optional dried mushrooms: Place the dried mushrooms in a bowl and pour on boiling water to cover. Let them sit 20 to 30 minutes. Drain and rinse thoroughly, then squeeze dry and chop. Heat the 2 teaspoons of butter in a small skillet and add the mushrooms and the garlic. Sauté for about 3 minutes and season with a little soy sauce. Remove from the heat and stir into the tomato sauce.

Cooking the eggplant: Preheat the oven to 450° F (230° C). Rinse the eggplant slices and pat dry with a towel (this is definitely the most tedious part of the operation). Place the slices on oiled baking sheets and brush the tops with a little olive oil. Bake 8 to 10 minutes, until cooked through and fragrant. Be careful not to burn them. Remove from the oven and turn down the oven to 375° F (190° C).

Rolling out the crust and assembling the torte: Roll out ⅔ of the piecrust (easiest between pieces of wax paper) and line the bottom and sides of a very well-buttered 10- to 12-inch (25- to 30-cm) springform pan or cake pan. (See general directions for whole-wheat crusts, page 42). Beat one of the eggs, brush the crust and prebake for 7 minutes in the heated oven (retain the remainder of the beaten egg for the top crust). Remove from the heat.

Layer ⅓ of the eggplant slices over the crust, slightly overlapping. Top this with a layer of ⅓ of the mozzarella, then a layer of ⅓ of the tomato sauce, then ⅓ each of the breadcrumbs and Parmesan. Repeat the layers 2 more times, ending with the sauce, breadcrumbs and Parmesan. Beat the remaining 3 eggs in another bowl and pour over the top of the torte (the beaten eggs will sink into the torte as it bakes and hold everything together).

Roll out the remaining dough and place it over the top of the torte. Fold over the edge and shape an attractive lip by gently pinching all the way around the rim of the pan.

Brush the top crust with the remaining beaten egg you used for the bottom crust and bake 1 hour, until golden brown. Let sit 15 to 20 minutes before cutting into wedges to serve.

To prepare ahead of time: The dough for the crust can be mixed up several days in advance and refrigerated or frozen. The tomato sauce will hold for 2 days in the refrigerator in a covered bowl. All of the ingredients can be prepared up to 1 day in advance. The entire torte can be assembled up to 1 day in advance and held in the refrigerator or freezer. Transfer directly to the preheated oven and bake 1 hour and 20 minutes, or until the crust is golden brown.

SERVES 8 GENEROUSLY

Sautéed Red and Yellow Peppers

THESE MAKE a gorgeous, light side dish. They go especially well with my richer entrées, like Deep-Dish Eggplant Torte in this menu or Green Lasagna With Spinach Filling (page 88), but they would go equally well with lighter fish dishes.

- 2 tablespoons olive oil
- 2 large sweet yellow peppers, halved, seeds removed, then cut into thin lengthwise strips
- 2 large sweet red peppers, halved, seeds removed, then cut into thin lengthwise

strips
1 to 2   cloves garlic, to taste, minced or put
          through a press
¼   teaspoon fresh thyme leaves (optional)
          Salt and freshly ground pepper, to taste

Heat the oil in a large skillet or wok and add the peppers and the garlic. Sauté over medium-high heat until crisp-tender, 10 to 15 minutes. Add the thyme and salt and pepper to taste and serve as a side dish.

SERVES 4 TO 6

Citrus and Date Gratin

❦

A BEAUTIFUL HOT dessert for a winter feast. The dates add the crowning touch. When you bake the gratin, they caramelize, and the combination of flavors is heavenly.

Note: If you use dried dates, make sure they're not too hard.

5   oranges
2   grapefruit
12   dates, as fresh as you can get them, pitted
      and quartered
5   large egg yolks
6   tablespoons mild-flavored honey
2   tablespoons rum
1   tablespoon vanilla
1   teaspoon ground cinnamon
½   cup (120 ml) crème fraîche (page 20)

Squeeze the juice from one orange and one grapefruit, strain and set the juice aside.

Remove the peel and zest from the remaining oranges and grapefruit and cut the fruit into quarters or eighths. Distribute, along with the dates, among 4 to 6 small gratin dishes, or toss together and place in a 1- or 2-quart (1 L or 2 L) gratin dish.

Heat the juice to the boiling point in a small saucepan. Meanwhile, beat together the egg yolks and honey until thick and lemon-colored. Slowly pour in the hot juice, beating. Return the mixture to the saucepan and place over medium heat. Heat through, stirring constantly with a wooden spoon, until the custard thickens and coats the spoon like thick cream. In the beginning, it will be foamy on the top, so it will be hard to see it thickening. To be safe, keep checking by removing it from the heat once wisps of steam begin to appear and spooning out a little. When thick, remove from the heat and stir in the rum, vanilla and cinnamon. Set the crème fraîche aside, covered.

Preheat the broiler 15 minutes before you wish to serve. Beat the crème fraîche in a bowl and beat in the custard sauce. Spoon the sauce over the fruit and place under the broiler for 3 to 6 minutes, until the sauce begins to brown. Remove from the heat and serve.

To prepare ahead of time: The custard sauce will hold for several hours or overnight in the refrigerator. Allow it to cool and cover tightly. The fruit can be prepared several hours before assembling and refrigerated.

SERVES 4 TO 6

March

❧

A French-American Menu

APERITIF: BEAUJOLAIS OR GAMAY PRIMEUR

CURLY ENDIVE SALAD WITH BAKED GOAT CHEESE

SOURDOUGH COUNTRY BREAD (PAGE 26)

PROVENÇAL-STYLE FISH CHOWDER

TEXAS CORNBREAD (PAGE 39)

PEAR CRISP WITH GINGER CRÈME ANGLAISE

WINE SUGGESTIONS: BOURGUEIL OR CHINON ROSÉ,
BANDOL ROSÉ OR RED DOMAINE TEMPIER

SERVES 6

March

I HAVE SERVED this meal at every season of the year, in France, San Francisco, Texas and New York, and it's always a hit. You can make the soup anywhere you can find fresh fish and vary the other ingredients according to season and availability. Any firm white-fleshed fish will do. In the United States, I've used Pacific red snapper, redfish and cod. In France, I garnish the soup with mussels, whereas in the States, I usually opt for clams. As for the vegetables, in fall and winter I use pumpkin, an idea I got from a Portuguese recipe, whereas in spring and summer, I add zucchini and sweet corn.

This menu is a perfect example of how I like to marry French and American gastronomy in a meal. The salad is clearly a traditional French dish, and it's an excellent beginning. The soup starts with the idea of a Manhattan-style chowder, with lots of tomatoes and potatoes, but the flavors are distinctly Provençal, with all the garlic, the hint of cayenne, the saffron and the orange peel. So in the end, the soup is more reminiscent of bouillabaisse than of clam chowder. But then I serve it with Texas Cornbread, which brings us back to the U.S.A., and cornbread couldn't be a better accompaniment for this dish. It always elicits a lot of table conversation. The French are enchanted with any bread that is like cake, and the Americans, ecstatic to be eating their beloved cornbread instead of baguettes, have questions and comments like: "How did you get it to be so light? It's not like my mother's" or "Why isn't it a brighter color yellow?" (answer: because of the whole-wheat flour).

The warm pear crisp with its sweet, nutty topping and ginger-flavored crème anglaise is especially popular with Americans and the British, Irish and Scots, who love "crumbles." I have also served apple pie for dessert with this soup and other kinds of cobblers or crisps, depending on the season and what's available.

One of the great advantages of this meal is that so much of it can be done in advance. The salad greens can be washed and dried as far ahead as the day before, the remaining vegetables and vinaigrette prepared hours in advance. The goat cheese is marinated for a day, so everything for the salad is ready to be put together just before you serve it. The breads will hold for a day or two if tightly wrapped, and the crème anglaise can be made a day in advance. You can do everything for the soup, right up to the addition of the fish and saffron, several hours before serving time. The vegetables take only about 15 minutes to cook, and the fish cooks so quickly that you can add it between courses. The mussel or clam garnish can be steamed hours before in the white wine. The pear crisp shouldn't sit too long, as the topping might get soggy, but it will hold for several hours and can be reheated.

Curly Endive Salad With Baked Goat Cheese

❀

I ALWAYS EAT THIS salad as my main course when I go to my local bistro, Le Bistro Henri, on the rue Princesse. Mine is a little different from Henri's because I don't use as much cheese; I don't want my guests to be too full for the next course. And I make sure to use the least salty goat cheese on the market. The ones to avoid are Bûcheron and the aged, harder goat cheeses. Generally, the soft, moist, fresh ones are less salty. In the United States, try local fresh goat cheeses. If you can't find curly endive or watercress, use other lettuces; that shouldn't stop you from making this dish. And if you're eating the salad as a main course, you could increase the cheese.

FOR THE CHEESE

12	½-inch (1.5-cm) thick rounds of fresh goat cheese
⅓	cup (80 ml) fruity olive oil
4	sprigs fresh thyme or ½ teaspoon dried
¼	teaspoon chopped fresh rosemary (optional)

FOR THE DRESSING

2 to 3	tablespoons red-wine vinegar, to taste
1	tablespoon fresh lemon juice
1	teaspoon Dijon mustard
1	small clove garlic, minced or put through a press (optional)
1	teaspoon chopped fresh tarragon or ¼ teaspoon dried
7	tablespoons olive oil (use the cheese marinade, adding additional oil, if necessary)
2	tablespoons walnut oil
	Salt and freshly ground pepper, to taste

FOR THE SALAD

12	Garlic Croutons (page 45), preferably made with sourdough bread
½	teaspoon fresh or dried thyme
½	large or 1 small curly endive, leaves separated and thoroughly washed and dried
2	generous handfuls watercress, stems trimmed
12 to 15	sprigs of fresh chervil, if available
1	sweet red pepper, seeded and sliced thin (optional)
¼	pound (115 g) mushrooms, cleaned and sliced thin (optional)

FOR THE GARNISH

12	radish roses or tiny radishes

Marinating the cheese: Marinate the rounds of goat cheese in the ⅓ cup (90 ml) olive oil for a day, along with the fresh or dried thyme and the optional rosemary. Turn from time to time.

Making the dressing: Mix together the vinegar, lemon juice, mustard, garlic and tarragon. Whisk in the oils and add salt and freshly ground pepper to taste.

Assembling the salad: Preheat the oven to 425° F (220° C). Place Garlic Croutons on a baking sheet and top with the marinated cheese. Sprinkle with ½ teaspoon thyme. Bake 6 minutes, until the cheese is bubbling. Meanwhile, toss the endive, watercress and chervil, if available, and optional red pepper and mushrooms, together with the dressing and distribute among 6 salad plates.

Top the salads with the croutons and hot cheese, garnish with radishes and serve.

To prepare ahead of time: The croutons can be toasted 1 day in advance. Store in a sealed plastic container. The endive and watercress can be washed and thoroughly dried up to 1 day in advance. Wrap in towels, then seal in plastic bags. You can prepare the remaining vegetables and hold them for several hours in the refrigerator. The cheese is marinated for 1 day (you can do this the night before), and the dressing will hold for several hours.

SERVES 6

Provençal-Style Fish Chowder

THIS SOUP (pictured on the front cover) is intensely satisfying. Even though I call it a chowder, it has a decidedly Mediterranean flavor, with all the garlic, the saffron and the special perfume of the orange peel, which is added close to the end of the cooking.

You can prepare this soup, up to the addition of the saffron, orange peel and fish, well in advance of serving it. This makes it a great dish for a dinner party, as the fumet and the tomato sauce with the vegetables are easy and straightforward. The orange peel and saffron can be added before you sit down to the first course, and the fish can be added between courses. The chowder, with cornbread or crusty Sourdough Country Bread (page 26), is a meal I never tire of and have served time and again at my Supper Club, to the delight of my guests.

FOR THE FUMET

1	pound (500 g) fish trimmings (heads and bones), rinsed
1	onion, quartered
1	carrot, sliced
1	stalk celery, sliced
1	leek, white part only, cleaned and sliced
2	cloves garlic, peeled
2	sprigs fresh parsley
1	bay leaf
1	sprig fresh thyme
1	quart (1 L) water
	Salt, to taste
1	cup (225 ml) dry white wine

FOR THE TOMATO STEW

1 to 2	tablespoons olive oil, as necessary
1	large onion, chopped
4	cloves garlic or more, to taste, minced or put through a press
2	28-ounce (765-g) cans tomatoes, with their juice, seeded and chopped
2	tablespoons tomato paste
1	tablespoon minced fresh basil or ½ to 1 teaspoon dried

½ to 1	teaspoon dried thyme
1	bay leaf
	Salt, to taste
¾	pound (350 g) new potatoes, diced
1	pound (500 g) pumpkin, peeled, seeded and diced, or zucchini, sliced
	Fresh corn kernels from 2 to 3 ears, if in season (optional)
	Pinch or two of cayenne or ¼ teaspoon crushed red pepper
	Freshly ground pepper, to taste

FOR THE MUSSELS AND CLAMS

½	pound (250 g) mussels or clams (enough for 4 per bowl)
1	cup (225 ml) dry white wine
½	cup (120 ml) water

FOR FINISHING THE SOUP

2	wide strips orange peel, without pith
	Generous pinch of saffron
	Additional water, if necessary
2 to 2 ½	pounds (1 kg to 1.25 kg) fish fillets or steaks, such as cod, striped bass, monkfish, tilefish, snapper or redfish, cut in 1-inch (2.5-cm) cubes (or a combination of several kinds)
3	tablespoons chopped fresh parsley
	Lemon wedges

Making the fumet: Combine the fish trimmings, quartered onion, carrot, celery, leek, garlic, parsley, bay leaf, thyme, water and salt in a large soup pot or saucepan and bring to a simmer over medium heat. Skim off all the foam that rises (the foam is bitter). Continue to skim until no foam remains, then cover, reduce the heat and simmer 15 minutes. Add the wine and simmer another 15 minutes, covered. Remove from the heat and strain at once through a fine sieve or a strainer lined with cheesecloth. Don't cook any longer than this or the fumet will be bitter.

Making the tomato stew: Heat the olive oil in a

large, heavy-bottomed soup pot or flameproof casserole and sauté the onion with the garlic until the onion is tender. Add the tomatoes, tomato paste, dried basil, if using (fresh goes in later), and thyme and simmer 15 minutes. Add the fumet, bay leaf and salt to taste. Bring to a simmer and cook, uncovered, for 30 minutes. Add the potatoes, cover, and simmer 10 to 15 minutes (you cover the soup now because you want to cook the vegetables without letting any more of the liquid evaporate), or until the potatoes are cooked through but still have some texture. Add the pumpkin or zucchini, the optional corn and fresh basil, if using. Cover and simmer another 15 minutes, or until the pumpkin is tender. Add cayenne and pepper and adjust seasonings, adding salt, garlic or more herbs, if you wish. At this point, you may remove the soup from the heat and let it sit until shortly before serving, when you will bring it back to a simmer and cook the fish.

Preparing the mussels or clams: While the stew is simmering, clean the mussels or clams well, in several rinses of cold water (see instructions for cleaning mussels, page 172). Bring the wine and water to a boil in a large lidded pot and add the mussels or clams. Steam 5 minutes, or until the shells open, shaking the pan once to distribute evenly. Remove from the heat, drain and set aside. Discard any that have not opened.

Finishing the soup: Fifteen to 20 minutes before you wish to serve, bring the soup to a simmer and add the orange peel and saffron. Adjust seasonings and add water if the broth seems too thick or if there's not enough of it to cover the seafood. If you add water, adjust the seasonings again. Add the fish, cover and simmer 10 minutes, until the flesh is opaque and falls apart. Serve at once, garnishing each bowl with mussels or clams, chopped fresh parsley and a lemon wedge.

To prepare ahead of time: The fumet, the tomato sauce base and the finished soup, up to the addition of the saffron, orange peel and fish, will all hold for several hours. The tomato sauce could even be made the day before and stored, covered, in the refrigerator.

SERVES 4 TO 6

Pear Crisp With Ginger Crème Anglaise

E VERYBODY LOVES a crisp or a crumble. This is such an American idea, but the crème anglaise, with its hint of ginger and the liqueur give it a special exotic twist. This is one of those scrumptious desserts that I find myself eating for breakfast (if any remains) the next day and picking at until there's none left. I love the rich flavor of the pecan topping.

FOR THE CRISP

¼ cup (45 g) currants
3 tablespoons pear liqueur or kirsch
½ cup (55 g) chopped pecans
½ cup (55 g) rolled oats
½ cup (55 g) whole-wheat pastry flour
¼ cup (30 g) raw brown sugar (Turbinado)

¼ teaspoon freshly grated nutmeg
¼ teaspoon salt
6 tablespoons (85 g) cold unsalted butter
2 teaspoons grated lemon zest
2 ½ pounds (1.25 kg) Bosc or Comice pears, peeled, cored and sliced
3 tablespoons fresh lemon juice
1 tablespoon mild-flavored honey
1 tablespoon cornstarch

FOR THE GINGER CRÈME ANGLAISE

4 large egg yolks
⅓ cup (80 ml) mild-flavored honey
1 ¼ cups (285 ml) low-fat milk
½ to ¾ teaspoon ground ginger, to taste
½ teaspoon vanilla

Making the fruit mixture, preparing the topping: Preheat the oven to 375° F (190° C). Butter a 2-quart (2-L) baking dish.

Place the currants in a bowl and toss with 2 tablespoons of the pear liqueur or kirsch. Let them sit while you prepare the pears and other ingredients.

Place the pecans in a dry skillet and toast over a medium flame just until they begin to brown and smell toasty, stirring constantly. Remove from the heat.

Mix together the oats, flour, raw brown sugar, nutmeg and salt. Cut in the butter and work to a crumbly consistency. Stir in the pecans and lemon zest (this can all be done in a food processor).

Toss together the pears, 2 tablespoons of the lemon juice, the currants and honey. Dissolve the cornstarch in the remaining 1 tablespoon each lemon juice and pear liqueur or kirsch and toss with the pears. Turn into the buttered baking dish. Sprinkle the topping over in an even layer.

Baking the crisp: Bake in the preheated oven for 35 to 45 minutes, until crisp and beginning to brown on the top. To finish browning the top, run the crisp under the broiler, watching closely, for 2 to 3 minutes. Serve warm, with the ginger crème anglaise.

Making the ginger crème anglaise: Beat the egg yolks until lemon-colored and add the honey. Beat until thick. Meanwhile, heat the milk in a heavy-bottomed saucepan to the simmering point. Being careful that it is not boiling, beat it into the egg-honey mixture. Return this mixture to the saucepan and heat over a medium-low flame, stirring constantly with a wooden spoon. Do not allow the mixture to boil. The crème anglaise is ready when it reaches the consistency of thick cream and coats both sides of your spoon evenly. Remove from the heat and strain into a bowl. Whisk in the ginger and vanilla.

To prepare ahead of time: The ginger crème anglaise can be made 1 day in advance. Cool, cover and refrigerate. Serve it cold or warm with the crisp. Do not bake the crisp too far ahead of time so the topping will remain crunchy. You can warm this in a low oven before serving.

SERVES 6

April

❧

A Salute to Spring

Aperitif: Sauvignon Touraine

Green Beans Vinaigrette

Sourdough Country Bread (page 26)

Cannelloni With Chard, Herb and Ricotta Filling

Pan-Fried Mushrooms

Strawberries and Oranges With Cointreau

Crisp Almond Cookies (page 77)

Wine Suggestions: Côtes-du-Rhône, Gigondas,
Coteaux du Tricastin

Serves 6

April

APRIL IN PARIS is a frustrating month: the weather is almost always cold and damp. You have a few warmish days of "false spring," enough to allow the trees to bud and to give you hope that the winter will end. But usually, it gets cool and nasty again and remains that way until mid-May.

So I tried to evoke the spring with this menu, beginning with a chilled, pale dry Sauvignon Blanc served as an aperitif. The green bean salad is the color of new leaves. The light, beautiful cannelloni, pale green with specks of parsley in the pasta, are filled with Swiss chard, an abundance of fresh parsley and a mixture of ricotta, fresh goat cheese and Parmesan, with more emphasis on the vegetables and herbs than on the cheese. The mushrooms served on the side have a meaty, savory quality that complements the soft cannelloni. And who can resist the first strawberries of the year? They look spectacular alongside the oranges and make a fine finale with the biscotti.

Green Beans Vinaigrette

❀

ONE OF MY FAVORITE bistros in Paris is a little place on the rue Princesse called Le Bistro Henri. It's a peppy neighborhood spot with a black and white tile floor and French doors that look out onto the narrow little street. Henri cooks everything to order on a two-burner stovetop behind a little counter. There isn't even a sign on the door; you just have to know about it. Henri has a prix-fixe menu with several choices of appetizers and main courses, all simple meat dishes. I always order the same things, both from the hors d'oeuvres section. I start with his salad of green beans and continue with a green salad topped with a generous portion of baked goat cheese on toasted Poilane bread (see my version on page 116). Henri serves his famous scalloped potatoes, a rich, buttery mixture of sliced potatoes and crème fraîche, baked until crisp on top, along with all orders, and this makes a great and filling dinner. I always drink the bistro's good Beaujolais or Bourgueil with this meal.

I think I appreciate Henri the most for his healthy green bean salad. Henri has never overcooked a bean. His vinaigrette is sharp and mustardy. Sometimes, I add toasted almonds to my green bean salad, and I hope it's as good as his.

FOR THE BEANS

½ cup (55 g) slivered almonds (optional)
  Salt, to taste
1 ½ pounds (750 g) tender green beans, trimmed and cut in half if very long

FOR THE VINAIGRETTE

5 tablespoons good-quality red-wine vinegar
2 teaspoons Dijon mustard
1 small clove garlic, minced or put through a press
  Salt and freshly ground pepper, to taste
¼ teaspoon dried tarragon
¾ cup (180 ml) olive oil, or use half olive oil, half safflower oil

FOR THE GARNISH

2 tablespoons chopped fresh parsley
  Fresh tomatoes, in season, cut into wedges

Making the bean salad: If you're using the almonds, roast them in a dry skillet over medium-high heat, stirring constantly, until they begin to smell toasty. Remove from the heat and transfer to a bowl.

Bring a large pot of water to a rolling boil. Add a generous amount of salt and the beans. As soon as the water comes back to the boil, count to 20, taste one bean, and if it tastes cooked but is still crunchy, drain at once and rinse with cold water. If you want the beans a little more done, cook another 30 seconds to 1 minute and drain. Set aside.

Making the vinaigrette: Mix together the ingredients for the dressing. Taste and add more vinegar or mustard, if you desire. Just before serving, toss with the beans, parsley and optional almonds. Garnish the salad, or each serving, with fresh tomato wedges, if using.

To prepare ahead of time: You can trim and blanch the beans 1 day ahead of time and hold them in a plastic bag in the refrigerator. The toasted almonds will keep for several days in a tightly covered jar. The dressing can be made several hours in advance and held in or out of the refrigerator.

SERVES 4 TO 6

Variation: **Green Bean Vinaigrette With Beet Garnish**
This is the version I served at my April Supper Club. I didn't want to repeat the tomatoes that were in the cannelloni sauce or the almonds in the biscotti, so I omitted the almonds and substituted steamed beets for tomatoes. Use 2 to 3 medium beets for this recipe; steam until tender and slice into very thin rounds. Toss with a few tablespoons of the vinaigrette. Surround the beans with the sliced beets. The contrast of colors is beautiful.

Cannelloni With Chard, Herb and Ricotta Filling

THESE DEMAND a lot of time, and I suggest you make them with a friend. I remember vividly the first time I made the cannelloni for the Supper Club. Siena Herrera, my assistant at the time, a beautiful, golden-haired French woman of Cuban origin who was studying to be a fashion designer, rolled and cut neat squares, all the same size (mine are never that even). I cooked the squares, and a woman who was renting a room in my apartment for a few weeks filled them with the chard, cheese and herb mixture I'd put together that afternoon. We worked late into the night and held the cannelloni in a covered dish in the refrigerator. I finished them with the sauce just before baking and serving. Upon tasting this dish the following evening, my assistants agreed that the labor of love had been worthwhile.

The cannelloni are light and springlike, with the taste of fresh herbs and chard. They can be made with parsley, spinach or whole-wheat pasta. I think the green-flecked parsley cannelloni are the prettiest.

Note: Dried commercial cannelloni can be substituted for the fresh.

FOR THE PASTA

3 egg Whole-Wheat Pasta, Spinach Pasta or Herb Pasta made with parsley (homemade, increased according to the note on page 40)
1 tablespoon salt
1 teaspoon vegetable or olive oil

FOR THE FILLING

1 pound (500 g) Swiss chard leaves (3 pounds, 1.5 kg, with stalks)
1 cup (30 g) finely chopped fresh Italian flat-leaf parsley
½ cup (15 g) finely chopped fresh basil, if available (use 1½ cups, 45 g, parsley in all if basil isn't available)
1 pound (500 g) part-skim ricotta
½ pound (250 g) fresh goat cheese, preferably not too salty

⅔ cup (70 g) freshly grated Parmesan (2 ½ ounces)
½ teaspoon dried thyme
½ to 1 teaspoon minced fresh rosemary or ¼ to ½ teaspoon dried, to taste
2 cloves garlic, minced or put through a press
⅛ teaspoon freshly grated nutmeg
2 large eggs, beaten

FOR THE TOMATO SAUCE

1 to 2 tablespoons olive oil, as necessary
1 small or medium onion, minced
3 large cloves garlic, minced or put through a press
3 pounds (1.5 kg) fresh tomatoes, peeled, seeded and chopped, or 3 28-ounce (765-g) cans
¼ teaspoon honey or sugar
Salt, to taste
1 to 2 tablespoons chopped fresh basil, if available, or ½ to 1 teaspoon dried, to taste
Pinch of ground cinnamon
Freshly ground pepper, to taste

FOR THE TOPPING

½ to 1 cup (55 g to 115 g) freshly grated Parmesan (2 to 4 ounces)
2 to 3 tablespoons chopped fresh parsley

If you are making a large quantity of the cannelloni and need to stack them, do so between sheets of aluminum foil, lightly oiled with olive oil, and heat the sauce separately on the stove. Sauce the cannelloni when you serve them. You must have the filling ready before you roll out and cook the pasta, since you must fill the pasta as soon as it is cooked. The entire dish is then baked in the oven.

Mixing up the pasta dough: Mix up the pasta dough of your choice, according to the directions on pages 40 to 42. Knead and allow it to rest 30 minutes while you make the filling.

Making the filling: Wash the chard, separate the leaves from the stalks, weigh out 1 pound (500 g), and place in a large, dry skillet. Cook over high heat without adding any additional liquid, just until it wilts. Remove from the pan, rinse with cold water, and squeeze very dry in a towel. Chop fine by hand or in a food processor, and blend together with the remaining filling ingredients, either in a food processor or in the bowl of an electric mixer, stirring well with a wooden spoon.

Rolling, cutting, cooking and filling the pasta: Roll the pasta out into long, wide sheets. Cut these into squares about 4 ½ by 5 ½ inches (12 x 15 cm). Allow them to dry for about 20 minutes on towels.

Bring a large pot of water to a rolling boil and add 1 tablespoon of salt and 1 teaspoon of oil. Have a bowlful of cold water next to the pot. Drop the pasta squares into the boiling water, a few at a time, and cook for about 30 seconds to 1 minute, or until they float up to the surface. Remove from the pot with a slotted spoon and place in the cold water to stop the cooking, then drain on a towel. Continue until you have cooked all the squares.

Oil a 3-quart (3-L) baking dish. Place 2 heaping tablespoons of filling along the longer edge of each sheet and roll it up. Place the cannelloni side by side in the baking dish, seam side up. (You may need 2 baking dishes.)

Making the tomato sauce: Heat 1 tablespoon of the olive oil in a heavy-bottomed Dutch oven or saucepan and sauté the onion and 1 clove of the garlic until the onion is golden and translucent. Add the tomatoes, honey or sugar, salt to taste and the remaining garlic and bring to a simmer. Simmer over medium heat, stirring occasionally, for 30 minutes. Add the basil and cinnamon and simmer another 20 minutes. Correct the salt and add freshly ground pepper to taste. For the best texture, puree through the medium blade of a food mill. Taste and adjust seasonings.

Final assembling and baking: Preheat the oven to 375° F (190° C). Top the cannelloni with a layer of tomato sauce, then a sprinkling of grated Parmesan. Bake for 20 to 30 minutes in the preheated oven, until the cheese is melted and the sauce is bubbling. Sprinkle with parsley and serve.

To prepare ahead of time: The tomato sauce can be made up to 1 day ahead of time but is best made the day you are serving.

The chard filling can be made 1 day ahead of time and held in a covered bowl in the refrigerator.

The cannelloni can be made and filled 1 day ahead of time and held in the refrigerator. Oil the baking dish or dishes well and cover tightly with lightly oiled foil.

Serves 6 (18 cannelloni)

Pan-Fried Mushrooms

THIS IS A CONVENIENT side dish and is especially good with hefty main dishes. Cultivated or fresh wild mushrooms are both suitable.

1	tablespoon unsalted butter
1	tablespoon olive oil
1 ½	pounds (750 g) cultivated or wild mushrooms (such as cèpes [porcini], chanterelles, oyster or a combination), cleaned, trimmed and thickly sliced or quartered
2	shallots, minced
3	cloves garlic, minced or put through a press
¼	cup (60 ml) dry white wine
2 to 3	tablespoons soy sauce
1	teaspoon fresh thyme or ½ teaspoon dried
1	teaspoon fresh rosemary or ½ teaspoon dried
	Salt and freshly ground pepper, to taste
2	tablespoons chopped fresh parsley (optional)

Heat the butter and oil in a large, heavy-bottomed skillet and add the mushrooms and shallots. Sauté over medium heat until the mushrooms begin to release their liquid, about 5 minutes. Add the garlic and sauté about 2 minutes, then add the wine and the soy sauce. Raise the heat and cook, stirring, until most of the liquid has evaporated, about 5 to 10 minutes. Lower the heat a little and add the herbs, salt and freshly ground pepper to taste. Cook, stirring, for another few minutes. Taste and adjust seasonings, adding more garlic, soy sauce or thyme or rosemary, if you wish. Remove from the heat, stir in the parsley and serve.

To prepare ahead of time: All the ingredients can be prepared and held in covered containers in the refrigerator for several hours. The entire dish will hold for several hours on top of the stove. In this case, don't add the parsley until you reheat the mushrooms.

SERVES 4 TO 6

Strawberries and Oranges With Cointreau

THIS IS A SALAD for early spring, when the strawberries are coming in and the oranges are going out. The colors are gorgeous, like the red and orange tulips that also appear at this time.

I like to use the blood oranges we get here, which come from North Africa and Israel, as well as navel oranges. The blood oranges are tart and dark red, the navels sweet and bright orange.

2   pints (750 g) ripe strawberries (1 ½ pounds), trimmed and quartered or cut in half
1   tablespoon mild-flavored honey
    Juice of 2 oranges

4   navel oranges, or 2 blood oranges and 3 navels, peeled, white pith removed, cut into wedges
¼   cup (60 ml) Cointreau
3   tablespoons chopped fresh mint

Prepare the strawberries and toss with the honey and orange juice. Cover and refrigerate for at least 1 hour.

Toss together the strawberries, oranges, Cointreau and mint. Refrigerate until ready to serve.

To prepare ahead of time: This can be prepared several hours before serving. Cover and chill.

SERVES 6

May

❧

A Mexican Fête

APERITIF: MARGARITAS (PAGE 50)

CEVICHE

CUMIN AND CORNMEAL BREAD (PAGE 31)

CHALUPAS OR TOSTADAS EXTRAORDINAIRES

PAN-FRIED ZUCCHINI WITH PARSLEY BUTTER

STRAWBERRY SORBET

TEXAS TEA CAKES (PAGE 99)

WINE SUGGESTIONS: BEAUJOLAIS, GAMAY TOURAINE OR MEXICAN BEER

SERVES 6

May

THIS IS MY STANDARD Tex-Mex buffet, and it never gets old. I have made this meal for 6 people, for my regular 25 Supper Club guests, for parties of 50 and 150. The larger buffets include more dishes (see menus on pages 167 and 171), but everything centers around the black-bean chalupas or tostadas.

I've made this menu so many times that I can practically do it with my eyes closed. For that reason, I often choose it when I know I'm going to be distracted by deadlines or out-of-town visitors.

Chalupas or Tostadas Extraordinaires show up at least once a year at the Supper Club, and they are my standard fare for catered events, whether large or small. They are convenient in that everything except the guacamole can be prepared hours in advance. I usually soak the beans two days before the dinner and cook and refry them the day before. They reheat easily in a moderate oven, and their flavor improves overnight.

At the Supper Club, my assistants and I make up the chalupas at the buffet and run them to the tables. But at larger events, the chalupa buffet is part of the party. My assistants and I stand behind long tables, making up the chalupas as guests move through the line.

I'll never forget the first time we catered a big *International Herald Tribune* staff party for 150 people. The party was on a large barge that left from just outside Paris and moved up the Seine, around the Île-St.-Louis and back, a four-hour ride. It was a very hot summer night in July 1983, and everybody was up for a party. The guests stood around drinking margaritas and eating crudités while we passed Mexican-Style Mussels on the Half Shell (page 172) for about an hour, until everybody was there. Then there was a great moment when the boat began to move, the Tex-Mex band I'd hired began to play, and we started serving chalupas. People moved through the line, then came back for seconds, and my crew and I didn't look up for a couple of hours.

When things slowed down a little, I went up on the top deck, just as the boat was passing under the ornate Pont Alexandre, Paris's most beautiful bridge. Everything was perfect at that moment: the air was soft and warm, the city was lit up, the chalupas were a hit, and I was doing a big catering job on a boat on the Seine in Paris.

Ceviche

❀

CEVICHES are made with various kinds of seafood; the traditional Mexican one, according to Diana Kennedy, calls for mackerel or sierra; other recipes call for bay scallops. But I prefer a light fish, like cod or whiting. Both of these fish have a mild, subtle flavor, and they are inexpensive.

Ceviche is always popular at my Supper Club. It isn't too piquant, as it often is in Mexico and Texas; I have to keep the conservative French palate in mind. I also don't want to interfere too much with all the other flavors in the dish. What distinguishes my ceviche from many others is the quantity of vegetables—the avocados, tomatoes, onions—which give it a variety of textures and fresh flavors.

Note: Do not make this dish unless your fish is very fresh.

1 ½ pounds (750 g) very fresh fish fillets, such as cod, red snapper, whiting or redfish
    Juice of 7 large limes (1 ½ to 2 cups, 350 ml to 450 ml)
1   small onion, sliced
1   clove garlic, minced or put through a press
1 to 2 fresh or canned jalapeño or serrano chili peppers, to taste, seeded and chopped
2   medium tomatoes, chopped
    Salt and freshly ground pepper, to taste
1   large or 2 small ripe avocados, peeled, seeded and diced
¼   cup (60 ml) olive oil
4   tablespoons chopped fresh cilantro

FOR THE PLATE

6   ounces (170 g) large spinach leaves, washed and stemmed or 1 head Boston or leaf lettuce
1   small avocado, peeled, seeded and sliced
    Thin slices of lime
2   tomatoes, sliced
2   ears corn, cooked and broken into 2-inch (5-cm) pieces (optional)
    Radish roses (optional)
    Fresh cilantro sprigs

Cut the fish fillets into ½-inch (1.5-cm) cubes and place in a bowl. Pour on the lime juice and toss together well. Marinate the fish in the lime juice, making sure it is completely submerged, for 7 hours, covered, in the refrigerator. The fish should be opaque.

Add the onion, garlic, chilies, chopped tomatoes, salt, pepper, diced avocado and olive oil and refrigerate another hour or more. Just before serving, toss with the chopped cilantro and adjust seasonings.

Line individual salad plates with leaves of spinach or lettuce. Top with the ceviche. Garnish with slices of avocado, lime and tomato, the optional radish roses and the optional corn on the cob. Sprinkle with additional sprigs of cilantro and serve.

To prepare ahead of time: This must be made at least 8 hours before serving.

SERVES 6

Chalupas or Tostadas Extraordinaires

❀

THIS RECIPE hasn't changed too much since I first published it in *The Vegetarian Feast*. The chalupas are still extraordinary; maybe even better than the original.

Refried Black Beans (page 51)
½   cup (115 g) part-skim ricotta or low-fat cottage cheese
½   cup (120 ml) plain low-fat yogurt

½	pound (250 g) white Cheddar
1	recipe Salsa Fresca (page 53) or more, to taste
½	cup (55 g) almonds
1	small head leaf or romaine lettuce
1	recipe Guacamole (page 52)
12	chalupa crisps (homemade, page 44) or store-bought tostadas

Soak the beans overnight, then cook and refry according to the recipe.

Whip the ricotta or cottage cheese in a food processor or mixer, and stir in the yogurt (don't blend them together or the mixture will be too runny). Grate the Cheddar. Hold in separate bowls, covered, in the refrigerator.

Make the salsa, cover and refrigerate until ready to serve.

Roast the almonds in a dry skillet over medium heat or in the oven, just until they begin to brown and smell toasty. Remove from the heat and chop, not too coarsely but not too finely (you need them for texture and a nutty taste). Set aside.

Wash the lettuce, dry it and cut it into ribbons. Refrigerate in a plastic bag.

Make the guacamole as close to serving time as possible and refrigerate, covered, until ready to serve.

Forty minutes before serving time, preheat the oven to 350° F (180° C). Douse the refried beans with a little cooking liquid and cover with foil.

Reheat for 30 minutes in the oven.

Assembling the chalupas or tostadas: A chalupa buffet is a lovely sight. Have the beans in an attractive baking dish and all the other ingredients in pretty bowls. Spread a generous spoonful of the refried beans on each chalupa or tostada. Top with a sprinkling of the grated cheese, then a spoonful of guacamole. Top the guacamole with a spoonful of the yogurt-ricotta mixture, then shredded lettuce, then a generous spoonful of salsa and finally a light sprinkling of chopped almonds. Serve 2 to a plate, and pass extra salsa on the side.

To prepare ahead of time: The beans will hold for up to 3 days, covered, in the refrigerator. They also freeze well. Place a layer of plastic or wax paper between the beans and the foil so the beans won't react with the aluminum, but remember to remove the plastic before you reheat them.

The ingredients for the salsa can be prepared 1 day in advance and held in covered containers in the refrigerator. The salsa can be assembled and held in the refrigerator for several hours. The cheese can be grated and the ricotta and yogurt mixed 1 day ahead of time. These can be refrigerated, covered, in the bowls you will be serving from. The chalupa crisps can be fried and the lettuce cut into ribbons several hours in advance.

SERVES 6

Pan-Fried Zucchini With Parsley Butter

T HIS SIMPLY PREPARED zucchini is a great accompaniment to more complicated main dishes.

1 ½	pounds (750 g) zucchini, sliced thin
1	tablespoon unsalted butter
	Salt and freshly ground pepper, to taste
2	tablespoons minced fresh parsley

Steam the zucchini until crisp-tender, about 5 minutes. It should just be starting to become translucent. Refresh under cold water. This can be done in advance and the zucchini held in a bowl.

Heat the butter in a wide skillet and add the zucchini. Sauté, stirring with a wooden spoon, until the squash is heated through. Add salt and freshly ground pepper to taste, stir in the parsley and serve.

SERVES 4 TO 6

Strawberry Sorbet

✿

T HIS IS A DISH for spring and summer, when strawberries are at their best. It's tangy and perfect after a rich or spicy meal (or any meal, for that matter).

½   cup (120 ml) mild-flavored honey
1 ⅔   cups (385 ml) water
3   pints strawberries, washed and hulled
     (2 ¼ pounds, 1 kg)
½   cup (120 ml) fresh orange juice, strained
3   tablespoons fresh lemon juice, strained
2   tablespoons crème de cassis liqueur
     Fresh mint for garnish

Combine the honey and water in a large saucepan (the honey boils up drastically) and bring to a simmer. Simmer 10 minutes and allow to cool.

Puree the strawberries in a food processor or blender until smooth. Add the orange juice, lemon juice, crème de cassis, and ⅔ of the honey syrup. Taste and add the rest of the syrup if the mixture isn't sweet enough. Freeze in an ice cream maker or a sorbetière, or still-freeze according to the instructions in the note on page 55.

Transfer to individual serving dishes, a mold or an attractive bowl, cover each serving dish or the bowl with plastic, then foil, and freeze. Work quickly so the mixture doesn't melt. Allow to soften in the refrigerator for 20 minutes before serving. Garnish each serving with fresh mint leaves.

To prepare ahead of time: The sorbet should be made at least 1 day in advance and will last for weeks in the freezer.

SERVES 6 TO 8

June

✿

An Early-Summer Menu

APERITIF: CHAMPAGNE AND GRAPEFRUIT JUICE PUNCH

ASIAN SALAD WITH HOMEMADE BUCKWHEAT PASTA

COUNTRY BREAD WITH OLIVES (PAGE 38)

POACHED FILLETS OF SOLE WITH PUREED TOMATO SAUCE

STEAMED ZUCCHINI

CONCASSÉE OF FRESH STRAWBERRIES

HONEY-LEMON REFRIGERATOR COOKIES (PAGE 55)

WINE SUGGESTIONS: SAUVIGNON TOURAINE, ENTRE-DEUX-MERS,
GRAVES BLANC, CHARDONNAY HAUT-POITOU

SERVES 4 TO 6

June

I REMEMBER WALKING around Paris on a rare and welcome warm June day in 1985, during one of those springtimes that was more like winter, envisaging what the plates would look like for each course of this dinner: pasta salad with a rainbow of green and red vegetables, served on a bed of lettuce; delicate fish fillets in a satiny tomato sauce, garnished with a steamed vegetable; something fruity and unexpected for dessert. Chilled white wine, yellow and white daisies on the table, colorful Italian pottery instead of my usual white porcelain. I sat in the sun at a sidewalk café on the boulevard Port-Royale, drank fresh lemonade and wrote shopping lists.

The sauce for the cold poached fish was an uncooked puree of tomato sauce, my version of a recipe I had come across years ago in Roy Andries de Groot's *Revolutionizing French Cooking*. The original recipe is by Michel Guérard. My sauce has additional herbs, a touch of balsamic vinegar and a julienne of orange zest, the finishing touch added at the end. It is a lively, easy dish. A simple steamed vegetable, zucchini, in this case—but green beans, fresh peas or snow peas would also be nice—is all you need to accompany the fish.

The salad is sublime, with delicate homemade noodles, pungent sauce, fresh cilantro, crisp, bright snow peas, shiny red peppers and a shrimp garnish. The delicious Concassée of Fresh Strawberries, served with honey-lemon cookies, makes a perfect finale to this meal.

Champagne and Grapefruit Juice Punch

❦

THIS IS THE PUNCH I always served in Austin, Texas, for my big parties. It's great because it seems you can drink a fair amount without becoming too inebriated, probably because of the large proportion of citrus juice.

1 quart (1 L) canned or bottled grapefruit juice

1 bottle dry Champagne
3 tablespoons crème de cassis liqueur
Ice cubes
Sliced citrus and strawberries for garnish

Mix together the grapefruit juice, Champagne and liqueur in a punch bowl. Chill with ice cubes, garnish with the fruit and serve.

SERVES 6

Asian Salad With Homemade Buckwheat Pasta

❦

A CONVENIENT SALAD for a dinner party because all the components can be prepared in advance. Just before serving, toss it with the dressing. It is as beautiful as it is delicious and could be eaten as a simple meal as well as a starter. You can, of course, buy the noodles, but I have given you my recipe in case you want to make them yourself.

FOR THE SALAD

Homemade Buckwheat Pasta (page 41) or ½ pound (250 g) commercial buckwheat noodles (also called soba; can be found in Japanese markets and natural-foods stores)
2 tablespoons sesame oil
½ pound (250 g) snow peas, trimmed
1 sweet red pepper, seeded and cut into thin strips
2 tablespoons minced chives
3 tablespoons minced fresh cilantro

FOR THE DRESSING

2 tablespoons fresh lemon juice
2 tablespoons cider vinegar or more, to taste
2 tablespoons water
1 tablespoon tamari or soy sauce
1 teaspoon dry sherry
1 teaspoon mild-flavored honey (optional)

1 teaspoon minced or grated fresh ginger
1 clove garlic, minced or put through a press
1 teaspoon sesame tahini
3 tablespoons safflower oil
3 tablespoons sesame oil
Salt and freshly ground pepper, to taste
Pinch of cayenne

FOR THE PLATES

Leaf lettuce
24 to 30 small shrimp, cooked and peeled, for garnish (optional)
Additional chopped fresh cilantro

Make the pasta and cook al dente, just until firm to the bite, and toss with the 2 tablespoons sesame oil. Set aside.

Steam the snow peas until crisp-tender and refresh under cold water (or you can blanch them, as for green beans; see page 73). Toss with the noodles and all the remaining salad ingredients. Chill until ready to serve, or serve at room temperature.

Mix together all the ingredients for the dressing in a blender until smooth. Adjust seasonings. Shortly before serving, toss with the noodles. Taste and adjust seasonings, adding more salt, pepper, soy sauce or cayenne, if you wish.

Line plates or a platter with the lettuce leaves.

Top with the salad, and place 4 to 6 shrimp on the top of each serving. Sprinkle with additional cilantro and serve.

To prepare ahead of time: The noodles can be made 1 to 2 days in advance and dried. They can be cooked several hours ahead of time, tossed with the sesame oil in a bowl and refrigerated. The dressing can be made 1 day in advance and refrigerated in a covered jar. The vegetables can be prepared several hours in advance and refrigerated in plastic bags or covered containers.

SERVES 4 TO 6

Poached Fillets of Sole With Pureed Tomato Sauce

❦

HERE IS ANOTHER perfect do-ahead dish for a dinner party. Every portion of it can (*must*) be prepared well in advance, unless you are serving the fish hot. Even then, it's just a question of 5 to 10 minutes' work. Since you are relying on ripe, fresh tomatoes, this is a spring or summer dish, and for this reason, I like to serve the fish at room temperature. I poach them in the morning, chill them, and an hour or so before serving, remove them from the refrigerator.

Everybody loves the flavor of the basil and the hint of orange in this elegant dish.

FOR THE FISH

Vinegar Court Bouillon (page 139)
1 to 1½ pounds (500 g to 750 g) sole fillets (allow 4 ounces, 115 g, per person)
2 to 3 teaspoons olive oil, for the serving dish
Salt and freshly ground pepper, to taste
Juice of ½ lemon
Thin strips of zest from ½ orange

FOR THE SAUCE

2 pounds (1 kg) tomatoes, peeled and seeded
2 large cloves garlic, peeled
2 tablespoons chopped fresh basil leaves
1 tablespoon fresh chervil leaves (or, if unavailable, use 3 tablespoons fresh basil in all)
1 tablespoon chopped fresh parsley
1 tablespoon balsamic vinegar or more, to taste
Salt and freshly ground pepper, to taste
3 tablespoons fruity olive oil (optional)

Thin strips of zest from ½ orange

First make Vinegar Court Bouillon and allow it to cool. If you are serving the fish cold, it doesn't matter whether you poach the fish or make the sauce first. If you are serving the fish hot, make the sauce first.

Preparing the fish: Rinse the fillets and pat them dry. Place them on a cutting board and slap with the flat side of a large knife. This breaks down the muscle fibers so they won't curl when you poach them. Make a few diagonal slashes, about ⅛ inch (0.25 cm) deep, across each one.

Spread 2 to 3 teaspoons olive oil over the bottom of an attractive flat or oval serving dish or casserole. Set aside.

Butter a deep, flat frying pan or flameproof gratin dish and add Vinegar Court Bouillon, which should be at room temperature or warm, but not too hot. Add the fish fillets in an even layer. Bring to a simmer over low heat. Never let the bouillon actually boil; it should be just trembling. When it reaches this point, count 5 minutes for each ½ inch (1.5 cm) of thickness in the layer of fish (fillets are usually ½ inch, 1.5 cm, thick). After 5 minutes, the fish should be opaque and should break apart easily with a fork. Carefully remove the fillets from the poaching liquid with a slotted spatula and place in the oiled casserole. Lightly salt and pepper, then sprinkle with the lemon juice and orange zest.

Preparing the sauce: Blend the tomatoes, garlic, half the basil, chervil, if available, parsley and the vinegar together in a food processor or blender until smooth. Add salt and freshly ground pepper to taste. If you wish, add a bit more balsamic vinegar.

Transfer the mixture to a large bowl, and using a wire whisk or an electric mixer, beat to incorporate air and lighten the sauce, while you slowly drizzle in the olive oil. This step gives the sauce a silky texture. Taste and correct seasonings. Set aside in the refrigerator in a covered bowl if serving the next day or at room temperature if serving in a few hours.

Shortly before serving, stir in the remaining basil and the orange zest. Correct seasonings.

If serving cold: Cover the fish with plastic or foil and refrigerate. An hour or two before serving, remove from the refrigerator. Pour on half the sauce and let sit at room temperature until ready to serve. At serving time, place the fillets and some of the sauce on each plate, and top with more sauce.

If serving hot: After poaching and sprinkling the fish with the lemon juice, orange zest, salt and pepper, garnish with about ⅓ of the sauce. Bring to the table and serve, topping each serving with another spoonful of sauce.

Note: You could also cool the fish in its poaching liquid. In this case, poach for only 3 to 4 minutes and remove the casserole from the heat. The fish will have a slightly more vinegary taste.

To prepare ahead of time: The sauce will hold for 1 day in the refrigerator; the flavors actually ripen overnight, although the last of the basil and orange zest should be added close to the time of serving. The fish can be poached in the morning for an evening meal and stored in the refrigerator. The Vinegar Court Bouillon can be made 1 to 2 days in advance and refrigerated in a covered bowl or jar.

SERVES 4 TO 6

Vinegar Court Bouillon

❧

THIS IS A GOOD poaching medium for fish if you are going to serve it cold, especially with an acid sauce like the one for the poached fillets of sole in this menu.

1 quart (1 L) water
½ cup (120 ml) good-quality red-wine
    vinegar
1 onion, sliced
2 leeks, cleaned and sliced
1 carrot, sliced
1 stalk celery, sliced
2 whole cloves garlic, peeled
1 sprig of fresh parsley

1 sprig of fresh thyme
1 bay leaf
1 tablespoon salt, or to taste
6 peppercorns

Combine all the ingredients except the peppercorns in a large saucepan or soup pot. Bring to a boil, reduce the heat, cover, and simmer 30 minutes. Add the peppercorns and simmer another 15 to 30 minutes. Strain and retain the broth. Use for poaching fish.

This will keep for 1 to 2 days in the refrigerator and can be frozen.

MAKES ABOUT 1 QUART (1 L)

Ravioli With Cheese and Wild Mushrooms
page 224

Lulu's Huge Vegetable and Fish Platter
page 212

143

Crepes Filled With Lemon Soufflé
page 221

Two July Menus

❦

For a Hot Evening

Crazy Salad With Tuna Tartare

Sourdough Country Bread (page 26)

Cold Steamed Fish Fillets With Tomato-Caper Sauce

New Potatoes in Foil

Peach Tart

Wine Suggestions: Sauvignon Touraine, Coteaux du Tricastin,
Côtes-du-Rhône or Châteauneuf-du-Pape Blanc

Serves 6

July

July in Paris can be crazy: it can start out cold and wet, then become very hot and humid. The first menu here is a meal for a hot night, and when I served this in 1986, hot weather was upon us. A few years before, for a July Supper Club, it had been cold for so long I felt like trying to force the summer with vegetables. That year, I served hot baked whitings with the same tomato-caper sauce I had served on the cold fish and several vegetable dishes.

Life in Paris is relaxed during July and August, with so many people out of town. My soirees often continue late into the night. It's still light when we sit down to dinner, and if it's balmy, guests linger on the balcony after the meal.

Crazy Salad With Tuna Tartare

❧

THIS IS a "crazy salad" because of all the different colors and ingredients: lettuce, sweet baby peas, brilliant red peppers and ripe tomatoes. I make it in early summer when there is a great variety of produce in the markets. You don't have to be limited to the ingredients here. It could be a "clean-out-the-refrigerator" salad. What makes it truly special, though, is the raw tuna, which is marinated for several hours in lemon juice, crushed garlic and olive oil, then tossed with diced avocado just before serving.

Note: You must use only very fresh tuna for this.

FOR THE TUNA TARTARE

¾	pound (350 g) very fresh tuna, skin and bones removed
3	cloves garlic, peeled
¼	cup (60 ml) fresh lemon juice
6	tablespoons olive oil
	Salt and freshly ground pepper to taste
	Leaves from 3 sprigs of fresh parsley, chopped
2	teaspoons chopped chives

FOR THE SALAD

1	large head or the equivalent of a combination of lettuces, such as red tip, romaine, Boston, oak leaf
1	cucumber, peeled and thinly sliced
1 to 2	sweet red peppers, seeded and thinly sliced
½	pound (250 g) fresh peas (unshelled weight), shelled
½	pound (250 g) carrots, peeled and grated
1	bunch radishes, cut in half lengthwise and thickly sliced
¼	pound (115 g) mushrooms, cleaned, trimmed and sliced
3 to 4	tomatoes, cut into wedges
4 to 6	tablespoons of one or more chopped fresh herbs such as tarragon, basil, chives, parsley, dill
1	cup (115 g) diced Garlic Croutons (page 45)

FOR THE DRESSING

	Juice of 1 medium or large lemon
¼	cup (60 ml) red-wine vinegar
1 to 2	cloves of the crushed garlic from the tuna marinade, to taste, minced or put through a press
1	heaping teaspoon Dijon mustard
	Salt and freshly ground pepper, to taste
¾ to 1	cup (180 ml to 225 ml) olive oil, to taste; or use half olive oil, half safflower or vegetable oil

FOR THE GARNISH

1	avocado

Making the tuna tartare: At least 3 hours before you wish to serve, cut the tuna into ½-inch (1.5-cm) dice. Crush the garlic with the flat side of a knife and combine in a bowl with the lemon juice, olive oil, salt and pepper to taste. Add the tuna, parsley and chives and toss thoroughly. Cover and refrigerate for 3 hours. Stir from time to time; taste and adjust seasonings.

Preparing the salad ingredients: Wash and dry the lettuces. Tear into large pieces and wrap in a towel, then in a plastic bag, and refrigerate until ready to use.

Prepare the remaining vegetables, herbs and the croutons and toss together in a large bowl.

Making the salad dressing: Combine the lemon juice and vinegar, the 1 to 2 cloves garlic from the tuna marinade, mustard, salt and pepper, and mix together. Whisk in the oil or oils and combine well.

Just before serving, dice the avocado and stir into the tuna. Toss with 2 tablespoons of the salad dressing.

To serve: If serving on individual plates, toss the lettuces in one bowl with half the dressing, and the other ingredients in a separate bowl with the other half. Line salad plates with the lettuce and top with the vegetable mixture. Top this with the tuna and avocado and serve. If you are serving the salad from a big bowl, toss together the lettuce and vegetable mixture, top with the tuna and avocado and serve.

To prepare ahead of time: The tuna must be prepared several hours in advance. The peas can be shelled and the croutons made 1 day in advance. Hold the peas in a plastic bag or container in the refrigerator and the croutons in a well-sealed container. The vegetables and salad dressing can be prepared several hours in advance. Refrigerate the vegetables in plastic bags or covered containers and the dressing in a jar or bowl.

Serves 6

Cold Steamed Fish Fillets With Tomato-Caper Sauce

❀

I'VE SERVED the sauce that goes with this fish with tuna, baked whitefish and chilled fillets of red snapper, redfish or cod. It's a zesty Mediterranean tomato sauce, pungent with garlic and capers. (See photograph, page 69.)

FOR THE TOMATO-CAPER SAUCE

1   tablespoon olive oil
1   small or ½ medium onion, finely chopped
½   cup (60 g) capers, rinsed and chopped in a food processor or mashed in a mortar and pestle
4 to 6   cloves garlic, chopped (can be mashed along with the capers)
2 ½   pounds (1.25 kg) tomatoes, seeded and chopped
      Pinch of sugar
      Salt and freshly ground pepper to taste
2 to 3   teaspoons chopped fresh basil
¼ to ½ teaspoon fresh thyme leaves or ¼ tsp dried

FOR THE FISH

6   red snapper or redfish fillets, about 6 ounces (170 g) each
      Salt and freshly ground pepper, to taste
1   large sprig of fresh basil for the steaming water

Making the sauce: Heat the olive oil in a large, heavy-bottomed skillet and add the onion. Sauté for a few minutes and add the capers and the garlic. Sauté, stirring, for 5 minutes, then add the tomatoes and a pinch of sugar. Cook over moderate heat, stirring occasionally, for 20 to 30 minutes. Season to taste with salt and freshly ground pepper, and stir in the basil and thyme. Allow to cool, then cover and chill.

Steaming the fish: First prepare the fillets by slapping them with the flat side of a knife to break down the muscle fibers so they don't curl when they are exposed to the heat. Score each fillet on the diagonal, 3 or 4 times, about ¼ inch (0.75 cm) deep. Lightly salt and pepper them and place on an oiled steaming rack. Bring a small amount of water, to which you have added a few leaves of fresh basil, to a boil in your steaming pot. Place the steaming rack over the boiling water, cover, and steam 5 minutes per ½-inch (1.5-cm) thickness. The fish should be opaque and flake easily with a fork. Immediately transfer the fillets to an oiled platter or casserole and allow them to cool. Cover and refrigerate until 30 minutes before serving time.

Thirty minutes before serving, remove the fish and the sauce from the refrigerator. The fish should be cold, but not so cold that you can't taste it. Serve each fillet partially covered with the sauce, with more sauce on the plate. This is excellent with potatoes or fresh pasta on the side.

To prepare ahead of time: The sauce can be made 1 day ahead. Cool, then transfer to a bowl or serving dish, cover and refrigerate. The fish can be steamed several hours in advance but should be bought the day you are serving it. Once steamed, cover and refrigerate.

Serves 6

New Potatoes in Foil

❧

IF YOU ARE INCREASING this recipe by a substantial amount, make several packets. If you crowd the potatoes, they take longer to bake. I learned this the hard way at the Supper Club, when my assistant, following my directions, removed the potatoes from the foil after 25 minutes and served them rock hard. I died a hundred deaths.

1 ½ pounds (750 g) new potatoes, the smaller the better
2 tablespoons unsalted butter or olive oil
    Salt and freshly ground pepper, to taste
2 sprigs of fresh thyme or ½ teaspoon dried
2 tablespoons chopped fresh parsley

Preheat the oven to 425° F (220° C).

Scrub the potatoes, dry, and cut in 1-inch (2.5-cm) pieces.

Cut a double-thick square of aluminum foil large enough to form a loose pouch for the potatoes. Butter or oil the foil generously and place the potatoes on top. Salt and pepper, add the thyme and remaining butter, and fold the foil over the potatoes. Crimp the edges of the foil together tightly. Bake in the oven 25 to 30 minutes. Remove from the oven and open the foil. Check to see that the potatoes are tender. If they are not, close and bake another 5 to 10 minutes. Remove from the foil, toss with the parsley in a serving dish and serve hot.

SERVES 6

Peach Tart

❧

THE TASTE OF this juicy peach tart, with its crunchy, almondy crust, is sublime. However, the crust underneath the fruit will get soggy very quickly. It's because whole-wheat pastries are more penetrable than those made with white flour. It helps considerably to brush it generously with beaten egg before you prebake it. But I recommend that you make this as close to serving time as possible.

    Sweet Almond Piecrust (page 43)
1 large egg, beaten
    Juice of 1 lemon
2 tablespoons mild-flavored honey
2 ½ pounds (1.25 kg) peaches (or a mixture of peaches and apricots), peeled, pitted and thinly sliced
2 tablespoons apricot preserves (optional)

Make the piecrust. Refrigerate until ready to prebake.

Preheat the oven to 375° F (190° C). Brush the crust generously with the beaten egg and prick with a fork in several places. Prebake 20 minutes, until the bottom is cooked through and the edges are beginning to brown. Remove from the oven.

Mix together the lemon juice and honey in a large bowl. Toss the sliced peaches or combination of peaches and apricots with the lemon-honey mixture. Arrange the fruit on the prebaked crust. Retain any liquid remaining in the bowl. Return the tart to the oven and bake another 10 to 15 minutes, or until the crust is brown and the fruit is heated through.

Transfer the liquid from the fruit to a saucepan and reduce over medium-high heat until you have a thick syrup. Add the optional apricot preserves and melt together with the syrup.

Remove the tart from the oven and brush the fruit gently with the syrup. Serve warm or cooled.

SERVES 8

July, continued:
For a Cooler Evening

❧

Vegetables à la Grecque

Country Bread With Olives (page 38)

Baked Whiting or Small Trout With Tomato-Caper Sauce

Pasta With Sweet Peas and Herb Butter

Peach Tart (page 150)

Wine Suggestions: Châteauneuf-du-Pape Blanc,
Sauvignon Touraine, Coteaux du Tricastin, Côtes-du-Rhône

Serves 6

Vegetables à la Grecque

THIS RECIPE was inspired by a dish I ate at the Paris restaurant l'Ambroisie my first year here. The vegetables are stewed in bouillon, with lots of crushed coriander seeds, then marinated in the same broth. The broth is later reduced and poured over the vegetables, and the dish is quite stunning and fragrant with the intensified flavors in the bouillon.

FOR THE BOUILLON/MARINADE

2 ½	cups (570 ml) water
1 ½	cups (350 ml) dry white wine
	Juice of 2 large lemons
2	tablespoons white-wine vinegar or sherry vinegar
½	cup (120 ml) olive oil
3	cloves garlic
12	peppercorns
1	tablespoon coriander seeds
1	bay leaf
4	sprigs of fresh parsley
½	teaspoon fennel seeds
½	teaspoon salt
1	large shallot, chopped
⅔	cup (115 g) raisins

FOR THE VEGETABLES

2 to 3	large globe artichokes
	Juice of about 2 lemons
1	1-pound (500 g) fennel bulb, cut lengthwise into eighths
20	small boiling onions, peeled
8	whole cloves garlic, peeled
1	small cauliflower, broken into florets
½	pound (250 g) carrots, peeled and cut into 3-inch (8-cm) spears
½	pound (250 g) zucchini, cut into 3-inch (8-cm) spears

FOR THE PLATES

Lettuce leaves (optional)
Sprigs of fresh chervil or chopped fresh parsley
Radish roses
Thin slices of lemon

Preparing the bouillon: Combine all the ingredients for the bouillon in a large flameproof casserole or stockpot and bring to a simmer. Simmer, covered, while you prepare the vegetables.

Preparing the vegetables: Cut off the stems of the artichokes, pull off all the tough outer leaves around the bottoms, and slice off the tops where the artichokes begin to curve inward. Rub with lemon juice to prevent discoloration. Trim the bottoms of the artichokes by rotating them against the sharp blade of a knife, so that all the tough green skin is cut away and the white fleshy part underneath the leaves is exposed. Rub these cut surfaces with lemon juice and drop the artichokes into a bowl of water acidulated with the juice of 1 lemon.

Drop the artichokes, fennel, onions and garlic cloves into the simmering bouillon. After 15 minutes, add the cauliflower and carrots. Add the zucchini spears after another 10 minutes, and simmer everything together for 10 minutes more.

Remove the vegetables from the bouillon and place in a bowl. Take out the artichoke bottoms, allow them to cool and cut in half. Using a small spoon, gently scoop out the chokes. Put the artichokes back in the bowl with the other vegetables, pour on the bouillon, cover and refrigerate for 2 hours or overnight.

Finishing the dish: Drain the vegetables and strain the marinade. Place the marinade in a saucepan and bring to a boil over high heat. Reduce by ⅔. If you wish, line individual plates with lettuce leaves. Distribute the vegetables in equal portions over the plates. Pour on the reduced marinade and garnish with sprigs of chervil or chopped fresh parsley, radish roses and thin slices of lemon. Serve.

To prepare ahead of time: This must be made a few hours in advance and will hold for 1 to 2 days in the refrigerator.

SERVES 6 TO 8 GENEROUSLY

Baked Whiting or Small Trout
With Tomato-Caper Sauce

❧

IN COOLER WEATHER, I serve the sauce and fish hot. Small whole whiting baked in a little white wine have a subtle taste and go nicely with the lusty sauce.

Tomato-Caper Sauce (page 149)
6   small whiting or small trout, cleaned,
        heads removed
     Salt and freshly ground pepper, to taste
½   cup (120 ml) dry white wine

First make the sauce and set it aside.

Preheat the oven to 425° F (220° C). Butter a rectangular or oval baking dish large enough for all the fish to fit in a single layer. Wipe the fish and pat dry with a dish towel. Lay them side by side, alternating head end to tail end, in the buttered baking dish. Salt and pepper lightly. Place the wine in a saucepan, bring to a simmer and pour over the fish. Cover with buttered parchment paper or foil and bake 10 to 15 minutes in the preheated oven, until the flesh is opaque and flakes easily with a fork. While the fish is baking, reheat the sauce. Serve the fish with some of the sauce on top and more on the side.

To prepare ahead of time: Just as for the Cold Steamed Fish Fillets With Tomato-Caper Sauce, the sauce will hold for 1 day in the refrigerator. The fish can be prepared in their baking dish several hours in advance, covered, and refrigerated. Remove from the refrigerator 30 minutes before baking.
SERVES 6

Pasta With Sweet Peas and Herb Butter

❧

THIS SIMPLE, fragrant pasta (pictured on page 105) is lovely as a side dish with fish, but it could also be served as a first course.

5   tablespoons softened unsalted butter
¼   cup (10 g) chopped fresh parsley
¼   cup (10 g) chopped fresh basil
2   tablespoons minced chives
1   small clove garlic, pureed or put through a
        press
     Salt, to taste
1   pound (500 g) fresh peas (unshelled
        weight)
1   tablespoon olive or vegetable oil
¾   pound (350 g) spaghettini

Make an herb butter by combining the butter, parsley, basil, chives and garlic. Add a little salt to taste.

Steam the peas until tender, 5 to 8 minutes. Refresh under cold water and set aside.

Bring a large pot of water to a rolling boil. Add 1 teaspoon of salt, 1 tablespoon of oil and the pasta. Cook al dente, just until firm to the bite. This will take 3 to 5 minutes, depending on the width, or seconds if it is fresh pasta. Drain and toss in a warm serving dish with the herb butter and peas. Serve at once.

To prepare ahead of time: The herb butter can be made several hours before serving time and held in the refrigerator. The noodles are cooked and tossed with the herb butter just before serving.
SERVES 4 TO 6

August

❀

More Mediterranean Flavors in a Late-Summer Menu

APERITIF: CRÉMANT DE BOURGOGNE OR CHAMPAGNE

PASTA PRIMAVERA WITH ROASTED RED PEPPERS AND GOAT CHEESE

COUNTRY BREAD WITH OLIVES (PAGE 38)

HERBED WHOLE-WHEAT BREAD (PAGE 37)

COLD POACHED FILLETS OF FISH WITH EGG-LEMON SAUCE

BAKED TOMATOES

STEAMED ZUCCHINI

MIXED PLUM AND APRICOT TART

WINE SUGGESTIONS: SANCERRE OR ANY OTHER SAUVIGNON WINE,
SUCH AS ENTRE-DEUX-MERS, QUINCY

SERVES 4

August

THE FIRST-COURSE pasta salad in this menu, with its Mediterranean flavors—sweet basil, roasted red peppers and goat cheese—is very different from the Asian pasta salad I served in June. Each course is as exquisite to look at as it is tasty. The fragrant pasta salad sparkles with bright peas, asparagus and roasted peppers. The colors in the main dish are pale and summery: lemon-sauced fish fillets topped with dark green sprigs of tarragon; baked tomatoes and barely steamed zucchini fanning the plate. The flavors of the savory olive and herb breads make a nice contrast to the delicately seasoned fish. The tart is a pinwheel of multicolored fruit.

I came upon the fish dish in Elizabeth David's *Summer Meals*. I like the dish with sole but prefer a slightly more substantial flatfish.

August is the time in France for irresistible plums. Apricots are sweet and abundant, and they look beautiful interspersed with the plums.

Pasta Primavera With Roasted Red Peppers and Goat Cheese

꘠

THE PASTA you use for this can be fresh or dried, and you can choose any shape you fancy. I've made the salad with fettuccine, thinner tagliarini, spiral pasta and spaghetti (see photograph on page 107).

FOR THE VEGETABLES AND HERBS

3 sweet red peppers
1 pound (500 g) fresh peas (unshelled weight)
1 pound (500 g) fresh asparagus
2 tablespoons olive oil
1 clove garlic, minced or put through a press
  Coarse salt
1 bunch fresh basil
½ cup (15 g) chopped fresh parsley, preferably flat-leaf

FOR THE PASTA AND THE REST OF THE DISH

3-egg (½ pound, 250 g) Spinach Pasta, Herb Pasta or Whole-Wheat Pasta (homemade, increased according to the note on page 40), or store-bought
5 tablespoons olive oil
1 clove garlic, minced or put through a press
4 ounces (115 g) fresh goat cheese, preferably not too salty, diced or crumbled
1 cup (115 g) freshly grated Parmesan (4 ounces)
  Salt and freshly ground pepper, to taste
  Radish roses for garnish

Preparing the vegetables: First roast 2 of the red peppers. Either roast them under a broiler or above a burner flame, turning until charred on all sides. Remove from the heat and place in a paper bag or damp towel. Allow to cool.

Meanwhile, shell the peas and cut the tips of the asparagus off, about 2 inches (5 cm) down from the top. Trim off the tough base of the asparagus and cut the remaining stalks into pieces about ½-inch (1.5-cm) long. Keep the tops separate from the stalks. Seed the remaining red pepper and cut into thin lengthwise strips, then cut these strips in half or into thirds.

When the roasted peppers are cool enough to handle, remove the skins, rinse under cool water, and pat dry. Remove the stems, seeds and membranes and cut into thin strips. Place in a bowl and toss with 2 tablespoons of olive oil, the minced or pressed clove of garlic, about ¼ teaspoon coarse salt and 8 large leaves of the basil, cut into slivers. Toss together, cover, and refrigerate for at least 1 hour.

Mince the remaining basil and the parsley and set aside. Steam the peas and the asparagus tips and stalks separately, just until crisp-tender, about 5 minutes for the asparagus, 5 to 10 minutes for the peas. Refresh under cold water and set aside.

Cooking the pasta: Bring a large pot of water to a boil and cook the pasta al dente, just until firm to the bite. Drain and toss with the 5 tablespoons olive oil, which you have mixed with 1 clove garlic, minced or put through a press. Refrigerate until shortly before ready to serve, or leave at room temperature if serving soon.

Assembling and serving the dish: Shortly before serving, toss the pasta with the steamed peas and asparagus stalks, the sliced raw pepper, the minced basil and parsley, goat cheese and Parmesan. Taste and adjust salt and pepper.

Serve on individual plates and top each portion with a spoonful of roasted red peppers. Arrange asparagus tops and a few radishes on the side and serve.

To prepare ahead of time: You can roast the red peppers and marinate them 1 day in advance. Refrigerate in a covered bowl. You can also prepare all the vegetables 1 day in advance. Store them in plastic bags or covered containers in the refrigerator. The pasta can be cooked several hours in advance; toss with the olive oil and garlic, cover and refrigerate until ready to toss with the remaining ingredients. The salad will hold, all assembled, for 1 or 2 hours.

SERVES 6

Cold Poached Fillets of Fish With Egg-Lemon Sauce

✿

IPREFER THIS dish cold, but you can also serve it hot. It can be made well in advance, and it's easy. The sweet-pungent tarragon sets off the tangy egg-lemon sauce. If fresh tarragon is difficult to find, substitute chopped fresh chervil, basil or parsley. Any white-fleshed flatfish, such as sole, flounder, haddock or turbot, will work. Accompany the fish with a baked tomato and a fan of steamed zucchini slices.

If you place your leftovers in a tureen and pour the leftover sauce over them, then refrigerate overnight, you'll have a lovely lunch the next day. The fumet will gelatinize, and the gelatin has a marvelous flavor.

FOR THE FUMET

Heads and bones of 2 large white-fleshed flatfish (1 pound, 500 g)
1 quart (1 L) water
1 onion, quartered
1 carrot, coarsely sliced
1 stalk celery, coarsely sliced
2 cloves garlic, peeled
1 leek, white part only, cleaned and sliced
4 peppercorns
Bouquet garni made with 1 bay leaf, 2 sprigs of fresh parsley and 1 sprig of fresh thyme
1 cup (225 ml) dry white wine
Salt, to taste

FOR THE FISH

8 fillets large white-fleshed flatfish, such as sole, haddock, flounder or turbot, skin removed (1 pound, 500 g in all)

FOR THE SAUCE

4 large egg yolks
Juice of 1 to 2 large lemons, to taste
2 tablespoons chopped fresh tarragon, basil, parsley or chervil

FOR THE GARNISH

Thin slices of lemon
Sprigs of fresh tarragon or parsley

Making the fumet: Combine the fish bones and heads in a large soup pot with the water, onion, carrot, celery, garlic, leek, peppercorns and bouquet garni. Bring to a boil. Skim off all the foam that rises (it is bitter), and when there is no longer any foam, cover and simmer over low heat for 15 minutes. Add the white wine and salt to taste, cover and simmer another 15 minutes. Drain and strain the stock through a dishtowel or a double layer of cheesecloth. Set aside and cool to lukewarm or colder.

Preparing and cooking the fish: Rinse the fish fillets and pat dry with paper towels. Using the flat side of a large knife, slap the fillets to break down the muscle fibers so they won't curl when you poach them. Now make 2 or 3 diagonal slashes, about ⅛ inch (0.5 cm) deep, across the fillets on the skin side.

Butter a flameproof casserole large enough to accommodate the fish fillets in one layer. Lay the fish fillets in the casserole and add 3 cups (340 g) of the fumet, or enough to cover the fish. Cover with a piece of buttered parchment and bring to a bare simmer over medium heat. Reduce the heat and poach the fish for 8 to 10 minutes, or 5 minutes for each ½ inch (1.5 cm) of thickness, until the fillets are opaque and flake easily. Remove the fish from the liquid with a slotted spatula and place on an attractive serving dish. Keep warm in a very low oven if serving hot.

Making the sauce: Strain the poaching liquid into a saucepan. Turn up the heat and reduce to about 1 cup (225 ml). Remove from the heat and cool a moment.

Beat together the egg yolks and lemon juice (use the juice of 1 lemon at first, then add more if you want a more lemony sauce); add a ladleful or so of the hot stock to this, stir together well and return the mixture to the remaining stock. Stir over low heat until the mixture reaches a creamy consistency, being careful not to bring to a simmer or the eggs will scramble. Remove from the heat and adjust the lemon juice, salt and pepper. Pour over the fish fillets, cover, and refrigerate until 15 to 30 minutes before you wish to serve, depending on how cold you want the fish to be.

To serve: Just before serving, sprinkle the tarragon over the fish. Serve 2 fillets per person, first spooning a little extra sauce over the plate underneath the fillet, then garnishing with a sprig of tarragon or parsley and a lemon slice.

If you wish to serve the dish hot, once the sauce is ready, pour it over the fish, sprinkle with the tarragon or other fresh herbs, and serve, garnishing as above.

Chill any leftovers in a tureen.

To prepare ahead of time: The fumet will hold for several hours. Strain it and hold in a covered pot. The entire dish should be made several hours in advance when you are serving it cold. Cover with plastic wrap and refrigerate.

SERVES 4

Baked Tomatoes

❀

6	medium or large firm, ripe tomatoes
	Salt and freshly ground pepper, to taste
	Olive oil
2	shallots, minced
2	tablespoons pesto (page 230) or chopped fresh herbs such as basil, thyme, parsley, rosemary, oregano

Preheat the oven to 375° F (190° C). Oil a baking dish.

Cut the stems out of the tomatoes. Salt and pepper lightly and drizzle on a little olive oil. Sprinkle with the minced shallots, and place a spoonful of pesto or chopped herbs in the cone-shaped cavity where you removed the stem.

Bake 20 to 30 minutes in the preheated oven, until the tomatoes are bubbling and the skin is beginning to shrivel. Spoon any of the juices accumulated in the pan over the tomatoes, and serve.

SERVES 6

Mixed Plum and Apricot Tart

❀

THERE ARE TWO techniques for this exquisite tart: in the first, the fruit is briefly baked on the prebaked pastry; and in the second, the assembled tart is run under the broiler, just until the tips of the fruit begin to caramelize. In either version, the fruit should not cook very long, or the plums will lose their lively colors. (See photograph on page 36.)

Sweet Almond Piecrust (page 43)
¾   pound (350 g) greengage plums

¾	pound (350 g) fresh purple plums or prunes (use 1 ½ pounds, 750 g, purple plums or prunes if you can't find greengages)
1	pound (500 g) fresh apricots
¼	cup (60 ml) plum brandy or kirsch
2	tablespoons mild-flavored honey
½	teaspoon vanilla
1	large egg
1	tablespoon apricot jam

Mix the pastry dough, wrap it in plastic, and refrigerate for several hours or overnight.

Cut the fruit in half or into wedges and discard the pits. Combine the plum brandy or kirsch, honey and vanilla in a large bowl and toss the fruit in this mixture. Marinate for 1 hour or more.

For method 1, in which the fruit is baked: Preheat the oven to 375° F (190° C). Roll out the piecrust and line a buttered 12- to 14-inch (30- to 35-cm) tart pan. Beat the egg and brush the surface of the pastry generously. Prick in several places with a fork and bake 20 minutes in the preheated oven, until the surface and edges are brown. Remove from the oven. Raise the oven temperature to 400° F (200° C).

Drain the fruit in a colander over a bowl. Place the liquid in a saucepan at least twice the volume of the liquid and bring it to a boil. Reduce this by half, and stir in the apricot jam.

Arrange the drained fruit in the prebaked piecrust, alternating colors and overlapping the fruit if necessary. Gently brush with the reduced marinade-apricot jam mixture.

Bake the tart for 10 to 12 minutes, until the crust is a rich brown color. Remove from the heat and brush the fruit gently again with the marinade. Serve cool or warm.

For method 2, using the broiler: Proceed as above, but bake the empty pastry shell for 30 minutes. After you arrange the drained fruit in the pastry shell, brush with the glaze and run the tart under the broiler for 4 to 5 minutes, just until the tips of the fruit are beginning to brown. Remove from the heat, gently brush again, and allow to cool or serve warm.

SERVES 8

Part Two

MENUS FROM SPECIAL OCCASIONS AND SPECIAL PEOPLE

Tex-Mex in Paris

I WAS KNOWN in Paris for my Tex-Mex meals long before I began my Supper Club. I have forced my friend Serge Orenbush to lug a *comal* (a Mexican griddle), a tortilla press and kilos of black beans up a mountain in the French Alps so I could make enchiladas during a week-long ski trip in Avoriaz; and I've dragged the same equipment and ingredients to Saint Moritz. I knew there would be a need for all those Mexican cooking supplies when I first packed them into my car in Austin 10 years ago, and since then, I've never come back from the United States without at least 10 pounds of black beans in my suitcase.

My reputation for Tex-Mex food in Paris began our first October here with a Migathon. "Migathon" is a term coined by my friends Maggie Megaw and Steve Monas; it was what they called the Mexican brunches they were in the habit of throwing in Austin before they moved to New York (where they continued the tradition). The main dish was always migas: Mexican-style eggs scrambled with onions, tomatoes, chili peppers and crisp strips of fried corn tortillas.

When we all came over to Paris in the fall of 1981, we hadn't been here for more than a month when we decided it was high time we gave a party. Why not introduce the Migathon to Paris? Each of us invited the few people we knew. I had come over with most of the ingredients we needed, and

Fauchon, the Paris equivalent of Balducci's, supplied the rest. The food was a big hit; nobody can dispute the genius of Steve's migas.

Two days after our brunch, I got a phone call from the wife of Lee Huebner, the publisher of the *International Herald Tribune.* My friend and colleague, Patricia Wells, had been at the brunch and had told her about our great Mexican food. Mrs. Huebner wanted to know if we would cater a birthday party for her husband that Friday. How could we resist? Yellow Rose Catering was born.

I've catered a number of Tex-Mex events since that first small dinner party. The most challenging have been the two *International Herald Tribune* staff parties held on a barge in July 1983 and 1984. These are terrific parties, although transporting food for 150 people in my Volkswagen is hell. The people who run the boat aren't too happy about letting caterers other than their own use the kitchen, so they limit our refrigerator and work space and don't even let us use their sponges or brooms. But we manage.

I always do my chalupa buffets for large groups, with Crudités With Goat Cheese and Herb Dip, and Mexican-Style Mussels on the Half Shell as hors d'oeuvres. In addition to the chalupas, I often serve a Mexican rice salad and green pepper "boats" filled with sautéed zucchini and diced red pepper. Dessert is usually a big watermelon fruit basket or fruit marinated in sweet white wine.

The Migathon

❧

APERITIF: MARGARITAS (PAGE 50)

TORTILLA CHIPS (PAGE 44)

STUFFED JALAPEÑOS

GUACAMOLE NACHOS (PAGE 96)

BLACK BEAN NACHOS (PAGE 50)

STEVE'S MIGAS

HOMEMADE TORTILLAS (PAGE 44)

MEXICAN RICE (PAGE 53)

REFRIED BLACK BEANS (PAGE 51)

WATERMELON FRUIT BASKET

TEXAS TEA CAKES (PAGE 99)

WINE SUGGESTIONS: BEAUJOLAIS, GAMAY TOURAINE,
GEWÜRTZTRAMINER OR MEXICAN BEER

SERVES 6

Stuffed Jalapeños

❀

Eating these is a challenge for those sensitive to heat, but it's a dream for others who like it hot.

6 canned pickled jalapeño peppers
¼ pound (115 g) part-skim ricotta
¼ pound (115 g) fresh goat cheese, preferably not too salty
Chopped fresh cilantro for garnish

Wearing rubber gloves so the peppers don't irritate your hands, cut the jalapeños in half and discard the seeds.

Mash the two cheeses together in a bowl. Put the mixture into a pastry bag and pipe it into the jalapeño shells (or fill them with a spoon). Arrange on a plate and garnish with the cilantro.

Serves 4 to 6

Steve's Migas

❀

We usually make two batches of migas, one hot and one mild, as tolerance for piquancy varies from palate to palate. Some cooks add cheese to their migas, but Steve insists it makes them "too busy."

12 large eggs
 Salt and freshly ground pepper, to taste
½ cup (120 ml) safflower or vegetable oil
6 corn tortillas, fresh or stale (for homemade, see page 44), cut into strips
1 small onion, minced
2 to 4 fresh or canned jalapeño or serrano peppers, to taste, seeded and chopped
4 medium-sized tomatoes (1 pound, 500 g), seeded and chopped
3 tablespoons unsalted butter
1 tablespoon chopped fresh cilantro

Beat the eggs lightly in a large bowl. Do not overbeat; you want both white and yellow in the resulting dish. Add salt and freshly ground pepper and set aside.

Heat the oil in a large, wide frying pan over high heat to 360° F (180° C). Add the tortilla strips and fry until they are crisp and golden brown. This should take only a few seconds. Drain on paper towels.

Discard all but 2 tablespoons of the oil and allow it to cool for a few minutes. Reduce heat to low. Add the onion and peppers and sauté until the onion is soft but not brown. Add the tomatoes and cook very briefly, about 1 minute. Season with a little salt, and transfer to a bowl.

Melt the butter in the frying pan over low heat and add the eggs. Cook slowly over low heat, stirring. When the eggs are somewhat set, stir in the onions, peppers and tomatoes. Just before the eggs are set, stir in the fried tortilla strips. Stir in the chopped fresh cilantro and serve at once.

Serves 6

Watermelon Fruit Basket

FEEL FREE to use whatever fruits are ripe and available. In the United States, I always add Thompson grapes, for color as well as for their sweet, juicy taste. In summer, cherries would be welcome. Sometimes I use peaches, but they tend to discolor and fall apart a bit. Kiwi fruit makes a nice addition.

1	small watermelon
½	cantaloupe, halved and seeded
½	honeydew melon, halved and seeded
½	pound (250 g) fresh apricots, halved and pitted
1	pint strawberries (¾ pound, 350 g), hulled and halved
½	small ripe pineapple
2	tablespoons fresh mint leaves

Making the watermelon basket: Set the watermelon on a table. If it seems unstable, you can cut a very fine sliver out of the bottom to ensure that it won't roll.

Draw a "handle" across the top of the watermelon. Cut down the sides of the handle, then cut the melon crosswise in half, stopping at the handle. Lift off the melon on either side of the handle, and cut away the flesh underneath; save the flesh. Remove the watermelon flesh from the bowl of the "basket" with a melon baller. Place in a bowl. With a small, sharp knife, scallop the edges of the basket, but not the handle. Refrigerate until shortly before serving.

Preparing the fruit: Seed the reserved watermelon flesh and make balls, using a melon baller; place the balls in a large bowl. Make melon balls of the cantaloupe and honeydew. Toss with the watermelon balls, apricots and strawberries. Quarter the pineapple, remove the core and skin and cut in 1-inch (2.5-cm) pieces. Toss with the other fruit. Retain 1 tablespoon of whole mint leaves and chop the remaining leaves. Toss the chopped mint with the fruit. Refrigerate the fruit separately from the watermelon basket.

Assembling the dessert: Shortly before serving, give the fruit a toss and fill the watermelon basket. Place it on a large platter and surround with the fruit that wouldn't fit into the basket. Garnish with the whole mint leaves.

To prepare ahead of time: The fruit will hold for several hours in the refrigerator.

SERVES 12

A Tex-Mex Buffet

❧

APERITIF: MARGARITAS (PAGE 50)

CRUDITÉS WITH GOAT CHEESE AND HERB DIP

MEXICAN-STYLE MUSSELS ON THE HALF SHELL

CHALUPAS OR TOSTADAS EXTRAORDINAIRES (PAGE 132)

SAUTÉED ZUCCHINI AND RED PEPPERS IN BELL PEPPER BOATS

MEXICAN RICE SALAD

WATERMELON FRUIT BASKET (PAGE 169)

MANGOES, PEACHES AND BERRIES IN SWEET WHITE WINE

TEXAS TEA CAKES (PAGE 99)

WINE SUGGESTIONS: BEAUJOLAIS, GAMAY TOURAINE, GEWÜRTZTRAMINER
OR MEXICAN BEER

SERVES 6

Crudités With Goat Cheese and Herb Dip

❧

A FRENCH-INSPIRED addition to this Mexican menu, the herbed goat cheese makes a spectacular opener for any meal.

3 to 4   pounds (1.5 kg to 2 kg) assorted vegetables in season, such as zucchini, broccoli, cauliflower, green beans, carrots, red and green peppers, cucumbers
½   pound (250 g) low-fat cottage cheese
¼   pound (115 g) fresh goat cheese, preferably not too salty
1   cup (225 ml) plain low-fat yogurt
1 to 2   cloves garlic, minced or put through a press (optional)
½   cup (15 g) or more, to taste, chopped fresh herbs, such as tarragon, basil, parsley, dill, chives
   Freshly ground pepper, to taste

Cut the zucchini into spears or rounds and break the broccoli and cauliflower into florets. Steam or blanch the zucchini, broccoli and green beans until bright green; peel and cut the carrots into rounds or sticks, cut the peppers into strips, the cucumbers into rounds or sticks.

Beat the cottage cheese and goat cheese together with a food processor or a mixer and stir in the yogurt. Don't use the food processor to stir in the yogurt or the mixture will be too runny. Combine well and stir in the optional garlic, herbs and freshly ground pepper. Transfer to a bowl, cover, and refrigerate until ready to use.

Arrange the vegetables attractively on a decorative platter. Place the dip in a bowl in the middle.

SERVES 12

Mexican-Style Mussels on the Half Shell

❧

THIS IS ONE of the tastiest mussel dishes I've ever had. But there's no getting around it: cleaning mussels is tedious. However, washing them carefully is essential for two important reasons. First of all, by handling the mussels individually, you will detect any with broken or open shells; these mussels are no longer alive and must be discarded. Second, there is nothing worse than gritty mussels—except gritty lettuce. I have assistants to help me when I make them for my Tex-Mex catering jobs. Even so, when I'm cooking for a large crowd, mussels can be a nightmare. I serve them anyway because they're so good, making just enough so everybody can eat 2 or 3 while they're waiting for the chalupas.

1   quart (1 L) mussels
4   tablespoons salt or vinegar
1   cup (225 ml) dry white wine

1   cup (225 ml) water
2   shallots or 1 onion, chopped
2   cloves garlic, crushed
   A few sprigs of parsley
   Double recipe of Salsa Fresca (page 53)
   Fresh cilantro for garnish

Cleaning the mussels: Place the mussels in a large bowl of cold water. Brush them with a wire brush and pull out their "beards."

Drain the water and fill the bowl again, adding 2 tablespoons salt or vinegar. Let the mussels sit in the water for 15 minutes. The mussels will spit out much of their sand. Drain, rinse in fresh water, brush the mussels once more, and discard any that have broken shells or are opened. Soak one more time for 15 minutes in fresh water with the remaining 2 tablespoons vinegar or salt, drain and rinse thoroughly.

Cooking the mussels: Combine the wine, 1 cup water, shallots or onion, garlic and parsley in a large pot and bring to a boil. Add the mussels, cover tightly and steam 5 minutes, shaking the pan halfway through to redistribute the mussels. They should open after 5 minutes. Drain the mussels, straining the cooking liquid into a bowl, and discard any that haven't opened. Set the strained liquid aside.

Assembling the dish: Combine all the ingredients for the salsa and adjust seasonings. Remove the mussels from their shells but retain the shells. Add the mussels to the salsa, along with ½ cup (120 ml) of their cooking liquid. Stir together, cover and chill for 1 hour or more. Rinse the shells.

To serve: Place a mussel on a half shell and spoon on some of the salsa. Garnish with fresh cilantro. Place on a platter and serve as finger food.

SERVES 6 AS AN HORS D'OEUVRE

Sautéed Zucchini and Red Peppers in Bell Pepper Boats

❀

THESE ARE A TREAT for the eye as well as the palate. The little specks of red pepper set off the glistening zucchini.

2   tablespoons olive or safflower oil
1   medium onion, minced
1 to 2   cloves garlic, minced or put through a press
1 ½   pounds (750 g) zucchini, diced small
1   large sweet red pepper, seeded and diced small
     Salt and freshly ground pepper, to taste
3   small sweet green or red peppers, cut in half lengthwise, seeds and membranes removed

Heat the oil and sauté the onion with 1 clove of the garlic until the onion is beginning to brown. Add the zucchini, diced red pepper and the remaining garlic and sauté over moderate heat, stirring, for about 15 minutes, until the zucchini is bright green and tender. Season to taste with salt and freshly ground pepper and remove from the heat.

Spoon into the red or green pepper shells and serve, or hold in a covered dish and heat through in a 325° F (170° C) oven for 20 minutes before serving.

To prepare ahead of time: The pepper boats can be assembled hours in advance and held in a covered dish. Reheat in the oven as directed above shortly before serving.

SERVES 4 TO 6

Mexican Rice Salad

❀

THIS IS A GREAT buffet salad for a few reasons beyond its wonderful taste and variety of textures. First of all, it's so colorful, with the saffron-tinted rice and the vegetables. Also, it has good staying power. It will hold for several hours in the refrigerator, but toss the green vegetables with the rice and cumin-flavored vinaigrette just before serving; otherwise, they will lose their bright color.

FOR THE SALAD

3   cups (750 ml) water
1 ½   cups (340 g) long-grain white rice or brown rice
½   teaspoon saffron threads
½   teaspoon salt
½   pound (250 g) green beans, trimmed and blanched

1 sweet red pepper, seeded and cut into thin strips
4 scallions, thinly sliced
5 tablespoons pine nuts or chopped almonds
1 small cucumber, peeled, seeded and chopped
5 radishes, thinly sliced

FOR THE DRESSING

3 tablespoons white-wine or cider vinegar
Juice of 1 large lemon
1 clove garlic, minced or put through a press
1 teaspoon Dijon mustard
1 teaspoon ground cumin
¾ cup (180 ml) safflower oil
¼ cup (60 ml) olive oil
Salt and freshly ground pepper, to taste
4 to 5 tablespoons chopped fresh cilantro

FOR THE PLATES

Leaf lettuce
3 to 4 tomatoes, cut into wedges
Radish roses

Making the salad: Bring the water to a boil and add the rice, saffron and salt. Cover, reduce the heat and cook al dente, just until firm to the bite, 20 to 25 minutes for white rice, 35 to 40 minutes for brown rice. Remove from the heat, drain off the excess water and cool.

Toss the rice with the vegetables and nuts.

Making the dressing: Mix together the vinegar, lemon juice, garlic, mustard and cumin for the dressing. Whisk in the oils and season to taste with salt and pepper. Taste and adjust seasonings.

Assembling the salad: Toss the rice-vegetable mixture with the dressing and the cilantro. Refrigerate for an hour or so. If you are holding the salad for several hours, keep the green beans separate and toss with the salad shortly before serving.

Arrange leaf lettuce on plates, then spoon the salad over the lettuce. Garnish with tomato wedges and radish roses.

To prepare ahead of time: The vegetables, rice and dressing can all be prepared 1 day in advance and refrigerated in separate plastic bags or containers. The salad, without the green vegetables, will hold for several hours and with the green vegetables for 1 hour.

SERVES 6 TO 8

Mangoes, Peaches and Berries in Sweet White Wine

Y OU CAN USE other fruits in season for this dish, such as melon and nectarines. The mango is especially nice. As for the choice of wine, it should be sweet like a Sauternes, but I've also used less expensive sweet wine. (See photograph on page 108.)

4 ripe peaches, pitted and sliced
2 mangoes, peeled and diced or sliced
1 pint strawberries (¾ pound, 350 g), hulled and halved, or other berries of your choice (blueberries, blackberries, raspberries or red currants, if you can find them)
1 full wineglass sweet white wine

Prepare the fruit and toss together. Pour on the wine, toss and chill. Remove from the refrigerator about 15 minutes before serving so the fruit won't be too cold.

To prepare ahead of time: This will hold for a couple of hours in the refrigerator.

SERVES 6

174

New Year's Eve (Le Réveillon) Chez Martha

❦

APERITIF: CHAMPAGNE

ENDIVE, APPLE AND WALNUT SALAD

MEXICAN BLACK-EYED PEA SALAD
OR
MEXICAN BEAN SALAD

FENNEL, LEMON AND MUSHROOM SALAD

BLINI WITH SALMON AND CAVIAR FILLING

HUMMUS

ASSORTED HOMEMADE BREADS

CRUDITÉS

ASSORTED CHEESES

TANGERINES AND ASSORTED DESSERTS (BROUGHT BY FRIENDS)

WINE SUGGESTIONS: CHAMPAGNE, GAMAY TOURAINE, BEAUJOLAIS

SERVES 6

New Year's Eve (Le Réveillon)
Chez Martha

I LOVE TO CELEBRATE and dance on New Year's Eve, but I hate to go out into the jammed Paris streets. My way of getting around that is to throw an annual New Year's Eve party. I provide the dance floor, and guests bring Champagne and something to eat. But I always prepare a spread as well, so the buffet is lavish.

I give this New Year's Eve party with a couple of friends, who invite their friends (who invite their friends) and help with the organization and some of the preparation. The number of people at the party grows every year: the last count was about 150. The estimate was based on the number of empty Champagne bottles left after everybody had gone home. My sister Melody lined them up in my long hallway between the entrance hall and the kitchen; 75 bottles made two long rows and a great Polaroid picture.

People begin arriving after 10:00, and by midnight, the party is peaking. But waves of arrivals continue throughout the night. Mine is just one in a long list of parties for the people who arrive after 12:00. Parisians usually go out on New Year's Eve with old friends. So if I invite one friend and she brings her boyfriend, they usually come with the rest of the group they've been out with all night. The party goes on until the following morning: the last to leave wait for the first metros to begin running.

Both of my two long tables in the big dining room serve as buffets at these events. One is for desserts; people bring beautiful cakes and tarts from Paris bakeries, and Peters Day, an American illustrator, makes his unparalleled tarte tatins in big copper pans. The other table is packed with colorful salads, cheeses, my breads and blini, crudités, dips and pâtés. In the middle of the room are two immense plastic tubs. A friend named Rob Anderson, who is a graphic designer, is "the iceman" every year. He picks up a 20-kilo sack of ice at Paris's one ice depot, and the ice and Champagne go into the tubs. Since everybody has been instructed to bring Champagne, and I have a substantial stash of my own, there is no danger of running out. There are always guests who take it upon themselves to be barmen for a while, and they don't stop popping corks.

Once I start dancing, I don't stop, so I choose foods that are festive and don't need tending, like the blini. The most important of the dishes I prepare are those containing black-eyed peas. In Texas, it is a tradition to eat black-eyed peas on New Year's Day for good luck (since people in Paris don't begin to arrive until after 10:00, most of the eating goes on after midnight), and being superstitious, I stick to it. Americans familiar with the custom, and that means all Southern and black Americans, are always thrilled to see the peas. But I don't prepare them in the traditional way, with ham hocks and greens. I make a Mexican-style salad with a cumin vinaigrette, with lots of fresh cilantro and crunchy green peppers. Sometimes I combine the black-eyed peas with other kinds of beans. As a black American dancer from South Chicago commented one year, "Except for my mother's, these are the best black-eyed peas I've ever tasted."

Endive, Apple and Walnut Salad

EAT THIS salad all through the winter. Endive is convenient to have on hand because it lasts longer in the refrigerator than other lettuces. I love the textures and sweet and nutty combination of flavors in this salad.

FOR THE SALAD

1	pound (500 g) Belgian endives
2	tart apples, cored and sliced
5 to 6	medium or large mushrooms, cleaned and sliced
6	tablespoons broken walnut pieces
2	ounces (55 g) Gruyère cheese, cut into thin slivers, or blue cheese, crumbled
2	tablespoons chopped fresh parsley

FOR THE DRESSING

2	tablespoons red-wine vinegar
3	tablespoons fresh lemon juice
1	teaspoon Dijon mustard
	Salt and freshly ground pepper, to taste
¼	teaspoon dried tarragon
5	tablespoons walnut oil
6 to 8	tablespoons olive or safflower oil, to taste

Wash the endives and pat them dry. Either cut them in thick slices or separate the leaves. If the leaves are still wet, dry them in a salad spinner. Toss with the other salad ingredients.

Mix together the vinegar, lemon juice, mustard, salt, pepper and tarragon. Whisk in the oils and combine thoroughly. Toss with the salad just before serving.

To prepare ahead of time: All the ingredients except the apples can be prepared several hours in advance (the apples should be cut at the last minute, or they will turn brown). Wrap the endives in paper towels and seal in plastic bags. Place the other ingredients in a tightly covered container. The dressing will hold for several hours.

SERVES 4

Mexican Black-Eyed Pea Salad

IN TEXAS, they prepare them with ham hocks, but I can't think of a better way to serve up black-eyed peas than bathed in this cumin-scented vinaigrette.

FOR THE BLACK-EYED PEAS

1	tablespoon safflower oil
1	large onion, chopped
3 to 4	cloves garlic, to taste, minced or put through a press
1	pound (500 g) black-eyed peas, washed and picked over
2	quarts (2 L) water
1	bay leaf
	Salt, to taste

FOR THE VINAIGRETTE

	Juice of 1 large lemon
¼	cup (60 ml) red-wine vinegar
1	clove garlic, minced or put through a press
1	heaping teaspoon Dijon mustard
1	teaspoon ground cumin
	Salt and freshly ground pepper, to taste
¾	cup (180 ml) safflower oil
¼	cup (60 ml) cooking liquid from the beans

FOR THE SALAD

2 to 3	tablespoons chopped fresh chives
¼	cup (10 g) chopped fresh cilantro
1	sweet green pepper, seeded and chopped

1 small sweet red pepper, seeded, half
    chopped, half cut into thin strips for
    garnish
    Boston or leaf lettuce

Cooking the peas: Heat 1 tablespoon safflower oil in a large, heavy-bottomed saucepan or Dutch oven and sauté the onion with 3 cloves of garlic until the onion is tender. Add the black-eyed peas and the water and bring to a boil. Reduce the heat, add the bay leaf, cover, and cook 45 minutes, or until the peas are tender but not mushy. Add salt and the remaining garlic clove, or to taste. Drain the peas over a bowl and retain the cooking liquid.

Making the vinaigrette: Mix together the lemon juice, vinegar, garlic, mustard, cumin, salt and pepper. Whisk in the safflower oil and ¼ cup (60 ml) liquid from the peas.

Assembling the salad: Place the peas in a bowl and toss with the dressing. Add the chives and fresh cilantro and refrigerate for 1 to 2 hours, unless you are serving the salad warm. Shortly before serving, toss with the chopped green and red peppers (the vinegar will dull the bright green of the pepper if they are in contact for too long). Taste and adjust seasonings, adding liquid from the peas, lemon juice or vinegar and salt and pepper, if desired.

Line a bowl or plates with the lettuce leaves and top with the peas. Garnish with strips of red pepper and serve.

To prepare ahead of time: The vinegar acts as a kind of preservative, so the peas can be cooked up to 3 days in advance and marinated in the dressing. Refrigerate in a covered bowl. The completed salad will hold for 1 to 2 hours in the refrigerator.

SERVES 6

Mexican Bean Salad

❀

THIS IS A MORE colorful version of the black-eyed pea salad (page 178). The different-colored beans contrast beautifully with one another, and the cumin vinaigrette and fresh cilantro give the dish a decidedly Mexican flavor. The fresh green and red peppers add crunchy texture. The first time I served this to the French, they were very impressed because they don't usually use dried beans.

FOR THE BEANS

½ cup (115 g) red or kidney beans, washed
    and picked over
½ cup (115 g) black beans, washed and picked
    over
½ cup (115 g) chickpeas (garbanzos), washed
    and picked over
1 tablespoon safflower oil
1 large onion, chopped
4 cloves garlic, minced or put through a
    press

2 quarts (2 L) plus 2 cups water
2 bay leaves
    Salt, to taste
½ cup (115 g) black-eyed peas, washed and
    picked over

FOR THE VINAIGRETTE

Juice of 1 large lemon
6 tablespoons red-wine vinegar
1 clove garlic, minced or put through a press
1 heaping teaspoon Dijon mustard
1 teaspoon ground cumin
    Salt and freshly ground pepper, to taste
¾ cup (180 ml) safflower oil
¼ cup (60 ml) liquid from the beans

FOR THE SALAD

2 to 3 tablespoons chopped chives
4 tablespoons chopped fresh cilantro
1 sweet green pepper, seeded and chopped

1　small sweet red pepper, seeded and half chopped, half cut into thin strips
Boston or leaf lettuce

Preparing and cooking the beans: Since black-eyed peas cook faster than the other beans, they will be cooked separately. They require no soaking.

Soak the other beans, in 4 times their volume of water, overnight or for at least 6 hours. Drain.

Heat 1 tablespoon safflower oil over medium heat in a large, heavy-bottomed saucepan or Dutch oven and sauté the onion with 3 cloves of garlic until the onion is tender. Add the soaked, drained beans and 2 quarts (2 L) water, raise the heat and bring to a boil. Reduce the heat, add 1 bay leaf, cover and cook 1 to 1½ hours, until the beans are tender but not mushy. Add salt to taste.

Meanwhile, in a separate pot, combine the black-eyed peas, the remaining 2 cups (450 ml) of water, the remaining garlic and bay leaf, and bring to a boil. Reduce the heat, cover, and cook 45 minutes, or until tender. Add salt to taste.

Drain all the beans over a bowl and retain their cooking liquid.

Making the vinaigrette: Mix together the lemon juice, vinegar, garlic, mustard, cumin, salt and pepper. Whisk in the safflower oil and ¼ cup (60 ml) liquid from the beans.

Assembling the salad: Place the beans in a bowl and toss with the dressing. Add the chives and fresh cilantro and refrigerate for 1 to 2 hours, unless you are serving the salad warm. Shortly before serving, toss with the chopped green and red peppers (the vinegar will dull the bright green of the peppers if they are in contact for too long). Taste and adjust seasonings, adding liquid from the beans, vinegar or salt and pepper, if desired.

Line a bowl or plates with the lettuce leaves and top with the beans. Garnish with strips of red pepper and serve.

To prepare ahead of time: See Mexican Black-Eyed Pea Salad (page 178).

SERVES 4 TO 6

Fennel, Lemon and Mushroom Salad

❧

FENNEL is such a refreshing vegetable. This salad is great for a buffet because it doesn't wilt.

FOR THE SALAD

2　pounds (1 kg) fennel bulbs, quartered and sliced thin
½　pound (250 g) mushrooms, cleaned and sliced thin
1　lemon, peel and white pith removed, sliced very thin
2　sweet red peppers, seeded and sliced
¼　cup (10 g) chopped fresh parsley

FOR THE DRESSING

¼　cup (60 ml) fresh lemon juice
2　tablespoons red-wine vinegar
1 to 2　teaspoons Dijon mustard, to taste

1　small clove garlic, minced or put through a press (optional)
Salt and freshly ground pepper, to taste
½　cup (120 ml) safflower or sunflower-seed oil
3　tablespoons olive oil

Mix together the fennel, mushrooms, lemon, red peppers and parsley.

Whisk together the lemon juice, vinegar, mustard, optional garlic, salt and freshly ground pepper. Whisk in the oils. Toss with the salad and serve.

To prepare ahead of time: This salad will hold for several hours in the refrigerator.

SERVES 6 TO 8

Blini With Salmon and Caviar Filling

❀

LOVE MAKING BLINI for parties because they hold very nicely, so I can make them well in advance. I freeze the leftovers and always have the makings for an impromptu cocktail party on hand. The filling couldn't be easier. When I serve blini as part of a buffet, as I do for New Year's Eve, I make small ones for finger food. The blini are on one platter, the egg and caviar filling on another and the smoked salmon on another.

Blini (page 45)
¾ pound (350 g) low-fat cottage cheese
⅔ cup (160 ml) plain low-fat yogurt
3 hard-boiled eggs, chopped
1 small onion, finely minced
1 small jar black lumpfish caviar
Salt and freshly ground pepper, to taste
½ pound (250 g) smoked salmon, thinly sliced

FOR THE GARNISH

Lemons, cut into wedges
Chopped chives
Fresh lemon juice, to taste

Make the blini and set aside.

Beat the cottage cheese in a food processor or electric mixer until smooth, and blend in the yogurt. Stir in the chopped hard-boiled eggs, onion and the caviar. Add salt and freshly ground pepper to taste.

To serve, top each blini with smoked salmon and the cheese-egg-caviar filling. Garnish with lemon wedges and chives and squeeze on lemon juice to taste.

SERVES 6 TO 8

Hummus

❀

I'VE MADE HUMMUS so many times I can practically do it with my eyes closed, yet I never tire of it. I always make sure I'm a little hungry when I make it because I can't resist tasting. Time and again, it gets raves from guests. This version is much less oily than the traditional one. I thin it with low-fat yogurt instead of olive oil. The secret ingredient here is the ground cumin. The hummus can be served on bread or piped onto rounds of cucumber and strips of sweet red and green pepper. I usually do both: I make platters of the cucumber and peppers, with the decorative hummus topping, and place the remainder in a bowl, decorated with olives, chopped parsley and cherry tomatoes or radishes. Next to the bowl are baskets with assorted breads.

½ pound (250 g) dried chickpeas (garbanzos), washed and picked over

8 cups (2 L) water
Salt, to taste
2 large cloves garlic
4 to 6 tablespoons fresh lemon juice, to taste
¼ cup (60 ml) olive oil
4 to 6 tablespoons sesame tahini, to taste
½ teaspoon ground cumin
¼ to ½ cup (60 ml to 120 ml) plain low-fat yogurt, depending on how stiff you want your hummus (stiff is easier to pipe; less stiff is more refined)

Soaking and cooking the chickpeas: Soak the chickpeas overnight in about 4 cups (1 L) of water. Use bottled water if your water is hard.

In the morning, drain them and combine in a large pot with another 4 cups (1 L) water. Bring to a boil, reduce the heat, cover, and simmer 2 hours, until the chickpeas are tender. Add 1 teaspoon of the salt at the end of the cooking time.

Making the hummus: Drain the beans and puree them in a food processor or blender or through a food mill, along with the garlic. Add the lemon juice, olive oil, sesame tahini, cumin, salt and yogurt, and blend until thoroughly smooth. Taste and adjust seasonings, adding more salt, garlic or lemon juice, if you wish. Transfer to a serving bowl and cover. Refrigerate until ready to serve.

To prepare ahead of time: Hummus will hold for 3 to 4 days in the refrigerator but is best the day after you make it. It can also be frozen.

SERVES 12

A Picnic on the Seine

❧

Tomatoes With Pesto

Niçoise Salad Hero Sandwiches

Vegetables and Eggs With Tapenade (page 62)

Ratatouille

Provençal Onion Pizza

Assorted Cheeses

Sourdough Country Bread (page 26)

Assorted Fruits

Wine Suggestions: Bandol or any other rosé
from the south of France such as Tavel or Côtes de Provence

Serves 6

A Picnic on the Seine

ON A WARM SUMMER NIGHT, I like to picnic on the Seine. This is where Paris looks most like illuminated pages in a beautifully illustrated fairy tale. I love to look at the back of Nôtre Dame, with its flying buttresses, and watch the tour boats go by. The light in Paris is at its best in the late evening, as the sun sets behind the cathedral. When the weather is good, the sky becomes pink and orange, sometimes streaked with gold. The buildings glow; it's magic. In the summer the sun sets late—between 9:30 and 11:00, depending on the month—and then you get twilight, followed by the Paris city lights and the moon. Nôtre Dame is a spectacle, highlighted regularly by ultra-bright pink-yellow lights from the tour boats. Somehow I'm not rattled by these lights or by the sound of the guides, who, heavily miked, point out all the monuments in good French and badly in other languages as they go by. I've taken many a tour boat myself and love to think of how many have made their tour, hour after hour, year after year, and how many people have looked at Paris from the middle of the river.

My picnic on the Seine is a real treat for summer visitors, and I like to take them on one soon after their arrival. If they are too jet-lagged the first night, I plan it, weather permitting, for their second. There will be much eating in restaurants later, and this is such a dreamy way to see the city. I pack up baskets with Provençal tablecloths, silverware, plates, wine, water and plastic cups and food that's easy to carry and eat: the Niçoise Salad Hero Sandwich, ratatouille, Vegetables and Eggs With Tapenade, Tomatoes With Pesto, Provençal Onion Pizza, fruit, cheese, bread. The dishes are almost all Provençal in spirit, probably because my earliest picnics in France were in Provence. Everyone takes a basket, and we either walk or take the number 87 or 63 bus up the Boulevard Saint-Germain to rue Cardinal Lemoine, then it's a short walk to the river.

Sometimes, of course, my picnics are spontaneous. Then my menu is a little different: bread, cheese, tomatoes, crudités and fruit. Maybe I'll stop at a charcuterie and get grated carrot salad and cooked artichokes. If I have an hour, I'll throw together a salade Niçoise. How can anything taste bad when you're in Paris, eating on the banks of the Seine in the soft summer evening light?

Packing a Picnic Basket

I've always wanted one of those elegant wicker picnic baskets with silver servers and china plates, but I still don't have one. I use my market baskets and L.L. Bean canvas shoulder bags for my Paris outings, and they serve me well.

Use one bag for plates, tablecloths, silverware and wine. Pack up salads in plastic containers, jars or bowls with tight-fitting lids. Set them in bags or baskets and lay the cheeses, fruits and bread—the crushable items—on top. Carry attractive platters and bowls separately and transfer the food to them once you've arrived at your picnic spot. For stuffed vegetables like Vegetables and Eggs With Tapenade (page 62), it may be neater to carry the filling separately and stuff the vegetables and eggs at the picnic.

PICNIC CHECKLIST

Plates
Forks, knives, bread knife, serving spoons
Napkins
Cups
Wine
Water
Corkscrew, bottle opener
Cutting board
Dishtowels
Trash bags
Serving bowls
Lightweight platters
Candles
Flashlight
Salt and pepper
Mustard

Tomatoes With Pesto

✿

THESE ARE LIKE Vegetables and Eggs With Tapenade (page 62), but filled with pesto instead.

6   medium or 12 small tomatoes
½   recipe pesto (page 230)

Cut the tops of the tomatoes off, about ½ inch (1.5 cm) down. Gently squeeze out the seeds. Spread with a generous helping of pesto.

To pack for a picnic: Place the tomatoes side by side in a shallow plastic container with a tight-fitting lid. Or don't fill the tomatoes until you reach your destination. Keep the hollowed-out tomatoes in one container and the pesto in another.

SERVES 6

Niçoise Salad Hero Sandwiches

✿

THE QUALITY of the bread will determine how good your sandwich is. If made on a banal, cottony baguette, the sandwich will be nothing to write home about. But with a crusty sourdough baguette or country loaf, it is truly mouth-watering.

FOR THE SANDWICH

3   baguettes or 6 roll-sized sourdough country breads
1   clove garlic, halved
    Olive oil
    Red-wine vinegar
1   small head Boston lettuce, leaves separated and washed, then broken into small pieces
½   pound (250 g) carrots, peeled and grated
1   pound (500 g) tomatoes, sliced
½   pound (250 g) tender green beans, trimmed and blanched
1   small cucumber, peeled, seeded and thinly sliced
24   imported black olives, halved and pitted
1   7½-ounce (200-g) can tuna packed in water, drained
12   anchovy fillets (optional)

FOR THE VINAIGRETTE

¼   cup (60 ml) red-wine vinegar
1   clove garlic, minced or put through a press
1   teaspoon Dijon mustard
2   tablespoons chopped fresh herbs
    Salt and freshly ground pepper, to taste
⅔   cup (160 ml) olive oil

FOR FINISHING THE SANDWICH

6   hard-boiled eggs, sliced

Making the sandwich: Cut the rolls or baguettes in half and scoop out some of the bread. Rub the inside of the bread halves with a cut clove of garlic and drizzle on a small amount of olive oil and vinegar. Toss the crumbs from the inside of the bread together with the vegetables, olives, tuna and anchovies.

Making the vinaigrette: Combine the vinegar, garlic, mustard, herbs, salt and pepper. Whisk in the olive oil. Toss with the salad.

Assembling the sandwich: Mound the salad in one half of the bread, lay egg slices over the salad, and top with the other half. Cut each sandwich into 3 equal pieces. Squeeze together well and wrap tightly in plastic or foil. Refrigerate for 1 hour before eating. **To prepare ahead of time:** These will hold for several hours in the refrigerator. Wrap them tightly as directed above.

SERVES 6

Ratatouille

MY STEPMOTHER used to make ratatouille for us when I was a teenager, and when I began cooking at the age of 17, it was one of the first dishes I asked her to teach me. I've changed my recipe again and again. The most memorable ratatouille I've ever eaten was in a restaurant in Cassis called Chez Gilbert. All the vegetables in Gilbert's ratatouille are coarsely chopped and glazed with their reduced cooking juices. The chef won't divulge his recipe, but in researching this dish, I found that food writer Richard Olney's version seems to come pretty close, and mine is based on his. My friend Lulu Peyraud, at the winery Domaine Tempier, makes another great ratatouille; she insists it's because she cooks it in an earthenware pot.

Ratatouille should be made the day before you wish to serve it. It is good hot or cold and is perfect for picnics or for the first course of a summer meal.

1	pound (500 g) eggplant, cubed
	Salt
6	tablespoons olive oil
1	pound (500 g) medium-sized onions, sliced
6	cloves garlic, minced or put through a press
½	pound (250 g) sweet red peppers, seeded and cut in half crosswise, then into wide strips
½	pound (250 g) sweet green peppers, seeded and cut in half crosswise, then into wide strips
6	ripe tomatoes (750 g), peeled and seeded (about 1 ½ pounds); 4 cut into wedges, the remainder chopped
	Freshly ground pepper, to taste
1	teaspoon dried oregano or a mixture of dried or fresh thyme and dried oregano
1	bay leaf
1	pound (500 g) zucchini, thickly sliced
3	tablespoons chopped fresh basil, in season
	Pinch of cayenne (optional)

FOR THE GARNISH

Chopped fresh basil or parsley
Vinaigrette or olive oil (for cold ratatouille)
Lettuce leaves (for cold ratatouille)
Ripe tomatoes, cut in quarters (for cold ratatouille)

Place the cubed eggplant in a colander and sprinkle with salt. Let sit 30 minutes while you prepare the other vegetables, then rinse and pat dry with paper towels.

Heat 3 tablespoons of the oil in a very large, heavy-bottomed flameproof casserole or Dutch oven and sauté the onion with half of the garlic over medium-low heat until the onion is softened and translucent. Add the remaining 3 tablespoons oil, the peppers and eggplant and continue to cook over medium-low heat for about 10 minutes, stirring with a wooden spoon. Add the tomato wedges, the remaining garlic, salt and pepper to taste, the dried herbs and bay leaf. Continue to cook over low heat, stirring the vegetables gently until they are almost submerged in their own liquid. Raise the heat and bring these juices to a boil, stirring, then immediately lower the heat, cover partially and simmer 1 hour, stirring occasionally. Add the zucchini, chopped tomatoes and basil, and continue to simmer another 20 to 30 minutes, or until the zucchini is tender but still bright green.

Place a colander over a bowl and drain the ratatouille. Allow it to drain 10 minutes, then return the vegetables to the casserole. Place the liquid in a saucepan and reduce it over high heat, stirring often, until syrupy. Pour the liquid back over the vegetables, stir, and simmer together for a few minutes. Taste and adjust salt, pepper and garlic. If you wish, add a small pinch of cayenne. Transfer to a bowl and cool. Cover and refrigerate overnight.

If you are serving the ratatouille hot, bring it back to a simmer over low heat. Serve, topping each helping with chopped fresh parsley or basil. If you are serving it cold, douse it, if you wish, with a mild vinaigrette or simply with a little olive oil and sprinkle on chopped fresh basil or parsley. Serve over lettuce leaves, garnished with tomato wedges.

SERVES 6

Provençal Onion Pizza

❧

THERE ARE MANY versions of this recipe. Some people make theirs in a pastry crust, while others use a pizza crust, which I prefer. Sometimes it is laid thickly with onions, other times the layer is thin. The important thing is to cook the onions until they become sweet and slightly caramelized.

FOR THE CRUST

2   teaspoons active dry yeast
¾   cup (180 ml) lukewarm water
¾   teaspoon salt
2   tablespoons olive oil
2   cups (225 g) whole-wheat flour or whole-wheat pastry flour or use half whole-wheat, half unbleached white
    Unbleached white flour, as necessary, for kneading

FOR THE FILLING

2   tablespoons olive oil or more, as necessary
1   tablespoon unsalted butter
4   pounds (2 kg) onions, sliced very thin
2   teaspoons mild-flavored honey
¼   cup (60 ml) dry red wine
¼   teaspoon dried thyme or more, to taste
    Salt and freshly ground pepper, to taste
1   small can anchovy fillets
⅓ to ½ cup (about 50 g) black Niçoise olives

Beginning the crust: Dissolve the yeast in the lukewarm water. Let it sit 10 minutes, or until the mixture begins to bubble. Stir in the salt and oil. Add the flour, 1 cup (115 g) at a time, and mix thoroughly, first with a whisk, and then, when it becomes too thick for a whisk, with a large wooden spoon. Turn the dough out onto a lightly floured board and knead for 10 minutes, adding only enough flour to keep it from sticking. If you work briskly and use a pastry scraper to manipulate the dough, it won't stick too much. Shape it into a ball, then place in a lightly oiled bowl, rounded side down first, then rounded side up. Cover with a damp towel or plastic wrap and set in a warm place to rise until doubled in bulk, 1 to 1 ½ hours.

Preparing the onions: While the dough rises, heat the olive oil and butter in a large frying pan over low heat. Add the onions and cook over low heat, stirring from time to time, until they are translucent. Add the honey, wine and thyme and cook gently, stirring occasionally, for 1 to 1 ½ hours, until the onions are golden brown and beginning to caramelize. Add salt and freshly ground pepper to taste. The onions should not brown or stick to the pan. Add oil or butter as needed.

When the dough has doubled in size, punch it down and let it rise another 40 minutes (the onions will still be cooking).

Baking the pizza: Preheat the oven to 450° F (230° C). Turn the dough out onto a lightly floured work surface. Roll out to about ¼ inch (0.75 cm) thick, or a little thinner. Oil a 12- to 14-inch (30- to 35-cm) pizza pan or tart pan and line it with the dough. Pinch a lip around the edge.

Prebake the crust for 7 to 10 minutes, until the surface is crisp and the edges are beginning to brown. Spread with the onions, then top with anchovies and olives and bake for 15 minutes, or until the crust is browned and crisp. Remove from the oven and serve hot, or cool and serve at room temperature.

To transport for a picnic: Keep it in the pizza pan, but cut into pieces. Cover tightly with foil.

Serves 8

Menus From
Christine's Provençal Paradise

❧

Sweet and Sour Red Peppers

Christine's Creamy Cucumber Salad

Salmon Trout or Trout in Foil

Steamed Potatoes or Fresh Pasta
(tossed with olive oil, fresh parsley, thyme, rosemary and sage)

Cherry Clafouti

Wine Suggestions: Sylvaner or Pinot Blanc, Bandol Rosé,
Côtes de Ventoux Rosé or Red, Côtes de Lubéron White or Red

Serves 6

Menus From
Christine's Provençal Paradise

THE RECIPES in this chapter are dishes I have learned from my landlady and dear friend, Christine. Christine Ruiz Picasso is the widow of Paulo Picasso, Pablo Picasso's first son. She is an extraordinary woman who knows much about life.

When you first meet Christine, you are immediately struck by her beauty: her wide-set, soft blue eyes, ever so slightly Oriental; her high, Slavic cheekbones; her clear, shining complexion, dark eyebrows and silver-gray hair; and her wide, sensuous mouth, from which issues a voice with the melodic timbre of a bell. She is so direct and so much fun that anyone with half a sense of humor can communicate with her. And God knows, she's been put to the test, for I am forever bringing non-French-speaking friends with me on my visits.

Christine is hilariously funny and even bawdy and, at the same time, has great refinement and sensitivity. She is tender, motherly and loving; honorable, sentimental and wise; both spiritual and down-to-earth. Nature and humanity are equally fascinating to her; nothing goes unnoticed.

I met Christine in July of 1980, when I was renting La Sara, the farmhouse near Bonnieux, in the Lubéron. The Lubéron is a chain of low mountains that runs through the Vaucluse, east of Avignon and about 40 kilometers north of Aix-en-Provence. One of the most beautiful areas in France, Bonnieux is on the northern slope of the Lubéron and looks out over a wide valley and smaller mountain chain, called the Petit Lubéron. The country here is dotted with vineyards and lavender fields, and the earth has a red-ocher hue. The perfection in the landscape, the rich colors—greens, reds and purples—and the amazing Provençal light always stop me in my tracks. As you move farther east, beyond a town called Apt and north into the hills, the land becomes more rugged: the lavender fields continue, but vineyards give way to pastures and grain crops. Most of the towns in the Vaucluse are Roman and medieval hill towns, and they look almost like carved outcroppings of the mountain rock.

By the end of the '70s, Christine had had enough of Paris. Her husband had died in 1975, and she was ready to begin a new life, alone and in the country. It was in this part of France that she had decided to make her home. The day after Christine moved into her extraordinary stone farmhouse, she invited us all for lunch. She didn't have any real furnishings yet, so we brought a picnic. Her friend Nina Engels led us there—a good thing, as we would never have found the place on our own. When we finally arrived, after twisting and turning up an unpaved road for what seemed like a long time, we found ourselves in "God's country." The house itself, a 300-year-old, three-story, rectangular mas—the term used in this area for the stone and stucco farmhouses you see everywhere—is quite grand, but it's the vast countryside that takes your breath away. To the south are the mountains of the Lubéron; closer, to the southwest, are hills and dales displaying a patchwork of fields, yellow with hay, purple with lavender, and many shades of green. The little town of Saint-Michel-l'Observatoire sits on one of these hills, just close enough to reassure you that you aren't completely cut off from humanity. East of the house, the land slopes upward to a small plateau and then abruptly up to a high ridge and another plateau. To the north, the Petit Lubéron, with its patchwork fields, slopes more gently upward, but directly behind the house, there is a dramatic canyon and divide, which Christine fondly calls her own Texas.

Little did I know, on that hot July afternoon as we sat around eating Cavaillon melons and Nina's onion tarts and famous chocolate cake, then climbed and walked along the ridge, that a year later, I would be moving into Christine's Paris apartment. And that was the beginning of a long and special friendship and a deep love that would be nurtured by my frequent, unforgettable visits to her Provençal home.

Christine has come into her own since moving to the Vaucluse. The land around her house is now a working farm. Her caretakers, Bernard and Brigitte LeBecq, are specialists in natural medicine and organic farming, and over the years, Bernard has been revitalizing the earth, denatured after years of neglect, and planting grain crops and vegetable gardens. A couple of years after Christine moved in, she and Bernard planted 350 truffle oaks on the middle plateau east of the house. These are small scrub oaks whose roots have been injected with microorganisms that will eventually spawn truffles. If all goes well, in five years the oaks will bear, providing Christine with not only an enviable larder, but also a handsome source of revenue. "I've been a lot of things in my life; first I was a ceramicist, then in Paris I had a hotel, and after that, I had a fancy button-and-accessories store," says Christine. "I will go out a *trufficultrice*."

Christine the Hostess

EVERY SUMMER, and at various times during the year, Christine has a house full of guests. She is the kind of hostess who will hardly let you lift a finger. Each day, while you are waking up or swimming in the pool, sunbathing or hiking, reading or touring the region, she produces three fabulous meals. Yet her efforts are invisible; it is as if there were two of her, one laughing by the pool with you or watering the garden and one in the kitchen. If the weather is fine, you eat outside at lunchtime under a big white parasol. Christine hammers the stand into the ground and opens the parasol over one of her two stone tables, made from the large, flat yellow-white stones of the region. At dinner, she sets candles in large blown-glass lanterns and serves dinner under the stars. If it's too windy, chilly or hot (as it can be on summer afternoons), you eat in her friendly dining room in front of the stucco hearth. Christine is a wonderful cook, and the meals are long and leisurely; great food, great conversation— even when half the people don't speak French—and always, much laughter.

Breakfast consists of tea or coffee, fresh-squeezed juice and toasted whole-wheat bread with the inimitable lavender honey from the region and Christine's homemade preserves: cherry, apricot, strawberry, plum, peach, marmalade.

Christine has a way with vegetables, and each year, she grows more in her garden. At lunch, we eat salads of homegrown lettuces tossed with herbs and baby onions, one or two vegetable dishes (usually Provençal or Mediterranean in character), freshly picked tomatoes, cold meats or one of the fragrant Iranian dishes she has learned from her architect, Nasrine. Summer lunches generally begin with sweet, juicy melons from Cavaillon and end with a fresh fruit salad or tart. We drink chilled white or rosé wine from the cooperative at Apt, light and refreshing Côtes de Lubéron or Côtes de Ventoux. Afterwards, we sleep.

At around 8:00 or 8:30, the "pink time" in the Vaucluse sky, we find ourselves at the table again, eating little olives from the region, watching the sunset and drinking aperitifs. Christine then performs her magic act again, and we set the table for dinner.

If we've eaten a big lunch, dinner is light—a green salad with roasted goat cheese and perhaps a fruit tart or clafouti. Usually, though, it's substantial: meat or fish (either poached in court bouillon or baked), potatoes from the garden or pasta tossed with whatever herbs and vegetables are on hand, salad and fruit or dessert. If we're having fish, we'll drink rosé from the region; otherwise, we'll drink the fruity, light red.

Like so many French women I've met, Christine imprints a recipe in her memory after having made it just once. How many times have I remarked at table, "This is great! How do you make it?" only to have her recite the exact recipe.

I've visited Christine's paradise at every season of the year. Summer is the most fun because of the sun, the pool, the purple lavender fields and the fact that you can eat outside morning, noon and night. But each season has its special charm. After a heavy blizzard in February, I was enchanted by the silence, the birds and the dazzling snow. Springtime explodes with wildflowers—fields of red poppies and broom—and bright yellow sunshine. In autumn, the light is the purest, as if the land and air had been swept clean after the hot August haze. The minute I arrive, I feel tranquil and expansive, and that's because of Christine just as much as the place.

Sweet and Sour Red Peppers

❀

CHRISTINE SERVES these beguiling red peppers on their own, and they are marvelous with no further embellishment. I have served them alone and as a salad over lettuce, garnished with avocado, radishes and herbs. When I have red peppers left over from a dinner or a catering job, this is how I preserve them. They will hold for weeks in the refrigerator.

3   cups (700 ml) water
½   cup (120 ml) good-quality sherry vinegar or Champagne vinegar
⅓   cup (80 ml) mild-flavored honey
2   onions, sliced

8   cloves garlic, sliced
2   bay leaves
½   teaspoon whole peppercorns
2   pounds (1 kg) sweet red peppers, cut in half, seeded, and cut into very wide strips
4   sprigs fresh thyme

Combine the water, vinegar, honey, onions, garlic, bay leaves and peppercorns in a large pot and bring to a boil. Add the cut peppers and thyme and cook over fairly high heat for 15 minutes. Remove from the heat, cool, cover and refrigerate.
SERVES 6

Christine's Creamy Cucumber Salad

❀

I HAVE A VIVID mental picture of Christine sitting outside and mincing cucumbers into a bowl of fromage blanc, a kind of creamy cottage cheese. This salad is a very simple combination, and I look forward to it every time I visit. What makes it special is the quality of the fromage blanc, the tiny cucumber dice and the abundant freshly ground pepper. Sometimes Christine also adds goat cheese.

In my American version, I've substituted cottage cheese and yogurt for the fromage blanc. I usually add the goat cheese too.

1   pound (500 g) creamy cottage cheese (can be low-fat)
2   cups (500 g) yogurt (use a thick yogurt, not a runny one)
¼   pound (115 g) crumbled fresh goat cheese, preferably not too salty or more, to taste (optional)

1   long European cucumber, peeled and finely minced or 3 regular cucumbers, peeled, seeded and finely minced
Salt and *lots* of freshly ground pepper
Fresh lemon juice (optional)
Chopped fresh mint or tarragon (optional)

Using the back of a wooden spoon, mash the cottage cheese in a bowl and mix in the yogurt. Crumble in the optional goat cheese. Add the cucumbers and lots of freshly ground pepper. Add salt to taste and lemon juice, if desired. You can also stir in chopped fresh mint or tarragon. Chill until ready to serve.

To prepare ahead of time: This will hold for 2 or 3 days in the refrigerator in a covered bowl.
SERVES 6 TO 8

Salmon Trout or Trout in Foil

❀

EVERY WEDNESDAY, Christine goes to a tiny village to buy fish from a good fishmonger who sells at the weekly market. She usually comes home with several small or one large pink-fleshed salmon trout. Sometimes she poaches the fish in court bouillon, but more often, she bakes it in foil with her special mixture of Provençal herbs. She insists that the herbs must include cracked fennel or otherwise the dish won't taste as good.

Note: Herbes de Provence is a mixture of thyme, rosemary and savory and can also include dried oregano or marjoram, basil and fennel. Make your own by mixing these herbs in equal proportions. Be sure to include the fennel.

6	salmon trout or trout, about ½ pound (250 g) each, cleaned
	Salt and freshly ground pepper, to taste
3	tablespoons unsalted butter
3	teaspoons herbes de Provence (see note), with cracked fennel
6	sprigs of fresh tarragon or rosemary, if available
3	lemons, sliced

Preheat the oven to 450° F (230° C).

Cut 6 sheets of heavy-duty aluminum foil or double sheets of thinner foil, about 12 inches (30 cm) square, and rub the dull side with some of the butter (or use olive oil).

Wipe the trout with paper towels and sprinkle them inside and outside with salt and freshly ground pepper. Place a lump of butter and ½ teaspoon of Herbes de Provence in each cavity. Add a sprig of tarragon or rosemary.

Lay each trout on a piece of foil and top with a few slices of lemon. Fold the foil up over the trout and crimp the edges together tightly. Place the packets in a baking dish and bake for 10 to 12 minutes, or until the flesh is opaque and flakes easily with a fork (open one packet and test with a fork). Remove from the foil, pour the juices over the fish and serve.

To prepare ahead of time: The packets can be assembled several hours ahead of time and held in the refrigerator.

SERVES 6

Cherry Clafouti

❀

A CLAFOUTI is a sort of cross between a flan and a fruit-filled pancake. Christine makes hers in June, when her cherry trees are full of fruit. She makes enormous clafoutis, which keep well, but with all the guests, they last only a couple of days. I've changed her recipe somewhat, substituting honey for sugar.

1	pound (500 g) dark red or black cherries
1 ¼	cups (285 ml) low-fat milk
5	tablespoons mild-flavored honey
3	large eggs
1	tablespoon vanilla
	Pinch of salt
⅔	cup (160 g) sifted unbleached white flour
1	tablespoon unsalted butter, for the baking dish
1	tablespoon brown or white sugar (optional)

Preheat the oven to 350° F (180° C). Butter a 12-inch (30-cm) tart pan or a 2-quart (2-L) baking dish.

Pit the cherries above a bowl. Place the pitted

cherries in a separate bowl and strain off any juices from the pits.

In a blender or electric mixer, blend together the milk, honey, juice from pitting the cherries, eggs, vanilla and salt. Add the flour and continue to blend together for 1 minute, until completely smooth.

Pour into the bowl with the cherries, mix together well and turn into the buttered baking dish. Bake 45 minutes to 1 hour, until puffed and browned, and a knife comes out clean when inserted. Remove from the oven and sprinkle the top with the optional sugar. Serve hot or warm, but not cold. The clafouti will fall a bit upon cooling.

SERVES 6 TO 8

More From Christine

❦

Artichokes With Tomatoes, Garlic and Provençal Herbs

Iranian Omelet With Parsley and Mint

Tossed Green Salad

Alsatian Apple Cake
or
Peaches and Apricots With Currants

Wine Suggestions: Sylvaner or Pinot Blanc, Bandol Rosé,
Côtes de Ventoux Rosé or Red, Côtes de Lubéron White or Red

Serves 8

Artichokes With Tomatoes, Garlic and Provençal Herbs

☙

This is a traditional Provençal dish (pictured on page 106) in which artichokes are simmered slowly in olive oil with tomatoes, onion, garlic and herbs, usually thyme, rosemary and bay leaf. Christine's are the best I've ever tasted. She uses an entire head of garlic, the cloves peeled and slightly crushed, and adds diced green or red peppers, which make for a particularly savory dish.

The first time I had this at Christine's, I went home and looked up recipes in eight different French cookbooks and found eight different versions. In certain cases, a glass of white wine is added; some call for mushrooms, others carrots. Each author was quite certain that his or her recipe was the authentic version. At any rate, none of the recipes sounded as good as Christine's, so finally, I just called to get her recipe.

16 small young purple artichokes or 8 globe artichokes
2 lemons, cut in half
3 tablespoons olive oil
4 medium-sized white onions, chopped
2 small heads garlic, cloves separated, crushed slightly and peeled
2 large sweet green or red bell peppers or 4 small, seeded and diced
3 pounds (1.5 kg) tomatoes or 3 28-ounce (765-g) cans, with juice
2 tablespoons tomato paste (optional)
4 sprigs of fresh thyme or ½ teaspoon dried
2 bay leaves
   Salt and freshly ground pepper, to taste
1 quart (1 L) simmering water

Trim the stems off the artichokes, cut off the very tops, trim off the spiny tips of the outer leaves with scissors and rub thoroughly with the cut lemon.

Heat the olive oil over medium heat in a large, heavy-bottomed flameproof casserole or Dutch oven and sauté the onions and garlic cloves until the onions begin to turn golden. Add the peppers and continue to sauté until they soften, about 5 minutes. Add the tomatoes and sauté about 10 minutes, until they have begun to release their juice and cook down. Stir in the optional tomato paste, then add the artichokes, thyme, bay leaves, salt and pepper and about 1 cup (225 ml) of simmering water. Cover and simmer 45 minutes to 1 hour, stirring occasionally and adding water from time to time if the liquid evaporates. When the artichokes are tender, taste and adjust seasonings and serve. This dish is also good at room temperature or chilled. It will hold for a few days in the refrigerator.

SERVES 8

Iranian Omelet With Parsley and Mint

☙

AN IRANIAN VERSION of a flat omelet, this one is filled with parsley and mint and contains pine nuts, currants and a little saffron. I've had these omelets with other herbs, notably chervil, and they are excellent with fresh walnuts. But Christine's version is the best I've tasted. The eggs are just barely set, and the chopped herbs retain their texture and fragrance. The omelet is even better served cold, a day later—the herbs hold their color and body—so it makes great picnic fare. This version, using 18 eggs, makes a very large omelet, so you'll have enough to serve 6 people and leftovers for lunch the next day.

It's important to mix the eggs and filling

ingredients 1 hour or more before you cook the omelet. Also don't chop the herbs too finely. "It should be like a vegetable omelet," says Christine.

2   large bunches parsley, stems removed (60 g to 90 g), about 2 to 3 cups
1   large bunch mint, stems removed (30 g to 45 g), 1 to 1 ½ cups
18 large eggs
½   cup (50 g) pine nuts
⅓   cup (50 g) dried currants
    About ½ teaspoon salt, or to taste
    Freshly ground pepper, to taste
¼   teaspoon powdered saffron
2   tablespoons olive oil

Wash and dry the herbs. Chop coarsely with a knife, not in a machine. (You want them to swell and absorb the egg.)

Beat the eggs in a large bowl. Mix in the herbs, pine nuts and currants, the salt, freshly ground pepper and saffron, then cover and set aside for 1 to 2 hours in a cool place. If storing in the refrigerator, bring to room temperature before cooking.

To cook, heat a deep, wide frying pan over medium-low heat and add 2 tablespoons olive oil. Stir the egg mixture briskly and pour it into the pan. Turn the flame to low and cook, lifting the edges and turning the pan until the omelet cooks on the bottom, like a Spanish omelet. Cover the pan, place on a flame tamer or asbestos pad if the flame seems too high (you don't want the bottom of the omelet to stick and burn before it's cooked through) and cook 20 minutes, or until set but still a little runny on the top.

Bring to the table, cut into wedges, and serve, passing salt and a pepper mill. Refrigerate whatever is left over for the following day.

SERVES 8 TO 10

Alsatian Apple Cake

❧

CHRISTINE MADE this moist cake during one of my winter visits. She had been snowed in, and the treacherous road up to her house had just been plowed the day before we arrived. I've never been so terrified in a car, as I slipped and slid up the road. I had no snow tires, and the sun was setting fast. Christine's house was a welcome sight. She kept us happy that weekend with her usual delicious meals, served at the dining room table in front of a warm fire, and we ate a great deal of her Alsatian Apple Cake.

FOR THE CAKE

1   tablespoon unsalted butter
4   pounds (2 kg) baking apples or Golden Delicious apples
3   large eggs
⅓   cup (80 ml) mild-flavored honey
¼   cup (60 ml) safflower or peanut oil
2   tablespoons low-fat milk
1   teaspoon vanilla

2   tablespoons rum
½   cup plus 2 heaping tablespoons (75 g) sifted unbleached white flour
1   tablespoon baking powder
1   teaspoon baking soda
    Pinch of salt

FOR THE TOPPING

1   large egg
2   tablespoons unsalted butter, melted
2   tablespoons brown sugar

Preheat the oven to 425° F (220° C). Generously butter a 12-inch (30-cm) cake pan or a 10-inch (25-cm) springform pan.

Peel, core and cut the apples into eighths. Place in a large bowl.

Mix together the eggs, honey, oil, milk, vanilla and rum. Mix in the flour, baking powder, baking soda and salt. Blend well and pour the batter over the apples. Toss everything together and turn into the buttered baking pan.

Bake 30 minutes. Meanwhile, mix together the topping ingredients. After 30 minutes, pour this topping over the cake and spread evenly. Return to the heat and bake another 10 minutes, until caramelized on the top. Cool in the pan on a rack. Serve warm or cool. The cake reheats well.

SERVES 8 GENEROUSLY

Peaches and Apricots With Currants

❁

A favorite summer dessert, the ripe juicy peaches and apricots contrast beautifully with the intense sweetness of the currants.

Juice of 2 lemons
2 tablespoons mild-flavored honey or 4 tablespoons sugar
8 to 12 firm, ripe peaches, sliced
8 to 12 firm, ripe apricots, sliced
6 tablespoons dried currants

Mix together the lemon juice and honey or sugar. Toss with the peaches, apricots and currants. Chill for 1 hour or more and serve.

SERVES 8 TO 12

Menus From the Domaine Tempier Winery

❧

Orange and Olive Salad With Cumin

Lulu's Grilled Fish

Lulu's Potato Gratin
or
Lulu's Potato Gratin With Sorrel

Fresh Fruit

Wine Suggestions: Bandol Rosés and Reds Domaine Tempier,
Côtes-du-Rhône, Chianti Classico

Serves 6

Menus From the Domaine Tempier Winery

I FIRST WENT TO the Bandol vineyard of Domaine Tempier on a sunny July day in 1980. Nathalie Waag, my landlady, was a great friend of Lulu Peyraud, the proprietress, and when she told Lulu about my interest in food, Lulu invited us both to lunch. Nathalie wrote me a note saying, "Lulu Peyraud, the best cook I know, would like you to come to lunch next Monday" and gave me directions. I didn't quite know who Lulu Peyraud was or what Domaine Tempier was; I thought it might be a restaurant. At any rate, early Monday morning I made the beautiful two-hour drive, through the Lubéron to Aix and onto the autoroute toward Toulon.

Located just west of Toulon, Bandol is a seaside town situated about 50 kilometers east of Marseilles, in the Var. In this part of France, the Mediterranean coast is lined with small villages, and medieval fortress towns pepper the hills. The hilly, vineyard-covered countryside is dotted with palm trees, and the sky in this part of France is often a wash of pinks, oranges, purples, blues, greens and golds.

I found Domaine Tempier, and as I drove up, I could see that this was going to be an extraordinary place. I got out of my car and found myself standing under an arbor in front of a 150-year-old stucco farmhouse surrounded by terraced vineyards. In front of the massive wooden door, a long table had been laid with white linen cloths and porcelain dishes. The receptionist told me that my hosts were at the *cave* and would be back shortly. I was happy to marvel at my surroundings while I waited for them.

Soon everybody appeared: Lulu and Lucien Peyraud, their sons Jean-Marie and François, with their wives, Catherine and Paule; the food writer Richard Olney and his sister-in-law Judith, also a food writer; a wine merchant from Berkeley; and Nathalie. Like many winemakers, the Peyrauds are vivacious and passionate. Their eyes twinkle with humor and love. Lulu is a tiny woman with red hair and sparkling blue eyes. Her luncheons are always celebrations, no matter how disparate the group and despite language barriers.

Lulu served garlic croutons with tapenade, while Lucien poured chilled Domaine Tempier rosé. A small fire had been prepared on the ground outside, using wood and dried vines from the vineyard, and over it, a huge copper caldron of fish and vegetable bouillon was heating. Lulu and her daughters-in-law emerged from the kitchen with large cork trays holding about ten different kinds of fish and shellfish. When the bouillon began to simmer, Lulu sprinkled in some saffron and added the fish. After a few minutes, Lulu and Paule removed the fish from the bouillon and put it back on the trays and ladled bouillon and vegetables into each bowl on the table.

Eating bouillabaisse at Domaine Tempier is a

ritual. First you eat the bouillon and vegetables (leeks, potatoes, carrots) with croutons and rouille, a reddish-colored, spicy mayonnaise; then you eat more bouillon, rouille and fish. There are so many different kinds of fish that you spend hours at the table, taking a little of one kind or another with each helping, washing each one down with vintage after vintage of the Peyrauds' wine. That day, the bouillabaisse was followed by fresh goat cheese and figs, then Cavaillon melons filled with apricot puree and almonds.

I told the Peyrauds that this was my first bouillabaisse and that I'd been wanting to have the real thing for quite some time. "Your first!" Lucien exclaimed. "This calls for Champagne!" And with that, a plastic Champagne bucket in the shape of a top hat appeared, with two bottles of pale pink Champagne.

Small wonder that since that dreamy afternoon, I've returned to Domaine Tempier at least once a year, and I'm never without its wine. Lucien Peyraud's dry, elegant rosés and fruity, ruby-hued reds are among the most talked about wines in Provence. There are only four appellations in Provence, and Bandol is one of them.

When I moved to Paris a year later, I immediately wrote to Lulu, asking if I could come for the vendanges, the grape harvest. Lulu wrote back at once, saying that my room would be waiting. I had been in Paris for barely two weeks when I got in my car and hurried down to Bandol.

The first day, I went to pick grapes in a spectacular hillside vineyard called La Tourtine. It was sunny as only a Provençal day can be, and I could see the shimmering Mediterranean. The mistral, which had sounded like the ocean the night before, had become a gentle, refreshing breeze, and the vineyard was fragrant with fennel, rosemary, thyme and mint. The luscious, dark purple-blue grapes, which we were not barred from eating as we picked, also had a wonderful aroma.

The hours passed quickly. François Peyraud, who supervises the agriculture at Domaine Tempier and directs the harvest, taught me how to use my sicateur, the small curved scissors used to clip off the grape clusters, and how to cut out the moldy and rotten grapes. I learned to reject the small clusters that grow off tertiary branches and aren't sweet enough and the small white and pink bunches that

aren't ripe. Carrying a bucket, called a sceau, I worked in a row by myself or with one other person. A crew of two men repeatedly provided empty buckets in exchange for our full ones, which they emptied into bins on a tractor. I was lulled by the constant sound of grapes falling into empty containers, the cries of "Sceau!" as the buckets filled and the tractor coming and going from the cave, where the wine is made.

I had done farm labor years ago in the United States. But this was very different. It wasn't just the surroundings; it was the mixture of tension and celebration everyone felt, workers and patrons alike. The vendanges is an extremely intense time. The year's labor and investment depend upon it entirely. No matter how good a winemaker is, the quality of his wine from year to year is determined by timing, weather and good luck. If the vendanges begin too early, the grapes won't be sweet enough; if they begin too late, there is a greater chance that foul weather will spoil the grapes. The sky that first day was as blue-violet as Wedgwood ceramic, bluer than I'd ever seen it. Yet Lucien, François and Jean-Marie regarded it with suspicion. "It's too clear; there should be clouds," François remarked. Only rain could follow such clear weather, and rain would destroy the grapes. Luckily, François was wrong, and the harvest proceeded under clement skies.

Lucien, François and Jean-Marie work with unbroken concentration during this time. They maintain their good humor, but the strain of the vendanges shows in their faces. Lucien, like a new mother, gets up every two hours during the night to record the temperature of the fermenting wine, which must not rise higher than 26° C (about 80° F). François is in the vineyards at 6:00 every morning, checking the vines to determine which grapes are most ready for harvesting. Jean-Marie, who supervises the vinification, never takes his mind off the process going on in the cave. He is always late for lunch and eats little.

Yet all of the Peyrauds arrive with smiling faces, ready for conversation and fun, at the long outdoor lunch table where workers and family gather together daily. For despite the rigors of the vendanges, this is the most festive time of year, full of promise. During the rest of the year, life goes on in a business-as-usual way; but during the harvest, with the influx of new workers and the mystery of this year's wine, there is always a feeling of novelty.

Nowhere is that more apparent than at Lulu's table. She, above all, adores *la fête*, and her meals reflect it. They are filling Provençal country fare, fragrant with garlic and olive oil, washed down with ice-cold well water and Domaine Tempier's table wine. I have learned much about fish cookery from Lulu because she always respects my vegetarian preference and prepares fish dishes for me. She serves lunch effortlessly to between 15 and 25 people every day during the *vendanges*. Like all great hostesses, she is organized, and it was a joy to go with her to the market every day and watch her find the best products and check off her lists.

After the market, we would go home to her beautiful kitchen, which still looks like the kitchen her grandmother built because all the appliances are hidden behind closet doors, and prepare the lunch in two hours. Paule, François' wife, would always be there to help, along with whatever other daughters or daughters-in-law were around. Every day, I would be inspired by a new dish, and I left Domaine Tempier with several additions to my repertoire.

At the end of the harvest, after the last grapes have been picked, there is a big bouillabaisse lunch. Like my first bouillabaisse at Domaine Tempier, it is always a party. It begins with rosé and a nice hors d'oeuvre like tapenade or brandade (salt cod puree); then all of the workers, their spouses, several neighbors, family members and guests sit down at a long table under the arbor for hours of bouillabaisse and wine tasting. Jean-Marie and the head *caviste* continually disappear and reappear with different vintages. There are guessing games as to the years. After the soup comes fruit or sorbet, then *marc*, the eau de vie made from the seeds and stems after the harvest. Lucien conducts a *dégustation*, or tasting, at the *cave* after lunch, and François sets up the still for making *marc*.

The afternoon before this lunch, Lulu goes down to the port, either at Bandol or nearby Sanary or Toulon, wherever she knows the fishermen will be arriving with a good catch. She comes back with kilos of fish, and she and her helpers begin work on the soup. Lulu cleans all the fish at her soapstone kitchen sink. In her opinion, it is essential to clean your own fish, because only then will you know if it is truly fresh. She saves the livers for the rouille, used to garnish the soup. The fish are, for the most part, Mediterranean species like rascasse, a succulent, white-fleshed member of the gurnard family that is unique to the Mediterranean; sea bass; several Mediterranean varieties of bream; John Dory; another member of the gurnard family called *galinette*; and red mullet. There are usually mussels and one or two varieties of crab as well.. While Lulu cleans and scales the fish, her assistants make scores of garlic croutons, toasting rounds of French bread in the oven and rubbing them with garlic; they also peel dozens of cloves of garlic for the rouille.

In addition to the beautiful fish that will be cooked at the last minute in the bouillon, Lulu buys several pounds of tiny rockfish (called *soupe de poisson* or *bouillabaisse*), which she uses for the fish fumet. She sautés these with garlic and onion in olive oil, then adds water, tomatoes and herbs and brings the mixture to a boil. After carefully skimming off all the foam, she simmers the fumet for about half an hour and presses it through a strainer. Later, she will use it for her bouillon. It is this bouillon, with its chunks of leeks, carrots and potatoes, that makes her bouillabaisse taste so good. I've eaten bouillabaisse in a few restaurants in the south of France, but I've never had one that tastes as good as Lulu's.

You really need the Mediterranean fish for a real *bouillabaisse à la Marseillaise*, both the tiny fish for the fumet and the larger ones for the soup. Instead, you can find a marvelous fish soup, my Provençal-Style Fish Chowder (page 117); it's not bouillabaisse, but it is good and much less trouble to make. At any rate, there is enough in these menus to make you happy.

Orange and Olive Salad With Cumin

❧

THE SECOND TIME I went to Domaine Tempier during the harvest, Lulu served this at lunch (pictured on page 141).

8 navel oranges, peeled and white pith removed, sliced

¾ cup (85 g) imported black olives, cut in half and pitted

1 red onion, sliced very thin

Juice of 1 medium-sized lemon

½ to 1 teaspoon ground cumin, to taste

Salt and freshly ground pepper, to taste

1 tablespoon olive oil

Toss together the oranges, olives and onion.

Mix together the lemon juice, cumin, salt and pepper, then whisk in the olive oil. Toss with the salad and serve.

SERVES 6

Lulu's Grilled Fish

❧

LULU HAS A LARGE GRILL outside her kitchen. She prefers cooking her fish outside over vine branches, so that her kitchen won't smell. I was always astounded by her knack for grilling 25 fish at a time without cooking any of them too long.

FOR THE FISH

6 whole individual-serving-size fish (each weighing about ¾ to 1 pound, 340 g to 500 g), such as sea bass, red snapper, porgy, mullet, or 3 larger fish, each weighing 1½ pounds (750 g), or 1 very large fish, about 4 pounds (2 kg)

Olive oil

Salt and freshly ground pepper, to taste

4 or 6 branches fennel or rosemary (or a combination)

Several sprigs of fresh savory, thyme or basil

1 ½ bay leaves, broken into pieces if using more than one fish

FOR THE SAUCE

3 tablespoons lemon juice or the liver and roe from the fish

3 small or 2 large cloves garlic

Salt and freshly ground pepper, to taste

¾ teaspoon dried savory

⅓ cup (80 ml) olive oil

3 tablespoons or more finely chopped fresh basil or parsley, to taste

Preparing the fish for grilling: Clean the fish but save the liver and roe, if you have it, for the sauce. Do not scale.

Prepare a grill with aromatic wood, such as mesquite (Lulu uses branches from her grapevines).

Rub the inside of the fish with a little oil, salt and freshly ground pepper. Fill the cavity or cavities with sprigs of the fresh herbs: fennel or rosemary, fresh savory, thyme or basil and the bay leaf.

Making the sauce: Pound together the lemon juice or fish liver and roe, garlic, salt, pepper and dried savory in a mortar and pestle. Add the olive oil, a tablespoon at a time, incorporating each spoonful into the sauce with the pestle. Adjust seasonings. Add the chopped fresh basil or parsley and continue to mash and mix together until you have a thick, fragrant sauce.

Grilling the fish: Grill the small fish for about 8 to 10 minutes or longer, if necessary (4 to 5 minutes for each ½ inch, 1.5 cm, of thickness), turning it halfway through. Grill medium-sized fish for 15 minutes or for 4 to 5 minutes per ½ inch, 1.5 cm, of thickness, measured at the thickest point.

Serve and pass the sauce separately.

SERVES 6

Lulu's Potato Gratin

❀

ALTHOUGH Provençal cooking is not characterized by the use of butter and cream, Lulu pulls out all the stops with her Potato Gratin. But feel free to substitute my lower-fat version below, if you wish.

- 1 clove garlic, peeled and cut in half
- 2 ½ tablespoons unsalted butter
- 1 thick slice of onion
  Salt and freshly ground pepper, to taste
- 2 ½ pounds (1.25 kg) Idaho russet potatoes, peeled and sliced very thin
- 2 cups (450 ml) crème fraîche (page 20)
- 1 ½ cups (170 g) grated Emmenthaler or Gruyère cheese (6 ounces)

Preheat the oven to 425° F (220° C). Rub a 2-quart (2-L) earthenware gratin dish with the cut clove of garlic, then with some of the butter.

Bring a large pot of water to a boil, add the onion slice and some salt and blanch the sliced potatoes for 5 minutes. Drain.

Spread half of the potato slices in the buttered gratin dish. Add salt and freshly ground pepper, then top with half of the crème fraîche and half of the cheese. Repeat the layers and dot the top with the remaining butter.

Bake in the preheated oven for 35 to 45 minutes, or until the top browns. Serve bubbling hot.

SERVES 6 TO 8

Lower-Fat Potato Gratin: Substitute 1 ½ cups (350 ml) skim milk and ½ cup (120 ml) crème fraîche for the 2 cups (450 ml) crème fraîche. Reduce the cheese to 1 cup (4 ounces, 115 g) or reduce to 1 ounce (30 g), which you will sprinkle over the top. Use olive oil for the baking dish and omit the butter.

Lulu's Potato Gratin With Sorrel

❀

THE ACIDITY of the sorrel goes nicely with the potatoes.

- 1 bunch fresh sorrel
- 2 additional tablespoons unsalted butter
- ½ cup (120 ml) additional crème fraîche
  Ingredients for the Lulu's Potato Gratin (above)

Wash the sorrel and remove the stems. Dry and chop. Heat the butter over medium heat in a skillet and sauté the sorrel for about 3 minutes. Remove from the heat and mix with the additional crème fraîche. Divide into two portions.

Make Lulu's Potato Gratin as directed above, but before topping the potatoes with the crème fraîche and the cheese, add a layer of the sorrel mixture.

More From Domaine Tempier

❧

Curly Endive Salad With Baked Goat Cheese (page 116)

Tuna or Swordfish With Tomato-Caper Sauce

Steamed Potatoes Tossed With Olive Oil and Fresh Herbs

Fresh Fruit

Serves 4 to 6

❧

Lulu's Huge Vegetable and Fish Platter
With Garlic Mayonnaise

Fresh Fruit Sorbets

Serves 10

Wine Suggestions: Bandol Rosés and Reds Domaine Tempier,
Côtes-du-Rhône or Chianti Classico

Tuna or Swordfish With Tomato-Caper Sauce

❧

I THINK THE MIXTURE of tomatoes, garlic and capers that I learned from Lulu and serve at the Supper Club with steamed fish fillets (page 149) and baked whiting (page 153), is even better with grilled tuna or swordfish.

Tomato-Caper Sauce (page 149)
4 to 6   tuna or swordfish steaks, about 1 inch (2.5 cm) thick
1   tablespoon olive oil

First make the sauce. This will hold for 1 to 2 days in the refrigerator.

Brush the fish steaks with olive oil and grill over aromatic wood for approximately 8 minutes, or 4 minutes per ½ inch (1.5 cm) of thickness, turning halfway through the cooking. Watch closely, because tuna and swordfish will become cotton-dry if you overcook them. The steaks should remain pink in the middle.

Remove from the heat and serve immediately, topped with the sauce.

SERVES 4 TO 6

Lulu's Huge Vegetable and Fish Platter With Garlic Mayonnaise

❧

SOMETIMES Lulu serves this festive meal (shown on page 143) instead of bouillabaisse at the end-of-the-harvest luncheon. It's a wise idea to wait until the grape picking is over, because aïoli is a garlic mayonnaise, and garlic is a known soporific. A siesta is often required afterwards.

The aïoli is served on a large platter with a colorful assortment of vegetables and fish. I was intrigued by some of Lulu's vegetable choices, in particular by the sweet potatoes and beets. They all work, though, and they are simply prepared and delicious.

FOR THE AÏOLI

2   egg yolks, at room temperature
½   teaspoon salt
¾   cup (180 ml) olive oil
¾   cup (180 ml) safflower or canola oil
5   cloves garlic, peeled
  Juice of 1 large lemon
  Freshly ground pepper or a pinch of cayenne

FOR THE COURT BOUILLON

1   quart (1 L) water
1   onion, sliced
2   leeks, cleaned and sliced
1   carrot, sliced
1   stalk celery, sliced
2   whole cloves garlic, peeled
1   sprig of fresh parsley
1   sprig of fresh thyme
1   bay leaf
1   teaspoon salt (more or less, to taste)
2   cups (450 ml) dry white wine
6   peppercorns

FOR THE FISH AND VEGETABLES

2   pounds (1 kg) fresh cod fillets
1   cauliflower, broken into florets and blanched
12   small artichokes, steamed until tender and halved lengthwise, chokes removed
½   pound (250 g) green beans, blanched

1 pound (500 g) carrots, peeled, quartered
   and blanched
1 pound (500 g) fennel bulbs, trimmed,
   quartered and steamed for 20 minutes
1 pound (500 g) beets, peeled, quartered and
   steamed until tender
6 small sweet potatoes, baked in their skins
   and halved
6 hard-boiled eggs, halved
6 tomatoes, halved

Making the aïoli: Place the egg yolks and salt in a food processor bowl or blender. Turn on the machine and very slowly drizzle in the oils in a thin, steady stream while blending. If you use a blender, you will have to stop it from time to time to stir down the mixture. Squeeze in the garlic through a press, or pound it to a paste in a mortar and pestle and mix in thoroughly. Add the lemon juice and pepper and mix well. Adjust the salt. Refrigerate until ready to serve.

Making the court bouillon: Combine all the ingredients for the court bouillon except the wine and peppercorns in a large saucepan or soup pot. Bring to a boil, reduce the heat, cover and simmer 15

minutes. Add the wine and peppercorns and simmer another 15 minutes. Strain and retain the broth. Cool.

Poaching the fish fillets: Slap with the flat side of a knife to break down the fibers, and score a few times on the diagonal. Butter a pan or casserole wide enough to accommodate the fillets and lay them in the pan. Cover with cold or tepid court bouillon and bring to a bare simmer. Do not boil. Cover and cook 5 minutes for each ½ inch (1.5 cm) of thickness. The fish should be opaque and flake easily with a fork. Remove from the liquid with a slotted spatula.

Assembling the dish: After preparing the vegetables, place on a large platter with the fish, interspersed with mounds of the aïoli. Pass the platter and allow guests to take portions of each vegetable and fish, with a mound of aïoli for dipping.

To prepare ahead of time: Everything—the mayonnaise, court bouillon, vegetables and the poached fish—will hold for 1 day in the refrigerator. Bring the vegetables to room temperature before serving, or serve warm.

SERVES AT LEAST 10

Part Three

MENUS FROM
SMALL DINNER PARTIES

Menus From Small Dinner Parties

THERE ARE certain dishes that are too time-consuming for me to consider making for 25 people. They're fine for 4, 6 or even 8 people but would be a nightmare if you had to multiply them by 3 or 4.

Cleaning mussels, for example, can be tedious, but they make a relatively easy meal for a small number of guests when prepared simply, steamed in white wine or cooked in a more complicated soup or fish dish. In winter, I sometimes invite a few friends over for just mussels and a salad.

Fresh pasta, too, is difficult for me to serve at a Supper Club, unless it's a baked dish like cannelloni (page 125) or lasagna (page 88) or unless it's used in a salad (pages 104 and 137). By the time I get it out to all 25 people, it has cooled too much, and there is always the danger of overcooking it. But for my small dinners, pasta is what I serve most often, either as a main dish or on the side.

And of course, I'd never serve a soufflé, whether savory or sweet, for 25. Soufflés fall too quickly, and it's too important for everybody to see them, so I save them for smaller dinners.

I serve these meals in my breakfast dining room, which opens onto the kitchen. It's a cozy, square room with French doors, on the courtyard side of the apartment. The walls are covered with burgundy fabric, and the round table seats seven people comfortably. For the Supper Club and big parties, we use this room for preparing food and arranging plates and platters; it is part of the bustling inner sanctum of the kitchen. Many of my guests don't even see this part of the house because it's separated from the living room by a long, narrow hallway. But at smaller dinners, my friends watch me cook and sometimes help me with last-minute details. I love the intimacy and relaxed atmosphere of these candle-lit events as much as the excitement and fanfare of the Supper Club.

An Informal Dinner
for Any Time of Year

❦

CAULIFLOWER GRATIN

ITALIAN-STYLE MUSSEL SOUP

TOSSED GREEN SALAD

SOURDOUGH COUNTRY BREAD (PAGE 26)

CREPES FILLED WITH LEMON SOUFFLÉ

WINE SUGGESTIONS: CÔTES-DU-RHÔNE, BANDOL OR CHIANTI CLASSICO

SERVES 6

Cauliflower Gratin

❦

THIS DISH was inspired by Alice Waters' recipe for artichoke bottoms with a similar sauce. I had intended to make the artichoke dish for a dinner, but when I got to the market, there were great big cauliflowers on sale, and my mouth began to water as I envisioned them prepared the same way.

This extremely easy dish can be assembled several hours in advance and popped into the oven 10 to 15 minutes before serving. I have used it as an appetizer, as I do here, as a side dish or as the main attraction at a light dinner or lunch.

1	large cauliflower, about 2 pounds (1 kg), or 2 small ones, broken into florets
3	tablespoons olive oil or safflower oil or less, to taste
¾	pound (350 g) fresh goat cheese, preferably not too salty
1	clove garlic
¼	cup (60 ml) low-fat milk or plain low-fat yogurt
1	teaspoon fresh thyme leaves or ½ teaspoon dried
	Freshly ground pepper, to taste
6	tablespoons fine, dry breadcrumbs

Preheat the oven to 450° F (230° C). Oil a gratin or baking dish large enough to accommodate all the cauliflower.

Steam the cauliflower 10 minutes, drain and toss with 2 tablespoons of the oil in the prepared baking dish.

In a food processor fitted with the steel blade or in a bowl using a wooden spoon, mash the goat cheese and blend it with the garlic and milk or yogurt and the thyme and freshly ground pepper until you have a smooth mixture.

Spread the goat cheese mixture over the cauliflower. Sprinkle on the breadcrumbs. At this point, the dish can be set aside or refrigerated until ready to bake.

Just before baking, drizzle on the remaining tablespoon of oil. Place in the oven and bake 10 to 15 minutes, until the breadcrumbs are browned and the dish is sizzling. Serve at once.

To prepare ahead of time: The entire dish can be prepared several hours in advance, up to the drizzling on of the last tablespoon of oil and the baking. Hold, covered, in the refrigerator.

SERVES 6

Italian-Style Mussel Soup

❦

HERE, MUSSELS are cooked in a gutsy tomato broth, slightly piquant because of the cayenne.

4	quarts (4 L) mussels, cleaned
2	tablespoons olive oil
4	large or 8 small shallots, chopped
4	cloves garlic, minced or put through a press
4	pounds (2 kg) tomatoes, chopped or 4 28-ounce (765-g) cans, with juice

¼	teaspoon dried thyme, to taste
¼ to ½	teaspoon dried oregano, to taste
2	cups (450 ml) dry white wine
	Pinch of cayenne
	Generous pinch of saffron threads
	Freshly ground pepper, to taste
	Salt, if necessary (the mussels release their own salt)
¼	cup (10 g) chopped fresh parsley

Clean the mussels according to the instructions

on page 172.

Heat the olive oil in a large flameproof casserole or soup pot large enough to accommodate all the mussels. Add the shallots and garlic and cook over low heat until the shallots are tender. Add the tomatoes and stir together well. Add the thyme and oregano, bring to a simmer, cover and cook 30 minutes. Add the white wine, cayenne, saffron and pepper and bring to a boil. Add the mussels, cover and cook 5 minutes, shaking the pot or stirring the mussels, whichever is easiest, at least once to ensure even cooking. After 5 minutes, the mussels should be opened; if not, cook a little longer, until they open. Immediately remove from the heat. Discarding any that refuse to open, spoon the mussels into wide soup bowls. Taste the broth and add salt only if necessary, then spoon over the mussels, sprinkle with parsley and serve.

SERVES 6 TO 8

Crepes Filled With Lemon Soufflé

❀

I WAS INTRODUCED to this showy dessert (pictured on page 144) when I ordered it at a Paris restaurant called Le Petit Montmorency. It makes a grand and unforgettable finale. Dessert crepes are filled with a very light lemon soufflé, baked in a hot oven for a short time and served on bright red strawberry puree (you could also use raspberry puree). It's not the kind of dessert I'd make for the Supper Club, but for a small dinner party, it's dramatic, served hot and puffed from the oven.

FOR THE CREPES

3 large eggs
½ cup (120 ml) water
½ cup (120 ml) low-fat milk
¼ cup (60 ml) Grand Marnier
2 tablespoons raw brown sugar (Turbinado)
Pinch of salt
⅞ cup (100 g) unbleached white flour
2 tablespoons unsalted butter, melted, or safflower oil, plus additional unsalted butter for the crepe pan

FOR THE STRAWBERRY PUREE

2 pints (750 g) fresh strawberries, hulled (1 ½ pounds)
Juice of ½ lemon
1 tablespoon mild-flavored honey or sugar

FOR THE SOUFFLÉ

1 tablespoon butter

6 tablespoons raw brown sugar (Turbinado)
1 tablespoon mild-flavored honey
⅓ cup (90 ml) plus 1 tablespoon fresh lemon juice
5 large egg whites
¼ teaspoon cream of tartar
Pinch of salt
Finely chopped zest of 2 lemons
1 teaspoon cornstarch
2 tablespoons unsalted butter for the dish

Making the crepes: Break the eggs into the bowl of a food processor fitted with the steel blade or into a blender and add the water, milk, Grand Marnier, sugar and salt. Turn on the processor or blender, and slowly add the flour and melted butter or oil. Blend thoroughly for 1 to 2 minutes. Let sit, in or out of the refrigerator, for at least 30 minutes before making the crepes.

Cook the crepes in a heavy steel or nonstick crepe pan. Heat the pan over a medium-high flame and brush with butter. It should sizzle and be just short of smoking. Lift up the pan with one hand, and with the other, pour in a scant ¼ cup (60 ml, or about 3 ½ tablespoons or a little less) batter. Swirl the pan to distribute the batter evenly and place over the heat. Cook for 1 to 2 minutes, until the edges brown and come away easily from the pan. Using a wooden spatula or a knife, turn the crepe over and cook 30 seconds or less on the other side. Turn onto a plate. Brush the pan and continue to make the crepes, stacking them as they are done, until you have used up all the batter.

If you are going to hold the crepes for more than a few hours in the refrigerator, stack them between pieces of wax paper or parchment. Freeze extra crepes and use for another purpose.

Making the strawberry puree: Puree the strawberries in a blender or food processor until smooth. Add the lemon juice and honey or sugar and set aside.

Making the soufflé batter: Preheat the oven to 425° F (220° C). Generously butter 1 large or 2 medium-sized gratin dishes, using about 1 tablespoon butter.

Dissolve the sugar and honey in the lemon juice in a 1-quart (1 L) saucepan. In a large bowl, beat the egg whites at low speed until they begin to foam. Add the cream of tartar and salt and continue to beat at high speed until stiff, shiny peaks form. Turn off the mixer.

Heat the lemon juice mixture over high heat until it comes to a boil (you need the large saucepan because the honey will bubble up dramatically and overflow in a small saucepan). Cover, with the lid not quite tight, and boil hard for 1 or 2 minutes, until the mixture reaches the soft-ball stage, 238° F (120° C).

Start beating the egg whites again at moderate speed and slowly dribble in the lemon-juice syrup. When it has all been added, turn up the speed to high and continue to beat until the egg whites are tepid and glossy and form stiff peaks when lifted with a spatula. Beat in the lemon zest and cornstarch and remove the beaters.

Filling, baking and serving the crepes: Place a crepe in the buttered gratin dish or dishes and spoon on 2 heaping tablespoons of the soufflé mixture. Gently fold the crepe in half over the mixture and push it to one end of the dish. Fill all the crepes like this, and dot the tops with the remaining 1 tablespoon butter, or they will stiffen in the oven.

Place the baking dishes in the preheated oven and bake 7 minutes, until the soufflé is puffed and just beginning to color on the edges.

Meanwhile, spoon the strawberry puree onto individual dessert plates.

When the crepes are ready, place 2 on each plate on top of the puree and serve at once.

To prepare ahead of time: The crepes can be prepared 1 day ahead of time and held in the refrigerator. They also freeze very well.

The strawberry puree can be made hours before you wish to serve it and held in the refrigerator. It can be served cold or at room temperature with the crepes.

The soufflé batter will hold for 30 minutes at room temperature. If it falls a little, beat again before using. The crepes must be assembled and baked right before serving and served immediately.

SERVES 4 TO 6 (16 TO 18 CREPES)

A Fall/Winter Ravioli Dinner

❧

RED CHICORY AND ENDIVE SALAD WITH WALNUTS

RAVIOLI WITH CHEESE AND WILD MUSHROOMS

SOURDOUGH COUNTRY BREAD (PAGE 26)

GREEN MUSCAT GRAPES MARINATED IN MUSCAT WINE
OR
COFFEE BAVARIAN CREAM WITH KAHLÚA

WINE SUGGESTIONS: CHIANTI CLASSICO OR BAROLO

SERVES 6

Red Chicory and Endive Salad With Walnuts

❀

THESE ARE the greens I love to eat in winter. They make a perfect marriage with walnuts and a nutty dressing.

FOR THE DRESSING

2 to 3   tablespoons balsamic vinegar, to taste
1   teaspoon Dijon mustard, to taste
  Salt and freshly ground pepper, to taste
3   tablespoons walnut oil
6   tablespoons low-fat yogurt

FOR THE SALAD

½   pound (250 g) endives (2 medium-sized), leaves separated, washed and dried

½   pound (250 g) red chicory or radicchio leaves, washed and dried
4   tablespoons broken walnut pieces
  Handful of chopped fresh parsley (optional)

Mix together the vinegar, mustard, salt and pepper. Whisk in the oil and yogurt; combine well.

Toss the endive and chicory with the walnuts, optional parsley and dressing just before serving.

To prepare ahead of time: The endive, chicory and parsley can be washed, dried and refrigerated in plastic bags and the dressing made hours before serving.

SERVES 6

Ravioli With Cheese and Wild Mushrooms

❀

RAVIOLI, in a way, is the first thing I ever cooked creatively. I was 15, it was canned ravioli, and I was on a co-ed camping trip in Europe. My friends and I embellished that dinner with slices of canned Vienna sausage. After I arrived home at the end of the summer, announcing that I was "really very European," I announced to my parents that I'd learned to make ravioli. My stepmother, who had spent two years in Rome, was beside herself with pride—until she learned what kind of ravioli I'd made. (Years later, in Austin, Texas, I did make handmade ravioli for my parents—and served it from a can.)

There is something very special about homemade ravioli. Perhaps it has to do with all those individual morsels, each filled and cut by loving hands. It is definitely a labor-of-love dish, one that you need time for. These cheese and wild mushroom ravioli (pictured on page 142) are inspired by some tortellini I tasted in Verona. You could also fill them with the chard, herb and cheese mixture used in the cannelloni on page 125 (omitting the

eggs, or the filling will be too wet), and toss them with the same tomato sauce used for the cannelloni. *Note:* You may end up with more pasta than filling. Freeze the remaining pasta dough, or roll out, cut and dry. You could also serve these ravioli in a chicken or mushroom broth, with a little parsley and freshly grated Parmesan.

If using the chard filling, heat the tomato sauce and toss with the ravioli just before serving, or place the ravioli in individual bowls or plates and spoon the tomato sauce over the top. Serve, passing additional freshly grated Parmesan.

FOR THE PASTA

3-egg pasta dough, made with part whole-wheat pastry flour, part unbleached white or all unbleached white flour, increased according to the note on page 40
Salt

FOR THE FILLING

1½   ounces (45 g) dried mushrooms, such as

porcini (1 ½ cups)

Boiling water to cover

1   tablespoon unsalted butter or olive oil

2   cloves garlic, minced or put through a
      press

1   teaspoon fresh thyme leaves or ½ teaspoon
      dried

1   teaspoon chopped fresh rosemary or ½
      teaspoon dried, crumbled

¾ pound (350 g) part-skim ricotta

1   cup (115 g) freshly grated Parmesan
      (¼ pound)

½ cup (55 g) freshly grated Romano pecorino
      (2 ounces)

Freshly ground pepper, to taste

FOR THE FINISHED RAVIOLI

4   tablespoons unsalted butter

1   tablespoon olive oil

2   tablespoons fresh sage leaves or 1 teaspoon
      dried

½ cup (55 g) freshly grated Parmesan

Make the pasta dough and allow it to rest while you make the filling.

Making the filling: Place the mushrooms in a bowl and pour on boiling water to cover. Let steep 15 to 30 minutes, until softened. Drain, retaining the soaking liquid, and rinse thoroughly. Squeeze dry and chop fine. Strain the soaking liquid through a fine strainer and reserve it.

Heat 1 tablespoon of butter or olive oil in a small skillet and sauté the mushrooms, along with the garlic, thyme and rosemary, for about 3 minutes, stirring. Remove from the heat.

Blend together the ricotta, Parmesan and Romano cheeses and stir in the mushrooms. Add freshly ground pepper to taste.

Filling and cutting the ravioli: Roll out the pasta dough in strips about 5 (13 cm) inches wide and 12 to 18 inches (30 cm to 45 cm) long. Roll and fill one strip at a time; otherwise, the dough will become too dry. Place the strips on a lightly floured table or board, and fold in half lengthwise, then unfold so that you have a crease down the middle. Measuring every 2 inches (5 cm), place heaping teaspoons of the filling on one side of the crease, all the way down the length of the pasta. Using a pastry brush, lightly moisten the dough around each mound of filling and fold the top half over. Carefully squeeze out any air pockets around the filling, then press down gently between each mound of filling and along the bottom.

Lightly flour the strip of ravioli. Using a special crimper-cutter for pasta, a pasta cutting wheel or a sharp knife, trim the bottom edge of the strip, then cut down between each ravioli. Place the ravioli on lightly floured baking sheets or on lightly floured parchment on top of baking sheets. Cover with plastic wrap and refrigerate until ready to cook.

Cooking the ravioli: Preheat the oven to 300° F (160° C). Oil a baking dish. Cook only partially in salted, simmering water to which you have added the reserved mushroom soaking liquid. The water should not be boiling rapidly, as this could cause the pockets to open. After 2 minutes, remove them with a slotted spoon and drain in a colander. The ravioli will finish cooking in the oven. Place in the oiled baking dish and keep warm in the medium-low oven until ready to serve.

Final heating and serving: Melt the butter and olive oil together in a saucepan, add the sage leaves, and stir together over low heat for about 3 minutes. Toss with the ravioli and serve at once, passing the freshly grated Parmesan.

To prepare ahead of time: The filling and the pasta dough can be made 1 day in advance. Wrap the pasta in plastic, place the filling in a covered bowl and refrigerate.

Unlike cannelloni, ravioli are filled before they are cooked. You can hold them in the refrigerator overnight, but do not cook them first. Place the assembled ravioli on lightly floured pieces of parchment, dust the tops so that they won't stick and cover with plastic. The ravioli can also be frozen. In this case, don't roll the dough quite as thin, because it becomes very brittle when it's frozen and tends to break when you handle it. Place on lightly floured pieces of parchment, flour the top, cover with plastic or parchment, then wrap in foil. Transfer frozen ravioli directly from the freezer to simmering water.

The ravioli can be cooked a couple of hours ahead of serving time and held in an oiled baking dish. Warm in the oven as indicated in the recipe.

SERVES 6 (ABOUT 80 TO 85 RAVIOLI)

Green Muscat Grapes Marinated in Muscat Wine

❧

GREEN MUSCAT GRAPES, with their distinctive sweet flavor, are my favorite European grapes. I have seen them in markets in New York and California, imported from Italy. The wine made from the Muscat grape is sweet and fruity and tastes exactly like the grape.

2 ½ pounds (1.25 kg) Muscat grapes

2 cups (450 ml) Muscat wine

Remove the grapes from their stems, cut them in half, and remove the seeds. Toss in the wine and refrigerate several hours before serving. Serve in bowls, with some of the wine spooned over the grapes.

SERVES 6

Coffee Bavarian Cream With Kahlúa

❧

THIS RECIPE is in my first cookbook, *The Vegetarian Feast.* It's such a good dessert, with a subtle coffee taste and a drop of mint which surprises the palate, that I often serve it at small dinner parties.

The dish involves several steps, so if you can, you should probably make it the day before you wish to serve it. It will hold in the refrigerator for a couple of days and needs at least 5 hours to set.

6 large eggs, plus 2 egg yolks, at room temperature
2 envelopes unflavored gelatin
½ cup (120 ml) strongly brewed coffee, such as espresso
⅔ cup (160 ml) mild-flavored honey
1 ½ cups (350 ml) low-fat milk
½ teaspoon peppermint extract
¼ cup (60 ml) Kahlúa liqueur, plus 1 to 2 tablespoons additional for the whipped cream
2 teaspoons brandy

1 teaspoon vanilla
¼ teaspoon cream of tartar
⅛ teaspoon salt
1 cup (225 ml) heavy cream, chilled

Making the custard: Separate the eggs, placing the whites in a large, very clean bowl and the yolks, plus the two extra, in a second bowl. (Discard the extra egg whites.)

Dissolve the gelatin in the coffee in a small, heavy-bottomed pan. Set it aside.

Beat the egg yolks and the honey together, using an electric mixer, until thick and lemon-colored.

Meanwhile, heat the milk in a heavy-bottomed saucepan over medium heat until you see the surface begin to tremble. Making sure it is not boiling, slowly pour the scalded milk into the egg-honey mixture, beating all the while.

Transfer the milk and eggs back into the saucepan and place over a very low flame or on a flame tamer over a low flame. Heat through, stirring, being careful not to let the mixture come to a boil, or the eggs will curdle. When the mixture reaches 168° F (75° C), small wisps of steam will appear and it will begin to thicken. It should coat both sides of a wooden spoon like cream. (This usually takes a while if you are as paranoid about having the heat too high as I am.) As soon as the mixture thickens, remove it from the heat and stir for a minute or so to cool.

Heat the coffee-gelatin mixture, stirring over very low heat to dissolve the crystals completely, then whisk it into the custard, being careful to scrape every last bit of it out of the bowl with a rubber spatula. Strain this mixture into a 3-quart (3 L) bowl and stir in the peppermint extract, Kahlúa, brandy and vanilla. Set aside.

Beating the egg whites: Begin beating the 6 egg whites. When they begin to foam, add the cream of tartar and the salt. Beat until they form stiff, shiny (but not dry) peaks, then stir ¼ of them into the custard and gently fold in the rest.

Beating the cream: Leaving ½ cup (120 ml) of the cream in the refrigerator to chill further, beat the remainder in a chilled 1-quart bowl (1 L), circulating your beater or whisk to incorporate as much air as possible. Beat the cream until doubled in volume and until it adheres softly to a spoon when lifted, but not until it is stiff.

Stir the custard so it begins to set evenly. If you don't do this, the gelatin will settle at the bottom. Allow it to cool for about 10 minutes, stirring every minute or so, then gently fold in the whipped cream. Pour the Bavarian cream into a soufflé dish or a mold of your choice or into individual ramekins. Cover well and refrigerate for at least 5 hours, or overnight. Keep chilled until ready to serve.

To serve: Just before serving time, whip the remaining cream and flavor it with the remaining 1 to 2 tablespoons (to taste) Kahlúa. Serve from the soufflé dish or in ramekins, or unmold by dipping the mold in hot water for a few seconds and reversing it onto a serving plate. Refrigerate for a few minutes again to set. Top with the Kahlúa-flavored whipped cream.

SERVES 6 TO 8

A Summer Pesto Dinner

✿

Fresh Homemade Pasta With Pesto

Baked Tomatoes (page 160)

Sourdough Country Bread (page 26)

Tossed Green Salad

Peaches in Red Wine With Honey and Cinnamon

Wine Suggestions: Gigondas, Bandol, Barolo or Chianti

Serves 4 to 6

Fresh Homemade Pasta With Pesto

❀

PESTO HAS BECOME so popular in the United States that in many cities, fancy delis and charcuteries sell it year-round. But it's easy to make yourself.

Toward the end of August, I begin to make large batches to freeze for small dinner parties. I try to make enough to get me through the winter. The women in the Saint-Germain market who sell the best, most opulent basil know me very well, as I rarely go by their stands without purchasing at least four generous bunches, enough for a double batch of pesto.

I began giving pesto dinners one summer when a number of friends and friends of friends were in from the United States. I would make up the pasta dough in the morning and roll it out right before I cooked it. Sometimes I'd make the pesto in the morning, other times my guests would join in, picking leaves off the stems. These were rather impromptu dinners—I was determined not to devote much time to them during the day—and everybody pitched in.

Sometimes I cook all the pasta at once and toss it with the sauce. I find, though, that when I have more than six people, the pasta stays hotter if I cook each batch separately (it takes only seconds), transfer the noodles to a warm plate, spoon on the pesto and run it out to the table. I tell everyone to begin eating as soon as they get their plate so it won't get cold. I've served it this way for up to 10 people.

FOR THE PESTO

2 cups (55 g), tightly packed fresh basil leaves (2 ounces)
2 tablespoons pine nuts or broken walnuts
2 large cloves garlic
¼ teaspoon salt, or more, to taste
½ cup (120 ml) fruity olive oil
½ cup (55 g) freshly grated Parmesan (2 ounces)
2 tablespoons freshly grated Romano pecorino
Freshly ground pepper

FOR THE PASTA AND SERVING

Fresh pasta, either whole-wheat, spinach or herb, for 4 to 6 people (pages 40 to 42), cut into fettuccine, tagliarini or spaghetti noodles
Salt
2 tablespoons butter, at room temperature

Making the pesto for immediate use: Place the basil, pine nuts or walnuts, garlic and salt in the bowl of a food processor, a blender or a mortar and pestle. Process or pound until finely chopped or pureed. Slowly add the olive oil and continue to process until the mixture is smooth and uniform. Stir in the cheeses and freshly ground pepper.

Making pesto for the freezer: Omit the cheeses. Stir in when you thaw the pesto and correct seasonings.

Cooking the pasta, serving: The pasta dough can be made before or after you make the pesto. Just before you serve the pesto, bring a large pot of salted water to a rolling boil. Have plates warming in the oven. Cook the pasta for just a few seconds, until al dente, just until firm to the bite. You can cook it all at once or cook individual servings. Remove from the boiling water with a large skimmer, place on a warm plate, and top with a generous spoonful of pesto (about 2 tablespoons) and a little bit of butter. The water on the pasta will thin out the pesto. Or drain the pasta in a colander, return it to the hot cooking pot and toss with butter and the pesto. Serve at once.

To prepare ahead of time: Pesto will hold for several days in the refrigerator and can be frozen. Of course, it is most fragrant when the basil is at its freshest.

The pasta dough will hold in the refrigerator for 1 day, and you can roll out the pasta and hold the noodles, dusting them well with flour, in the refrigerator or dry or freeze them.

SERVES 4 TO 6

Peaches in Red Wine With Honey and Cinnamon

CHILLED RIPE PEACHES in spiced, honey-sweetened wine are the perfect finale to this summer meal.

6	firm, ripe peaches
2	cups (450 ml) full-bodied red wine
3 to 4	tablespoons mild-flavored honey, to taste
½	teaspoon ground cinnamon or more, to taste
1	teaspoon vanilla

Fresh mint for garnish

Blanch the peaches, run them under cold water and remove their skins.

Heat the wine to a simmer and remove from the heat. Stir in the honey, cinnamon and vanilla. Pour into a bowl and slice in the peaches. Refrigerate for several hours.

Serve cold, garnished with fresh mint.

SERVES 6

Index